Disclaimer

This publication contains the opinions and the ideas of the author. It is sold with the understanding that neither the author nor the publisher is engaged in rendering legal, tax, investment, insurance, financial, accounting, or other professional advice or services. It is sold with the understanding that neither the author nor the publisher is engaged in providing health advice. If a reader requires such advice or services, a competent professional should be consulted. Relevant laws vary from state to state. The strategies outlined in this book may not be suitable for every individual, and are not guaranteed or warranted to produce any particular results.

No warranty is made with respect to the accuracy or completeness of the information contained herein, and both the author and the publisher specifically disclaim any responsibility for any liability, loss, or risk, personal or otherwise, which is incurred as a consequence, directly or indirectly, of the use and application of any of the contents of this book. All characters in the book are fictional. Any resemblance to persons living or dead is purely coincidental.

D1732929

Dedication

This book is dedicated to the people who help others live their best, healthiest lives.

Acknowledgements

Special thanks to my wonderful wife, Autumn, who supports my eccentric, eclectic dreams unconditionally (even when they're nerdy).

Thank you to my parents for the decades of love and encouragement, and for inspiring me to teach in my own way.

Shout out to my family and friends for bringing joy and meaning to my life.

Thanks to my sister-in-law Britni for the clever graphic design (mrswickens.xo@gmail.com). If people judge this book by its cover, I'll be sitting pretty.

Thank you to my copy editor/proofreader Dana Nichols for the expertise, and for helping make my ideas legible.

Thank you to my therapist for helping me free my mind and find fulfillment.

Section 1: Learning the "Why" of Financial Health 6

Section 2: Financial Essentials (Flour) 59

Section 3: Building a Winning Game Plan (Liquid and Flavor) 102

Section 4: Ten task finale 194

Your best life is a healthy life 210

Appendix: Terminology crash course 211

Healthy Dough

Ingredients for the financial health you crave

Section 1: Learning the "Why" of Financial Health

Chapter 1: Welcome!

You are about to become extremely *rich. Plus you'll be a world-class musician, your hair will look nicer, your jokes will finally be funnier, and your vertical leap will improve by seven inches. All you have to do is invest exactly how I tell you, and you'll have mountains of cash before your next dental checkup. And if you double down with our extra special bonus offer, you'll be a renowned underwear model by Tuesday. Don't worry, you'll have enough cash to buy off the paparazzi. Everyone except me is a liar, and I never even exaggerate. I'm going to make you so mysterious and wealthy that your favorite musical artist will offer to play a 20-song set at your next birthday party. Oh, and did I mention that you'll be able to speak the languages of other animals? The time to buy is running out! Get rich now!*

Are you sick of being lied to yet? Thank goodness! That's all the time I'll spend on false promises, unlike a lot of other financial materials you may be exposed to on any given day. This book isn't a get-rich-quick scheme, so hey, sorry if that's what you were seeking. That said, I think you should stick around, because solid financial education is worth your time.

Healthy Dough is a financial philosophy focused on wellness. Money should be a healthy and positive part of your life. You're going to learn how your finances *affect* and are *affected by* the rest of your life, and how you can develop consistent, sustainable financial success.

You may already know that "dough" is slang for money, but that's not the only inspiration behind the title. Dough used in cooking or baking requires two basic ingredients: flour and liquid. Add in some extra flavor, and you can create whatever you desire. *Healthy Dough* also calls for a few basic ingredients. You will acquire the knowledge (flour), skill (liquid), and strategy (flavor) to create the financial health you crave.

To get us started, I want to take some time in this first section to show gratitude and get you excited to learn. Thank you for supporting my book and my brand. I genuinely believe that by developing your financial health you're helping yourself, your loved ones, and your community — regardless of your current socioeconomic status. I also appreciate you helping me toward achieving my dreams. I'm thrilled at the possibility of my thoughts and ideas providing value to the world around me (and let's be honest, I hope to make some dough in the process).

In general terms, an asset is something of use or value, and an *investment* is a class of asset that can improve or protect your cash flows. Assets come in many forms, such as cash, investments, property, equipment, vehicles, marketable goods, and even intangible valuables such as knowledge. *Investing* is the act of exchanging resources to acquire resources of greater benefit. As you read this book, you're investing in an asset — look at you go! Do you even need me? You are giving up money and time to purchase and read this book, in exchange for knowledge that will improve, protect, or otherwise enhance your cash flows. Your financial education is an asset with obvious use and value, and I believe the benefits of reading this book will outweigh the costs. You're going to learn how to earn and save enough money to buy whatever fancy possessions you may want, and be grounded enough to realize you probably don't need them.

At the time this book is being written, I am an active certified public accountant (CPA) with a background in auditing, corporate accounting, and financial reporting. To paint myself deeper into the dork corner, I've decided to be a financial author as well. I became interested in personal finance as a teenager, and took to applying the concepts and strategies as quickly as I could find opportunities to do so. I love learning different perspectives and philosophies, and have had an absolute blast developing and verbalizing my own. I'm not going to promise you a simple plan to make you wealthy, primarily because I'm not a liar. However, I am someone with passion, novel ideas, and a belief that a person's overall health — including financial health — is more important than wealth.

Full disclaimer: though health and finance are discussed in this book, I am not a financial advisor nor a licensed expert in any branch of health. The content of this book is general in nature, and is peppered with my personal opinions and philosophies. I'm happy to share my observations and experiences, and what's worked (and failed) for me during my journey.

While I'm not yet wealthy enough to quit my day job, I've been fortunate to consistently meet my financial goals throughout my adult life. I attribute my success to a thoroughly developed personal finance acumen and thoughtful decision-making, which I've applied to my financial choices. The same mentality I apply to money has helped me make nonfinancial life choices in a healthy way as well (most of the time). My goal isn't to convince you that you need me, my brand, or some product to be financially savvy; it's actually quite the opposite. I want to provide you with basic financial tools and concepts, and help you realize that *you* can develop your own sustainable financial success.

I hope to share the fundamentals of personal finance in a way that is approachable, applicable, and entertaining. This book is intended to make financial concepts accessible to the masses, and package them in a way that incorporates unique ideas, experiences, and philosophies along the way. The content is conceptual because the world changes too fast to spend time on too many specifics. I want you to be informed and adaptable, so that you can cut your own path through the jungle of financial decision-making. This book may be your first hack at the brush, or maybe it's a new machete that'll help clear your existing path. Regardless of your experience, demographics, total health, or current knowledge base, I believe this book can help you achieve the financial health you crave.

I'm a proud native of the Pacific Northwest, having lived in the south Puget Sound region my entire life. As you'll uncover in some of my analogies, fitness, sports, and music are among my favorite things in life. I also love animals, humor, and the beautiful earth we've been so lucky to enjoy. I spend as much time as I can outside of work doing the things I love, with my favorites being exercising (especially wandering around outside), playing guitar, and spending time with my amazing roster of loved ones.

I've always tried to soak up as much financial perspective as I can, and have learned from a broad array of examples. Some of my favorite people in the world are wealthy, financially healthy, and consistently kind; the type of people who inspire others to be their best. I've observed other wealthy people who believe that human value is scaled to asset value, and they treat people according to that falsehood; they've helped guide me on what *not* to do once I'm rich. My viewpoints have been equally influenced by individuals who are hard-working and good-natured, but struggle to effectively manage their money. I've learned that just as badly as I want to avoid snobbery, I want to avoid being financially unprepared. All these encounters led me to begin studying personal finance for two main reasons: the desire for financial success, and the belief that basic financial education can change lives. The world is full of wonderful people whose days are disrupted by financial struggles, as well as wealthy people who could benefit from a change in perspective. Whether they need to spend less, express gratitude, earn more, find fulfillment, or grow their money, certain barriers keep people of all income levels from achieving financial health.

My main inspiration to create *Healthy Dough* is having seen good people create bad financial situations, and having observed the way that financial ailments negatively impacted their well-being. Financial education is my way of helping prevent unforced errors and promoting happy, healthy lives. I want to empower people to control their financial health rather than letting it control them. I know it's possible because I've applied the practices in my own life, much to the gain of my overall health and wellness. Throughout this book, I happily share some of my personal stories — including the ones in which we get to laugh at my own follies a bit.

The other greatest influence on this project has been my quest to master my own health. I've gone through periods of my life where I've been in subpar health in a variety of ways, many of which could have been avoidable. At times I've struggled with my physical health, and I've survived my fair share of mental health and social health struggles as well. In my adult life I've been fortunate to have traditional financial success, but have definitely had periods where my financial *health* could improve. I've learned to understand the "why" of various difficulties, and have chosen to turn my challenges into strengths. I want to teach you to do the same thing, because you are also capable of taking care of your financial health and overall well-being.

There are four values that support the mentality and lifestyle that *Healthy Dough* promotes. They are:

Lifelong Learning

Learn every single day, and your life will be stimulating and meaningful in ways money can't buy. Learn from every experience and every person you encounter. Learn from the wonderful and the terrible. Don't forget to learn from yourself. You're never going to run out of things to learn — so learn to love it.

Tenacity and Toughness

Embrace every day like a kid running an obstacle course. Hustle, sweat, climb, fall, run, crawl, and laugh through the whole experience. Not every performance can be a personal best, but you'll get as far as you want to go if you show up for yourself every chance you get. Adversity is the sugar that sweetens victory.

Toughness is the energy you have available to conquer challenges.

Resilient people find and create energy to endure and succeed, because they know what they're after. Purpose. Positivity. Gratitude. Determination. These things will give you the energy to be tough. Find reasons to be tough, and you may realize you're tougher than you think.

There's toughness in brute strength, and there's toughness in flexibility.

"Water can flow, or it can crash. Be water, my friend." — Bruce Lee

Continuous Improvement

Invest in yourself. Make yourself proud. Smile at every challenge, and be thankful for the chance to grow. Self-mastery sits on the horizon no matter where you stand, so you might as well start heading that way.

"There is nothing noble in being superior to your fellow man; true nobility is being superior to your former self." — Ernest Hemingway

Love and Kindness

Find purpose in living for love, compassion, and respect. Be kind to everyone. Love your people, love your world, and love yourself.

This book is for everyone. The need for financial health applies to all races, regions, ethnicities, religions, orientations, political parties, genders, occupations, and age groups — you get the point.

The Declaration of Healthy Dough

Embark on this educational endeavor by first embracing one important fact: your life is guided by *your* choices, and *your* effort. Thus, I present the Declaration of Healthy Dough. Read it and believe it. Even if you're not into rah-rah stuff, read it at least once, and think about it. Heck, write your own version if you want, but please take my point that you are in control of your life.

I am the one in control of my health, finances, and happiness. I invest in myself because I'm worth the cost. I am tough enough to be honest and accountable, even when it sucks. I'm good enough today, and I'll be even better tomorrow. I will be grateful for my success, and better for my struggles. No one owes me a damn thing, and I like it that way. I am responsible for my mistakes and errors, and that's great news, because it means I'm also in control of how I address them. I will never truly fail because I will never stop trying. Wellness is more important than wealth, but I can have both. I choose to invest in my health today, because health is freedom.

Concepts > Instructions

If you're looking for an infomercial or a get-rich-quick pamphlet, you're going to be disappointed with this book. Like, ending-up-5-inches-shorter-than-your-older-brothers disappointed (and trust me, that's frustrating). One of my favorite quotes can be attributed to one of my dad's best friends, the late high school football coach Eric Allen, who regularly said, "If it were easy, everyone would do it." If there were step-by-step instructions on how to get rich, don't you think everyone would do it?

Sorry, but there are no mindless scripts or automations to follow in order to attain your financial goals. I'm not saying that anyone who claims to have the secret scheme to help you achieve your dreams is a liar; but I'd be amazed if they passed a polygraph test. In order to reach your goals, accept that concepts are more important than instructions.

There are roughly 43 quintillion possible Rubik's Cube combinations on a 3-by-3-by-3 cube. That is 43,000,000,000,000,000,000 — or in other words, 43 billion times 1 billion. It would take over a trillion years to write down individual instructions to solve each possible combination. And even that would only be possible if each set of instructions only took one second to write, with no breaks between. So then, how in the world do people solve Rubik's Cubes consistently, and sometimes in under a minute? It's because they understand the concepts. There are not written instructions on how to solve each individual combination, but those in the know are able to look at a cube and apply their knowledge.

Managing finances is like solving a Rubik's Cube. First off, there are no exact written steps in order to achieve financial goals, because there are infinite combinations of factors including starting place, opportunity, and actual results. We need to understand financial concepts in order to look at the "cube" in front of us, think critically, and apply our knowledge properly. You will consistently reach your goals if *you* understand what you're doing. For that reason, as I've mentioned, my approach in this book is far more conceptual than instructional.

In Section 1, we'll start with a deep dive into financial health and why it matters. You'll learn about the intersections of health and finance and the importance of investing in yourself. In Section 2 we pick up the "flour" of *Healthy Dough*, and gain the foundational knowledge required to make quality financial decisions. We will explore critical financial terms and concepts, and hopefully not pass out from boredom. Power through it and absorb as much as possible, but don't linger – you can always refer back to this section as needed while you work through the rest of the book. Once you've crossed the desert of core financial concepts, you'll be rewarded with the liquid and flavor (skill and strategy) provided in Section 3. You'll learn how to build a winning game plan and make your finances a positive and healthy part of your life. By the time you reach Section 4, you'll have everything you need to make *Healthy Dough*. I'll send you off with ten actionable steps that will help you achieve the financial health you crave. I've also tagged on an Appendix containing more key definitions. If you come across a term you don't yet understand, my hope is that you can flip to the Appendix and get what you need.

Let's go!

The presentation of the materials should be applicable and useful to everyone, but may be especially useful to those who are new to the game, or are looking for a fresh perspective. Thank you for choosing to invest in yourself and invest in me. Let's get going!

Chapter 2: Stan and Stella: teaching us why financial health matters

How did you come across this book, and what was your goal when you started reading? Do you think financial education will improve your life? Are you just reading it to appease someone who gifted it to you? Do you want to build generational wealth and throw yacht parties like P. Diddy? Regardless of what brought you here, it's a savvy move to learn more about money. But why does it even matter?

In order to explain the concept of financial health and why it's so important, I'm going to share a tale that shows the amazing impact that daily decision-making plays in sustainable financial success. "Stan and Stella" is a fictional story based on true events. Well, it's based on observations of the different ways people handle money, and how they play out in the real world. It will demonstrate the severity of the trouble caused by borrowing money to live outside your means, and the prosperity of keeping things simple.

Before we continue, please note that this story contains oversimplification related to salaries, debt and lease approval, cost of living, and credit card contracts; but don't let that undermine the value of this parable. The reality of overspending and compounding interest is still very accurately depicted here.

There may be terminology and concepts in the story that you're not certain of yet, such as principal, interest, Roth 401(k), employer match, credit rating, and social health. Later sections — especially "The Essentials" — explain these, and more, in adequate detail. At the risk of sounding annoying, I don't mind if you feel a little overwhelmed by some of the financial lingo in the story. It actually proves one of the core beliefs of *Healthy Dough*, which is that you need to be able to speak the language of finance to understand what you see and hear. It may be fun to re-read "Stan and Stella" once you've read the rest of the book, since you may be able to dust off a few hidden gems that you missed the first time.

Enough preamble. Let's meet your new pals!

Stan and Stella

Stan and Stella are friends who live in the same city. They recently graduated from college, where they became close through mutual friends. Stan is generally a pretty nice guy, albeit a little outwardly cocky for some people's tastes, and sometimes he may take himself too seriously. He loves having the latest and greatest things, and tends to use possessions as a way to gauge his quality of life. He gets bored and anxious if he's not being entertained. Like many people, he struggles with self-esteem, but doesn't really want to admit it — he is a dude, after all. A lot of Stan's college friends came from wealthy families, and he loved getting to use their vacation homes during spring break. Stan really wants to be rich so he can enjoy the finer things in life. He believes that he *deserves* luxury, because he works hard and it's important to him. He believes money is the ultimate measure of success.

Stella is balanced and steady, though she's not without her own challenges and adversity. She tries to be self-aware, having decided as a teenager that it was too stressful to try to seem happy and impressive for others 24 hours a day. She is hardworking and thoughtful, and had similar grades to Stan when they were in school together. She is kind to everyone, and has a few close friends she trusts unfailingly. She's the type of person who delivers handmade cards to show love and gratitude. Stella really enjoys traveling and going out with friends, but she also knows how to enjoy life without spending money. She understands the need to make sacrifices and tough decisions to meet her goals — financial or otherwise.

Stan and Stella snapshot: Visiting your friends

Imagine that you're close friends with both Stan and Stella. It's been about a year since you all graduated from college together, and you're visiting from out of town for a couple of nights.

Stella throws a little shindig for you and some other friends on the first night of your trip, and you stay on her couch that night. Her place just outside the city seems like a perfect spot to start out, and you have a great time while you catch up with friends. Not much pomp or circumstance, but you look forward to visiting again sometime, one hundred percent.

You spend the next day with Stan, and crash on his couch for night two. You're shocked by how nice his urban apartment is, especially for someone just starting out in their career. You enjoy zipping around the city in his nice new car as he chauffeurs you to his favorite local attractions and restaurants. You have a blast hitting the town, and look forward to your next visit.

Now that you've visited both of your friends and experienced their lifestyles firsthand, who do you think has more money: Stan or Stella? Stan certainly provided you with a day in the high life. He drives a flashy car, lives in the cool part of town, and dines like he's a television food critic. Meanwhile, Stella displays a more modest lifestyle and she's more content to socialize without spending a bunch. She is *way* financially healthier Stan. Why does a modest lifestyle lead to better finances than a lifestyle of luxury? The Paradox of Wealth.

The Paradox of Wealth

The more you spend, the less you save. The less you spend, the more you save. The more you save, the wealthier you are. A luxurious lifestyle may *look* like wealth, but it's quite often the exact opposite.

The long version

How do people with seemingly similar circumstances end up with such financial disparity? The short answer is: choices. The differences in their behaviors and values are what gives them disparate results. Stan and Stella have entered the market in nearly identical circumstances, but Stan has made choices that leave him on the wrong side of $0. Meanwhile, Stella lives within her means, and thrives as a result. Let's paint in more details about Stan and Stella and learn even more from their story.

Stan and Stella go to the market

Let's rewind and start the long version of the story one month after you, Stan, and Stella graduate college. Now that they're done with school, Stan and Stella are entering the workforce as full-fledged adults. They laugh about how old they've become, and crack up at the commercial series about young adults turning into their parents if they buy a certain brand of insurance. They are about to start work at the same company downtown, and each will earn $54,000 per year. Net of taxes, they'll receive $1,700 per semimonthly paycheck, adding up to a monthly net pay of $3,400.

Stan and Stella are each starting their careers with $500 of graduation gift money in the bank, and no other marketable assets. Their only other possessions are home goods and furniture acquired during college. They each have about $30,000 in student loan debt that requires monthly payments of $325 for 10 years. They both need to find a place to live and secure a mode of transportation to travel to their office and other destinations. They'll also need to figure out how to forage for food now that they can't just walk down to the dining hall three times a day. They'll both be required to make other routine financial decisions.

Stan knows that he wants to live in a hip neighborhood right in the heart of the city, since he expects to spend lots of time "out." Apartments usually require up-front deposits of at least one or two months of rent at the time of signing, but he doesn't have that kind of cash. Instead, he finds a building that's running a zero-deposit special, and signs a 12-month lease that costs $1,400 per month. He negotiates a mid-month payment cadence so that he can pay his rent after his first paycheck of each month (starting with the first one). With housing secured, he sets off to find a vehicle. Stan views vehicles as a barometer to measure wealth and success, and he'd like to have both of those things, like, yesterday. Stan visits one dealership, set on buying a new rig even before he gets a sniff of new rubber tires. He feels like a teething puppy looking at a giant basket of chew toys; he just needs to decide which one to chomp down on. Within an hour he is signing for an 84-month (seven-year) auto loan that will cost him a $500 monthly car payment. He tried to borrow more, but his lack of employment history and credit history made that impossible. He even had to fluff his application a little bit by saying that he lives with his parents rent-free — his reasoning being that it was kind of true earlier in the week, before he signed his apartment lease agreement. He doesn't see any moral dilemma; he deserves a nice car, and that's that.

Stan wakes up on his first day of work in a flashy apartment, feeling quite pleased to be enjoying the benefits of professional life before ever clocking in. He begins to build his daily routine, which includes starting the day with a delicious mocha from the coffee shop on the first floor of his building. He doesn't mind that it's expensive and takes much longer than brewing his own, because he feels more professional when the public sees him loitering in his business casual. He lives close enough to the office to walk, bike, or bus to work, but if he did that, how would people know he has a nice car? He thinks preparing his own food is boring, so he dines out at least once a day. Between his coffee and dining out, his daily food costs are about $30 per day ($900 per month). Stan spends about $475 per month on other assorted things, such as his cell phone, home internet, car insurance, and so on.

Stella's car-buying process is about as riveting as a monotone history lecture. Keeping her monthly net pay front of mind, she thinks she can easily swing a $200 per month car payment and still meet her other financial goals (more on those later). She shops around for a few days and buys a reliable used car that's mostly depreciated and gets great mileage. Stella takes out a 60-month (five-year) auto loan that will cost her the $200 per month she'd planned on. She'd have preferred to pay cash, but she doesn't have enough, and even though she doesn't want to take on another loan, she needs a car now. Because of this compromise, she commits to keeping the car for as long as she possibly can; it's merely a tool in her mind.

Stella lives rent-free with her parents during her first month of work. She'd much rather have had her own place right away, but didn't find anything in her price range during her initial search and had no interest in overspending. She's decided to tough it out and be appreciative to have the option to live with her parents temporarily, even though it makes her commute a little longer. Her patience is rewarded when she finds the right place at the right price. Her new apartment is just outside of town. She signs a 12-month lease costing $1,000 per month with no up-front deposits. Nothing fancy, but it's nice, safe, and close enough to where she will spend most of her time.

Stella is pretty low-maintenance about food and beverages. She uses her coffee maker or drinks office coffee every day, packs a lunch to work, and only goes out to eat for special occasions. She learns to cook, and has fun reinventing the recipes her parents brought with them when they moved to the United States. Her daily food bill is about $12 per day ($360 per month). Stella spends $515 on other assorted things, such as her cell phone, home internet, and car insurance — pretty much exactly the same costs as Stan, but slightly more each month because she also pays for a gym membership and gives to her favorite charity.

Stan and Stella side-by-side

Figure 1-1 shows Stan and Stella's typical monthly financial picture in the first year of their careers.

Figure 1-1

Monthly Finances - Year 1

	Stan	Stella
Gross pay	$4,500	$4,500
Net pay	$3,400	$3,400
Housing	$1,400	$1,000
Student loan	325	325
Vehicle	500	200
Food	900	360
Other expenses	475	515
Total expenses	$3,600	$2,400
Margin	$ (200)	$ 1,000

Stan stumbles

As you can see in the table, Stan's monthly net pay is $3,400, but each month he spends $3,600. How in the world does that work? Is he a magician? Well, no. Stan took out a credit card as soon as he got his first paycheck. He has minimal credit history, but was able to get a credit card with a limit of $3,000 and 24% annual interest rate (compounding monthly), with no minimum monthly payments required. Stan puts $200 on his credit card during month one, because he spends $200 more than he earned. His spending is exactly the same in month two, so he has to put another $200 on his card. Oh well, it's just another $200, right? Wrong. Stan gets to pay a little extra since he didn't pay off his month one balance during month two. If Stan had paid off his month one expenses on time in month two, he wouldn't be charged any interest; however, since he does *not* pay his bill, he's penalized with the contractual interest charge. The interest charge is only $4, so Stan shrugs it off. But what will happen if he keeps overspending, not making payments, and letting his balance grow?

The Buildup

You've probably heard of Albert Einstein, the famous physicist who bent our minds and transformed science with the theory of relativity. Even *he* was impressed by the exponential power of compounding interest, and referred to it as the "eighth wonder of the world." The good news for us is that it's much less complicated than astrophysical theories about time and space. You can easily learn the concepts and use them to your advantage. Unfortunately, some people learn the hard way. Stan is one of those people.

Figure 1-2

Stan's Credit Card Build Up

Month	Beginning Balance	Additions	Payments	Interest	Ending Balance	Monthly Change
Mo0	-	-	-	-	-	-
Mo1	-	200	-	-	200	200
Mo2	200	200	-	4	404	204
Mo3	404	200	-	8	612	208
Mo4	612	200	-	12	824	212
Mo5	824	200	-	16	1,041	216
Mo6	1,041	200	-	21	1,262	221
Mo7	1,262	200	-	25	1,487	225
Mo8	1,487	200	-	30	1,717	230
Mo9	1,717	200	-	34	1,951	234
Mo10	1,951	200	-	39	2,190	239
Mo11	2,190	200	-	44	2,434	244
Mo12	2,434	200	-	49	2,682	249
Mo13	2,682	200	-	54	2,936	254
Mo14	2,936	5	-	59	3,000	64

Stan continues to spend $200 more than he earns for as long as he can, which includes that weekend you visit him and Stella. As shown in the Figure 1-2 above, Stan can add $200 per month on his card for 13 months. Based on his excess spending alone, Stan's $3,000 credit card limit could handle 15 months of his $200 per month deficit — so why is his card declined at lunch on the first day of month 14? The answer is, accumulation of compounding interest. Stan is broke. He hasn't saved a single penny in the first year of his career, and he still has bills to pay, student loans, 70 more car payments he can't afford, and now $3,000 in nonessential consumer debt on his credit card. Whoops! Tough break, Stanimal. That's the reality of overspending, debt, and compounding interest.

Compounding interest means that the entire balance owed — including any portion that relates to previously accrued interest — is subject to interest. The $3,000 balance on his card consists of $2,605 in actual spending, and $395 in interest. Notice how his interest expense increases each month as his balance grows. Interest is the cost of borrowing money and not paying it back, and there's a reason his bank has a nice lobby. By month 13, his $200 addition and $0 paydown results in an increased balance of $254, consisting of the $200 he overspent that month, plus $54 in new interest on his prior balances. Stan is faced with the harsh reality that his card is maxed out, and thus unusable. He has to find a way to borrow more money to sustain his lifestyle, or immediately change his spending habits in order to avoid bankruptcy.

The Paydown

In an act of desperation, Stan applies for another credit card, but the bank swats away his application like it's a bloodthirsty mosquito. Why? Because he has trashed his credit rating by maxing out his one and only credit card. He's paid his auto loan and student loans on time, but no one wants to lend him more money. Would you trust someone to pay *you* back if they already had to borrow money from someone else every month? Stan has two choices — get a higher paying job (which is easier said than done), or alter his spending. Since Stan has much more control over his spending than he does his salary, Stan backs off on his luxury lifestyle so he can get out of debt.

Unfortunately, Stan had signed another 12-month lease renewal for his apartment in month 13, and there is an expensive termination fee that he doesn't have cash for. Because of his shortsighted contract signing, he can't even afford to downsize to a cheaper apartment. He can't sell his car, because he owes more than he could sell it for and doesn't have cash to cover the difference. Stella had warned him that brand new cars tend to depreciate in value significantly in their first few years, but Stan wasn't expecting to be in this situation. And his student loans are not optional — he has to continue paying them each month or further destroy his credit.

Stan realizes his best route back to zero is to cut back on discretionary spending. He cuts his food bill by 25% by eating in and making his own coffee more often. He also cuts down on other spending where he can, such as downgrading his internet and cell phone packages, to reduce other expenses by about 16%. He starts telling his friends he can't hit their favorite spots for dinner or drinks, knowing he can't afford to go. By doing these things, he cuts his spending by $300 per month, which means he's spending $100 less than what he earns each month. Unfortunately, he isn't actually saving that $100 — he's just now paying for his prior purchases, plus the cost of interest.

Figure 1-3	
Monthly Finances - Month 15+	
	Stan
Gross pay	$4,500
Net pay	$3,400
Housing	$1,400
Student loan	325
Vehicle	500
Food	675
Other expenses	400
Total expenses	$3,300
Margin	$ 100

Stan is not only stressed about his financial debacles, he's gained unhealthy weight from drinking mochas and dining out, and feels awful. Consequently, he isn't sleeping well. He realizes that he let his material desires get the best of him, and he's embarrassed to be in the position he's in. He symbolically cuts his credit card in half and shares the ceremony on social media for some reason.

He maxed out his card in just over a year. But how long will it take him to pay it down if he uses his entire $100 monthly margin to pay down his old balance? Sadly, it's going to take him an entire presidential term to pay it back. That's right, four more years. Since his entire balance still accrues interest each month, it will take significantly longer to get back to where he started. He feels like he's fallen down a ravine. His momentum took him down fast, and the same gravity is going to make it really hard to climb back up to where he fell from. When he finally makes his first credit card payment in month 15, he's charged $60 of interest during the month. With the $60 of interest added to his balance the same month he makes his first $100 payment, his balance only actually decreases by $40. That's right: at this point, only 40% of his payment is actually decreasing his balance. He has other options to lower his expenses so that he can pay down his debt faster, but he feels that he's already sacrificed enough. He keeps his expenses the same for the next few years, and slogs along with his $100 per month payments until his balance is finally paid off. At the end of month 61, after 14 months of spending more than he earned and 47 months of spending *less* than he earned, Stan's credit card debt is finally paid off.

Stan has worked for five full years, still has a wheelbarrow full of other debt, and hasn't saved a penny. How did Stella do during that same stretch?

Stella saves

Stella wants to take care of the money she earns, because she thinks doing so will present her with more freedom, flexibility, and comfort than living outside her means. As soon as she learns her salary and signs her employment offer letter, she uses it to draft a budget for the first year of her career. She uses an online paycheck calculator to determine what her after-tax pay should be, and plans her expense structure so that each month she will spend $1,000 less than that number. She only considers apartments and vehicles that fit her established budget, and picks her favorite among those options rather than letting her overall favorites dictate her budget. As I mentioned, she waits patiently to find an apartment that meets her needs and her price range, even though it means living with her parents for a month. She feels sort of silly sleeping in her childhood bedroom during the first month of her career, but she'd feel much sillier if her pride made her sign an irresponsible deal. She reminds herself that waiting a month to get an apartment gives her a jump start on her cash savings.

Stella sets thoughtful financial goals and works toward them. Her first goal is to establish an emergency cash savings worth three to six months of living expenses, just in case she hits hard times for one reason or another. Stella's budget indicates that her monthly expenses will be $2,400 per month, which means her emergency savings needs to be between $7,200 and $14,400. She decides that $850 of her monthly margin should go to emergency savings.

Stella is also eager to contribute toward her Roth 401(k) retirement account, knowing that she does indeed want to retire someday. She learns that Roth investment earnings are never taxed, and after seeing that almost 25% of her monthly paychecks are withheld to pay various taxes, she likes the idea of decades of tax-free growth throughout her career. She is thrilled to discover that her company will match her retirement contributions up to 3% of her gross pay, so she plans to contribute a *minimum* of 3% of her gross pay to earn the match. She treats the company match as if it's an optional 3% tax-free raise, and happily takes the option. Free money, *woo-hoo!* She settles on a Roth contribution of $150 per month during year one, since it's enough to earn the full employer match while still making her emergency cash savings her top priority.

She meets her emergency savings goal by the end of year one, since her $11,700 account balance could cover nearly five months' worth of living expenses. She has earned 6% in her Roth 401(k) during the year and receives $1,620 in employer match in month 12, leaving her with a retirement balance of $3,470 at the end of year one. It doesn't seem like much now, but she beams as she calculates how this initial investment will pay off. She determines that if her investment continues to earn 6% for 40 years, the amount she saved this first year will become 11 times larger by the time she hopes to retire, and it will never be taxed. She marks her first year of finances in the win column, and updates her goals for year two.

Since Stella's emergency fund is well-established at the end of year one, she decides to update her savings strategy. She considers the benefits and opportunity costs of the various options available to her, and comes up with a plan that she's comfortable with. She bumps her retirement contributions to $500 per month — about 17% of her gross pay. This leaves her with $500 of other cash savings to play with. The importance (and joy) of home ownership is something that Stella's parents instilled in her from an early age, so she decides to start saving cash toward a down payment on a home. She also considers making extra principal payments on her auto loan or student loan, but decides that hanging onto her cash is a better fit for now. This is because even though she could reduce her interest costs by accelerating her debt paydown, her interest rates aren't too bad.

Stella continues the same saving and investment strategy for years two through five of her career, and earns 6% annually in her Roth 401(k). She deals with a normal share of life stressors along the way, but never loses a second of sleep worrying about money (or what people think of her old car). Most of Stella's free time is spent walking, hiking, socializing, and reading.

By the end of the fifth year of her professional career, Stella has $35,700 in the bank. She has contributed $25,800 to her Roth 401(k), which has a balance of $38,562. Between her contributions, the employer match, and the 6% annual earnings, her account is worth approximately 50% more than what she's contributed. She has consistently met her financial goals, and is off to a nifty start.

Five-year checkup

So far we've mainly focused on Stan and Stella's income and expenses, but haven't talked much about their personal balance sheets, which show measures of their financial positions at various points in time. Stan and Stella each earn the same salary, and entered the workforce in a practically identical financial position. They started off with $500 in the bank and $29,947 in student loans, but made different choices for five years. Let's take a look at how their decisions impacted their net worth over those five years, or 60 months.

Figure 1-4						
	Stan's Personal Balance Sheet					
	Month 0	Month 12	Month 24	Month 36	Month 48	Month 60
Assets						
Cash	500	500	500	500	500	500
Investments	-	-	-	-	-	-
Vehicle	36,580	31,093	27,984	25,186	22,667	20,400
Total assets	37,080	31,593	28,484	25,686	23,167	20,900
Liabilities						
Auto loan	36,580	31,959	27,150	22,145	16,936	11,514
Student loan	29,947	27,636	25,195	22,617	19,893	17,015
Other debt	-	2,682	2,562	1,908	1,078	26
Total liabilities	66,527	62,277	54,907	46,670	37,907	28,555
Net worth (defecit)	(29,447)	(30,684)	(26,423)	(20,984)	(14,740)	(7,655)

As you can see in his balance sheet, at the end of five years, Stan's debt is still greater than the value of his assets (see Figure 1-4). His debt balance at the end of year five is equal to over half of his gross annual pay, and continues to bear interest. He's decreased his liabilities by paying his auto and student loans on time, but he doesn't save or invest, and his vehicle has depreciated in value. He still has two years of car payments left, and will finally be able to pay off his credit card debt in month 61. He will have paid more than $2,000 in interest on the $2,605 he overspent in the first 14 months of his career. He's missed out on five years of investment growth and employer contributions, so his investment balance is equal to my chances of becoming an Olympic sprinter: exactly zero. He's earned $270,000 in five years, and only increased his net worth by $21,792 in that same span.

Figure 1-5

Stella's Personal Balance Sheet

	Month 0	Month 12	Month 24	Month 36	Month 48	Month 60
Assets						
Cash	500	11,700	17,700	23,700	29,700	35,700
Investments	-	3,470	11,472	19,968	28,987	38,562
Vehicle	10,860	10,317	9,801	9,311	8,845	8,403
Total assets	11,360	25,487	38,973	52,979	67,532	82,665
Liabilities						
Auto loan	10,860	8,858	6,774	4,606	2,349	-
Student loan	29,947	27,636	25,195	22,617	19,893	17,015
Other debt	-	-	-	-	-	-
Total liabilities	40,807	36,494	31,969	27,223	22,242	17,015
Net worth (defecit)	(29,447)	(11,007)	7,004	25,756	45,290	65,650

As you can see in Stella's balance sheet (Figure 1-5), sometime in the middle of her second year of employment she achieves her first badge toward financial independence: her assets exceed her liabilities, meaning she has positive net worth. Many of her friends will wait 10, 20, maybe even a lifetime of years before they achieve net financial worth. But she lived within her means and took advantage of basic financial strategies, and can smile at her accomplishment. By the end of year five, Stella has completely paid off her car, meaning her monthly expenses will decrease $200 per month until she needs a new car. This lowers her monthly expenses to $2,200, which means her three-month emergency savings floor is lowered to $6,600. She realizes she has flexibility with the $29,100 in other cash she has saved. She could continue to consider the full amount as her home savings nest egg, or even excess emergency savings. She could pay off her remaining student loan balance, which would eliminate five years of future interest expense, and lower her monthly expenses by $325 per month. Being debt-free five years into her career could be pretty neat. And if she did pay off her student loan, she'd still have over $12,000 in excess of her emergency savings floor. That money could be used to buy a newer car in cash, or simply kept as the emergency and home savings it started off as. She could set aside a few thousand dollars for the overseas vacation she's dreamed about since she was a girl. She needs to figure out what she wants to do, but it feels incredible to have options. She earned $270,000 in five years, and increased her net worth by nearly $100,000 in that same time period.

Figure 1-6 summarizes and compares how Stan and Stella's net worth changed over time. Even though they made the exact same amount of money, Stan is still in the hole and Stella is off to a roaring start. Stella's financial value is higher than Stan's by $73,305, which greatly exceeds an entire year of their gross earnings. Stan may have the nicer apartment and cooler car, but Stella is *way* wealthier than Stan.

Figure 1-6
Net Worth Over Time

Year	Stan	Stella	Difference
0	(29,447)	(29,447)	-
1	(30,684)	(11,007)	19,677
2	(26,423)	7,004	33,427
3	(20,984)	25,756	46,740
4	(14,740)	45,290	60,030
5	(7,655)	65,650	73,305

Stella is not only wealthier than Stan, she is financially *healthier* too. First off, she actually *is* financially healthy, because she achieved her goals without sabotaging other areas of her life. Some folks do well with money but never have true financial health, because the pursuit of money is a net negative in their life. But not Stella. Her finances did not cause her undue stress, she never felt the pressure of being overcome by debt, and she never had to sacrifice any quality of life in order to save. This was mostly because she knew that quality of life isn't determined by possessions, but by health and fulfillment. Stella had financial success and slept great, but her buddy Stan did not.

Stan's financial follies impacted his mental health and physical health for four years, mostly due to stress and associated sleep loss. That, and he had some serious dieting to do after dining with the restraint of a blue ribbon hog. Stan also ended up missing out on four years of things that were important for his social health, since he was too broke to join activities with friends on special occasions. Five years after starting his job, he was embarrassed and overwhelmed, and it took about four years of improved habits to pay off one year of bad habits. To summarize, the fallout of his financial mistakes kind of, well, sucked.

Why did Stan struggle?

Stan is an amalgam of financially unhealthy people I've observed throughout my life. Some of these people have been rich, and some have been in tremendous debt. I'm not trying to mock actual individuals by way of this fictitious composite character Stan, but my intention is to use him as a very real example of how tough life can get when people make unforced errors with their finances. I'm also trying to get your wheels turning on the interconnectivity of financial health with other factors of well-being such as self-esteem, anxiety, and physical health. The next sections are all about exactly that.

Tucked into descriptions of Stan were clues that his spending decisions were influenced by certain views and behavioral patterns of his life. You may have identified that Stan craved external validation, as demonstrated by his swagger and his ache to flaunt the nicest things. In short, Stan got a disproportionate amount of his confidence from external sources, such as possessions and the perceptions of others.

Allowing the perceived opinions of others to dictate self-worth is a trait of poor social health. Stan spent his money foolishly not just out of ignorance, but insecurity as well; he hoped that spending money would increase *his* value. Sorry Stanley, but that plan was about as effective as rock climbing in oven mitts. Even if Stan had won the lottery and become independently wealthy, he may not have ever achieved financial health, because he overvalued money and possessions. Even as a millionaire, he would likely still have had an unhealthy fear of parting with his money; a fear that his life wouldn't mean much without it; that he wouldn't have value without wealth. He thought of money and success as synonymous, rather than merely being correlated. It's also worth reiterating that in his descent into being broke, Stan wasn't physically or mentally healthy either. Outsourced nutrition doesn't help people stay in shape, and he was so stressed about debt that he couldn't sleep. Stan may not be real, but his story is very much alive in the real world.

Concluding on Stan and Stella

I hope that the examples of Stan and Stella have helped demonstrate how much control you have over financial choices, and the scary consequences of choosing poorly. I think most people aspire to be like Stella, but can think of times when they've been more like Stan (myself included). The story is meant to provide an initial look into how finances impact health and quality of life, because that's really what this book is about.

Chapter 3: Financial Health

Financial health – the goal of financial education

Healthy Dough is designed to help you achieve financial health. Financial health is a state of being in which finances are consistently a positive part of your life. While there can be overlap, it is not the same thing as wealth.

Wealth is numerical, and largely theoretical. The wealth of an individual is a valuation of the money, goods, and resources within their control, reduced by amounts that they owe to others. Financial valuation doesn't offer a clear answer as to whether the control of those things, or the means of acquiring them, is part of a meaningful or quality life. Some wealthy people have earned their money by achieving their dreams, and are fulfilled by using their resources to provide value to the world. Other wealthy people are completely miserable, and need to pull their heads out of their assets. When it comes to finances, I believe in health over wealth. An unhealthy financial life doesn't mean being poor, it means that money is a negative part of life. I contend that letting money dominate your daily life is a trait of poor financial health, no matter how wealthy you may be.

Your financial well-being has an extremely high impact on the quality of your life. And the good news is, financial health can be achieved by anyone. I repeat: financial health can be achieved by anyone. It's not a numerical target, and it's not a social status. What financial health really means is to have enough resources to be reasonably self-reliant; it means that finance is a sufficiently functioning component of your life; and it means that money supports your health, wellness, fulfillment, and life's quality.

One of the worst misconceptions I observe is that people think financial education is solely about getting rich. Sure, that's why some folks get into it — heck, that's why I started studying! But I'm experienced enough now to understand that a more worthy function of financial ed is to be adequately prepared to make money a positive part of life, for whatever goals you may have. Being equipped with this basic foundation of knowledge can improve your daily life in a variety of ways that don't actually cost money. On the other side of the coin, ignorance of the financial world can cause serious problems that ripple beyond yourself. Lucky for us, inexperience is easy to cure.

Anyone can gain or lose their financial independence, regardless of where they started or where they are now. Wealthy folks may have a bigger safety net, but if they were ready to part with it, I bet they could find someone willing to accept *all* of their money and possessions with about 10 seconds of notice. I would, wouldn't you? It's tougher to squander true financial health once you have it, due to the stout habits required to build it. The person in your friend group whose salary is lowest might also be the most financially healthy, and the person who earns the most might not be financially healthy at all — it just depends on their mindset, choices, and circumstances. Financial health is possible across a broad and varied range of salaries, spending habits, interests, and needs. Lifestyle and mindset are the real differentiators in how finances affect quality of life.

I'm not trying to ridicule people who buy fancy things, or people who are truly wealthy, especially considering that I intend to achieve independent wealth in my lifetime. Instead, I want to clarify that sometimes people seek wealth for unhealthy reasons, and that the floor of financial success is simply having enough to assure basic needs are met now and later. Humans can have an unhealthy obsession with obtaining more money and more things, even when those things may not add real value to their lives. Some of those people are broke, some are wealthy, and the rest fall in between. Personally, I hope I wind up wealthy, but I am liberated by knowing I really don't *need* to be. I want to be rich for two reasons: freedom and generosity. I dream of the flexibility to do exactly what I feel like doing, with the ability to give both time and resources. Sounds cool, right?

Healthy Dough is different than traditional financial education because it focuses on the intersection of health and finance. There are clear links between financial health and more traditional measures of total health, such as the Wellness Triangle (physical, mental, and social health). I have found that financial health is extremely correlated with these three facets of life. Financial health impacts, and is impacted *by*, the other components of health and well-being. In a subsequent section, I'll use real life examples to demonstrate this point. I've learned that the interactions between health and finance have an extremely high impact on the quality of daily life, and this philosophy energizes me to share my observations with you.

Characteristics of strong financial health

On the following pages we will discuss characteristics of strong financial health. As you study each category, evaluate yourself as you are right now, and think about where you want to end up.

Basic knowledge of personal finance

A person with strong financial health needs a basic knowledge of financial concepts, terminology, best practices, and strategies. This is something that will be covered in a later section, and I consider it to be the "flour" in *Healthy Dough*. Without a baseline of financial knowledge, it will be very difficult to build and maintain a strong financial situation. You need to be able to speak the language to make informed decisions. Imagine yourself at an international restaurant, looking at a menu written in a language you can't read, realizing you have no idea what you're about to order, kicking yourself for assuming the menu would have pictures, and determining that your only option is to hold up the menu and do the "point and pray." The potential consequences could be bad enough on date night; they're way too severe for something as important as your means of survival. You need functional knowledge and the ability to speak the language. Financial health implies sustainability, and even a colossal trust fund won't endure someone who doesn't know how, or care, to maintain it.

Adequate attention

Building and maintaining strong financial health takes some effort, but the pursuit shouldn't dominate daily life. A financially healthy individual is thoughtful about money and financial matters, but doesn't fixate on them. Your finances merely need to be given adequate attention and priority. Basic tasks such as budgeting, monitoring, and goal setting can go a long way.

Fixating on finances may seem like a productive pursuit, but it's not healthy in the bigger picture of life. I'm a number crunching nerd with goals and vision and anxiety about general preparedness, so I personally have to be very careful in this area. Obsession is typically not a healthy behavior, even if it's focused on positive things like goals and dreams. Constantly checking bank balances and investment performance, incessantly reading headlines and making micro-adjustments, and centering your whole brain around money isn't necessary. Really, it can even be counterproductive. Too little focus on finances is irresponsible; too much focus on finances is unhealthy.

Resources to meet basic needs

A person with strong financial health has resources to meet the basic needs of themselves and their dependents. The ability to accommodate basic needs such as nutrition and shelter should be reasonably assured to someone who is in a quality financial position.

Ethically sourced and responsible

The resources of a financially healthy individual are acquired in ways that are ethical and responsible. Money should be obtained legally and without the intent to screw anyone else over. You can be healthy, and even wealthy, without cheating or hurting anyone. Even if you're hot enough to be in "Ocean's Eleven" (or any other iteration of the gang), try not to make a career out of theft and deceit.

Picture a healthy economy like an old-growth evergreen forest. The giant trees all bend and maneuver ever so slightly over time, jockeying for the most prosperous position among the rest of the woodland. The ancient trees are simply reaching for the sun and taking the opportunities that they can; they're not intentionally trying to block out their neighbors from sunlight. Healthy individuals pursue prosperity in the same way; they thrive by simply taking their own opportunities to reach for the sun. They can have plenty of their own resources without sabotaging anyone.

Well-planned

A person with financial health has a plan in place to not run out of money at any point, including during working years and in retirement. They know that the best way to ensure liquidity is to prioritize planning through budgeting, goal setting, career planning, and thoughtful investing. The first steps toward retirement begin when you start working, and they don't end until you die, so plan accordingly.

Money maturity

Financial matters can be emotional, and rightfully so. Money and possessions are capable of pulling so firmly on our emotions because we associate them with security, safety, success, and our future. A person with strong financial health acknowledges the way that emotions add nuance to purchasing decisions, and also has the maturity to understand and respond to how they're feeling. They don't try to solve their mental, social, or emotional health challenges with money. Someone who is financially healthy is not likely to experience disproportionate emotions associated with the valuation of money and things. Money maturity comes down to making choices that properly incorporate both the brain and the heart.

On the other side, someone who tries to solve personal issues with money and possessions is not likely grounded when it comes to finances, and needs to improve this aspect of their overall health. A cliché example of this is the midlife crisis sports car. Having a sports car can be fun, but it's expensive and unlikely to solve most underlying problems related to middle age. Doing 90 with the top down just moves a person through the present, not back in time. Someone with money maturity understands how to deal with things in a manner that directly addresses the issue, rather than distracting from it.

Grateful, but growing; mindful, but motivated

Think of your present and future like a long walk in deep snow. Most of your focus is on the steps right in front of you, because it's easy to stumble if you're looking too far ahead. As you find your stride, you can allow yourself to soak up your immediate surroundings. Enjoy all of the beauty you see, but not at the expense of your footing. Take time here and there to pause and observe what you're approaching, and what's far ahead. Confirm that you're still going the direction that you've been intending. Allow yourself to dream of the joy your destination will deliver, but don't expect it to be more meaningful than the walk.

In modern culture, we often tromp through the trail, thinking only of the destination, and forget to soak up the present. I admit that I'm a repeat offender in constantly looking ahead and ignoring what's around me in a given moment (literally and figuratively). The recent boom of mindfulness practices is an important reaction to the busy, distracted, anxious lives people in our culture tend to lead. Finances are one of many areas in which gratefulness and mindfulness are necessary. A person with financial health is proud and appreciative of their financial stability, and works to protect it

— but that doesn't mean that they think they're "done" developing their financial life. Being content with present circumstances is no excuse to assume that your financial goals have been met forever. Unfortunately, when it comes to finances, "It ain't over till it's over." A retirement from a career doesn't mean a retirement from focusing on financial matters — it just means you aren't working anymore. For better or worse, we need to mind our money until we no longer have basic needs to meet. A person with financial health is aware and present in their daily life, but understands the need for continued growth and protection. They have a healthy balance of enjoying the present and looking to the future. Grateful, but growing; mindful, but motivated.

Some people aren't content with any amount of money, even extreme independent wealth. Think about the ultrarich — does their money seem to make them happy, or are they living proof that wealth isn't necessarily fulfilling? Whether they're hoarding billions or demanding their 16th birthday be televised, I speculate that many have very little daily appreciation for the wealth they have. They don't appreciate the present, they're not grateful, and they always think they deserve more. These are examples of when even the ultrarich have poor financial health, and need to pull their heads out of their assets.

Eye for value

A person with financial health primarily spends money on things that add value to their life in some way. They may validate spending money on investing in assets, wellness, or even fulfillment. They don't spend money on things that don't add value to their life, and they understand that value is not necessarily a monetary term. Value is about benefit, and you can gain value without breaking the bank. It's much easier to save when you find ways to have fun and enjoy life without spending money. I believe simply going for a walk with someone is a deeper and cheaper way to bond compared with going to a fancy restaurant together. The pleasant experience of fine dining may add some value to your day, but it can't compete with building real connections with yourself, nature, and your loved ones.

Consistent quality

When finances are consistently a positive part of a person's life, they have strong financial health. The attainment and use of resources such as money, land, and material things can be a net positive in your life. This means that the benefits of having or using these resources are greater than any negativity encountered in acquiring them. In other words, don't ruin your life trying to get rich. Strive for financial health in ways that allow you to experience a free and balanced life.

The Fourth Circle of Health

We live in a time in which the interconnectivity of health, in all its forms, is accepted as scientific fact. Reactions to this reality have expanded the scope of health care and introduced huge changes to societal and cultural norms. Slowly but surely, the world has adapted to embrace the Wellness Triangle: the idea that our well-being is the cumulative product of physical, mental, and social health.

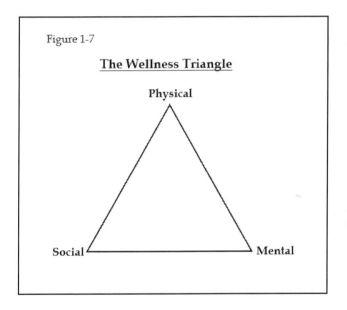

Figure 1-7

The Wellness Triangle

Physical

Social

Mental

I learned about the Wellness Triangle (drawn from memory in Figure 1-7) in high school health class, and it's been camped out in my brain ever since. The idea may seem simple now, but when it was introduced 25 years ago it probably made a splash on par with a breaching humpback. Notice the symbolism in the lines of the triangle, connecting each corner of health to the other two. Whether you call it the Wellness Triangle, Health Triangle, Triangle of Wellness, Triangle of Truth, Equilateral Equilibrium, or simply "total health," the concept is the same: physical, mental, and social health each contribute to complete and balanced wellness.

Until the 1990's, the term "health" was often only associated with physical health. Then we were illuminated by the Wellness Triangle, which indicated there's more to us than just thumbs and teeth. Imagine human beings as machines, with physical health relating to hardware, and mental and social health similar to software. Physical health may be measured by the functionality and performance of the body, such as the heart, lungs, muscles, teeth, bones, joints, tendons, ligaments, skin, other organs, and hormones. Physical health indicators are likely to have a numerical measurement, making them easy to compare and benchmark. You can measure blood pressure, weight, bone density, blood sugar, triglycerides, and so on.

Before I give a high-level summary of *mental health,* I should clarify that this overview is simply my own interpretation and understanding of the topic. This is based on my grade school classwork and my own experiences, and I am not a licensed expert. Please seek out resources to educate yourself thoroughly on mental health to best understand how it impacts yourself and others. That said, here's my crack at a synopsis.

Mental health is a more abstract and less measurable aspect of health and wellness by nature. For that reason, I think it's easiest to provide examples of both balanced and unbalanced mental health. In my view, an individual is likely to have balanced mental health if they are able to process emotions and stress without feeling debilitated, and if they generally feel "OK" day to day. A mentally balanced person may realize that while not every day is perfect, adversity is a surmountable part of life. I can't really comment much beyond that. A person with *unbalanced* mental health may experience undue difficulty processing emotions and stress. They may feel inadequate or hopeless. They may be affected by congenital conditions such as bipolar disorder or schizophrenia, or non-congenital conditions such as depression, anxiety, or post-traumatic stress disorder. Day-to-day life can be very difficult when these challenges are present.

Social health relates to how an individual interacts with society. To put it another way, social health encompasses the ways relationships impact wellness. This includes friendships, intimate relationships, relationships with coworkers, interactions with strangers, and family relationships.

As the triangle tells us, physical, mental, and social wellness are interconnected. Social and mental health can impact physical health. Physical health can impact mental and social health. Social and mental health are extremely correlated. Consider the following examples:

Depression and anxiety (mental health) can each negatively impact sleep patterns, which negatively affect hormones, leading to unhealthy weight gain (physical health). A concussion (physical health) may impact the brain in a way that leads to short-term or long-term changes in behavior, such as mood swings (mental health), therefore making it difficult to interact with others (social health). An unhealthy relationship (social health) may lead to undue stress, resulting in a daily life that's hard to manage (mental health).

One of my favorite anecdotes about interconnected health comes from singer-songwriter superstar Adele, who preaches the amazing benefits of focusing on balanced wellness. When discussing her weight loss of over 100 pounds, she explained that it wasn't really about weight, but about feeling better. Her story is an example of a total life transformation with a side benefit of losing a significant amount of unwanted weight. She found that being active and making her body strong improved her mental health and self-esteem. Just as importantly, she was clear that she did it for herself. She wasn't trying to be "good enough" for anyone else, and wasn't succumbing to social pressures that teach women to desperately seek aesthetic approval. She chose to make her day-to-day life the way she wanted it to be, because she knew she deserved to feel good. By doing so, she captained a convincing victory in favor of wellness.

Total health connection

For those wondering when we'll shift back to personal finance, my response is a common phrase best spoken by Rafiki, the cartoon mandrill shaman from *The Lion King*: "It is time!" Simply put, health and finance are inseparably linked. I believe that finances affect and are affected by physical, mental, and social health. Personal finance is so important in the modern world that financial health has emerged as a true requirement for balanced wellness, and has inspired me to expand on the Wellness Triangle. I think that financial health has become the *Fourth Circle of Health*.

As you continue reading, consider the overlapping sections of the diagram shown in Figure 1-8. Can you think of any examples where financial health crosses over to affect mental or social health? Or the intersection between physical health and financial health? Can you think of an example to plot in the very center of the diagram, where all four health factors are in play?

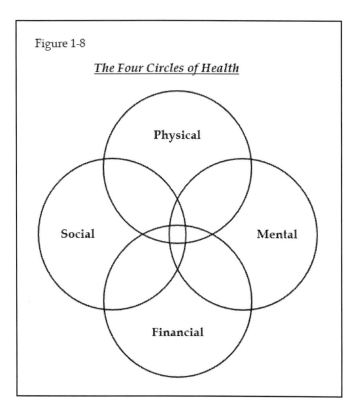

Figure 1-8

The Four Circles of Health

Physical

Social

Mental

Financial

Let's grab the low-hanging fruit to get started. Have you ever heard anyone say that they're stressed out about their finances? Have *you* ever stressed out about finances? Have you (or anyone you know) ever been stressed out by work, and is work your primary means of acquiring money? In recurring studies conducted by the American Psychological Association (APA), Americans list money and work among their top stressors. In the "Stress in America" survey conducted in 2022, the APA reported that 66% of Americans were stressed out about money, and 66% were stressed out about work (also worth noting is that 49% were stressed about personal health concerns).[i] The funny thing about money is that most people have to work for it – it isn't optional. My conclusions from these survey results are that the majority of American households have to work for money, and work is stressful, and so are finances. Ouch. The correlation between financial health and stress levels (mental health) is undeniable.

Now that you are starting to see what I mean about the *Fourth Circle of Health*, let's review some more examples.

Financial health x Physical health

An individual in poor physical health will likely have higher than average medical expenses, which will negatively impact their financial health. Some medical issues may be congenital and unavoidable, but many are highly preventable.

The most prevalent form of financially costly physical health issues can be found in obesity statistics, since obesity is strongly correlated with major health conditions. According to the Centers for Disease Control and Prevention (CDC), obesity-related conditions include heart disease, stroke, type 2 diabetes, and certain types of cancer. The estimated annual medical cost of obesity in the United States was $147 billion in 2008, and medical costs for people who had obesity were $1,429 higher than medical costs for people with healthy weight. [ii] Obesity rates have been increasing over time, despite being considered highly preventable in most cases. From 1999-2000 through 2017-18, U.S. obesity prevalence increased from 30.5% to 42.4%. I'll openly admit that for about seven years during that time range, I was part of that statistic. Now, I can happily say that I've made lifestyle changes to keep the weight off for good, and that my health care costs have gone down as a result.

In addition to increased expenses associated with poor physical health, an individual with poor financial health may not even be able to afford *access* to care, which can perpetuate preventable physical health issues, or make it impossible to treat ailments of any kind (the same could be said for mental health). In fact, the leading cause of bankruptcy in the United States is medical expenses.[iii]

Financial health x Mental health

An individual who struggles with mental health issues may find it more difficult to maintain steady employment, which has an obvious negative impact on financial health. Some mental health challenges may also adversely affect decision making and rationalization, leading to poor financial habits. I want to acknowledge again that mental health is remarkably complex, and while some disorders make it impossible to maintain traditional employment, others do not. There are less disruptive mental health issues for which mitigating strategies and specialized services that come with treatment may be able to help an individual function more easily at work.

Poor financial health can also *lead* to mental health challenges such as depression, anxiety, and low self-esteem. Unfortunately, mental health care typically costs money, making the challenge even harder for individuals to address.

Financial health x Social health

The most preventable financial nightmares can be caused by social health issues, because of two things: *people and lifestyle.* Try to think of a friend, family member, married couple, or coworker who derives their self-esteem by spending money on luxury. I bet it wasn't hard to come up with at least one. Financial disaster may await those who choose social circles where hemorrhaging money on nonessentials is not only tolerated, but *required.* I've known people who cut friends out of their social circle for skipping a night on the town or friendcation. I've known people who literally gave away their lunch money because they thought it was the only way to make friends. I've known people who thought the only reason people liked them was because they paid for everything. Okay, so in some cases, that may be true — but that doesn't mean it's healthy!

It's also extremely important to note that one of the top causes of bankruptcy in the United States, in addition to medical expenses, is divorce. The even scarier part is that according to a recent study, the fifth leading cause of divorce is financial issues.[iv] Dang, double whammy! In some cases, couples have divorced at least in part due to financial problems, and wind up bankrupt by the time the lawyers get paid. On the other side of the coin, some individuals don't feel able to leave unhealthy or abusive partnerships for a number of reasons, the fear of making ends meet being one of them. A toxic cocktail is created when bad finances blend with bad relationships.

There are other readily observable examples of the correlations and even causation of multifaceted issues involving financial health. But before we go further, I want to clarify that health and fitness are not the same thing.

Health and fitness are not the same thing

Health and fitness are often lumped together, and while they may have a strong correlation, they aren't synonymous. Fitness is about capability. Think about the general usage of the term "physical fitness," and how it describes the *ability* to achieve physical feats. It takes physical fitness to run a marathon, play sports professionally, go on a weeklong backpacking trip, lifeguard at a public beach, or serve as a combat soldier. But is a person who is physically fit also guaranteed to be physically healthy? Consider that the same individuals I just listed with great physical fitness could have challenges with physical *health*. For example: a marathon runner with an eating disorder; a professional athlete abusing drugs to cope with the pressure; a backpacker with a vitamin deficiency; a lifeguard with skin cancer; a deployed combat soldier with a history of heat stroke. These examples are all sadly quite feasible, and you may even have anecdotal history observing or *experiencing* similar disconnects between health and fitness. I've certainly misinterpreted health and fitness in my personal life, much to my own expense. Fitness is about ability; health is about balance, function, and sustainability. A healthy person is more likely to be fit, and a fit person may be more likely to be healthy, but health and fitness are empirically distinct.

Let's expand on the example of a professional athlete facing a substance abuse disorder that erodes their actual health. It's a regrettably common occurrence among athletes who are miraculously fit and physically capable, but have serious health concerns due to addiction. And it's not just physical health, but mental, social, and financial health that are impacted as well. More than once, I've read headlines about athletes who have died young in the presence of substance abuse. In such cases, the causes of death are commonly reported as organ failure, overdose, impaired driving, or suicide. Regardless of whether or not they are paid millions of dollars to play their favorite game, the strain of professional sports affects more than just an athlete's body. In addition to the pressure of having a job in general, expectations from fans and the media are intense. Such interactions can be severely socially unhealthy, ranging from being worshipped like modern mythology to receiving death threats for not doing a good enough job. *Ace Ventura: Pet Detective* taught us how hard it can be to miss a field goal in the United States ("Laces *out*").

Some athletes make the mistake of turning to substances in an attempt to cope, and some try to gain an edge. Some party too hard once the velvet ropes start opening; some abuse anabolic steroids to try to improve performance. Others drink too much when the grind won't stop, and nothing seems good enough for anyone; and others pick up a nasty new pill addiction after a knee surgery. Maybe they've even struggled since they were a kid. I speculate that most elite athletes who lose their millions of earnings do so because of unbalanced mental and social health. My point is, health and fitness are not the same thing. Keep an eye out and make sure you don't get them confused.

My fitness follies

As a millennial born in the early 1990s, I'm culturally obligated to talk and write about myself even if no one asks. As such, I want to share some personal experiences that have contributed to the philosophies of *Healthy Dough*. I'm going to recount some of the monumental times when I confused health and fitness in all *Four Circles* of my health — physical, mental, social, and financial — and what I wish I knew at the time. My hope in doing this is to demonstrate my credibility, lack of judgement on others, and honesty regarding the topic of health versus fitness. Honesty and accountability shine the sunlight that fuels personal growth. Lies and excuses are the only manure in the world that can't grow squat.

I've always had a life full of love and opportunity, just as I do now; but I've often struggled to take care of my *Four Circles of Health*, and I own all accountability for that now. Looking back, I wish I'd understood total wellness and taken care of myself sooner. I wish I had the same perspectives then that give me so much more comfort now, in the current stage of my life. I hope my stories inspire you to take a deep look at how you want your financial health to impact your life.

Feel free to wince or chuckle at my mistakes — some are actually kind of funny (but only now, after I've found ways to manage myself and prevent similar patterns). These are topics that I still have to sort through and categorize at any given point in my life; but I feel grateful to have come up with a framework that allows me to do so. I'm also grateful to be able to share the same framework with you. This is my story.

I decided at an early age that I was going to be rich. One of my earliest memories of childhood is explaining to my parents that I'd buy them a house on the water once I was wealthy. My 8-year-old self was quite certain I'd earn my money juggling three simultaneous careers: pilot, author, and marine biologist. Creative writing and sea life were my true passions at the time, but the reason I wanted to fly was because the only pilot I knew had a three-story house with a water view. As time went on I found my greatest aptitude was in arithmetic, and was probably not going to be in aviation. My career dreams became more practical with age, and I decided to use my fascination and skill with numbers to my advantage. It seemed like a logical path to the arbitrary affluence I intended to achieve. Eventually, I sought a career in financial business.

Let's jump to my early adult life, starting with when I was in college and narrowing down a specific career choice. I had earned good grades in college, was a student organization president, and worked in addition to attending school. My professors had explained that a high percentage of financial executives are CPAs with an audit background, and I wanted to be a CFO. The work sounded semi-interesting and promised to pay handsomely. So, I decided to become a CPA and picked a high-demand career as an auditor. In the infancy of my adulthood, I was pretty traditionally successful. I worked hard to position myself to be a high earner, and was actively recruited by the top firms in my market. I accepted my first professional job in the fall of my senior year, a year in advance of my start date. The state of Washington requires CPA candidates to have earned five years of college credits to sit for the licensing exam, and I finished those five years of coursework in 47 months. Not bad for a kid who failed a high school history class and earned a "D" in 11th grade English (more on that later).

I had some great times in college, but from day one I was fixated on completing school so I could move on to a "better" part of my life when I could be rich. I dreamed of how nice it was going to be to no longer be a broke college student. I knew that soon I'd be able to earn enough money to spend on fun things in addition to being able to survive, save, and invest. It was going to be cool, and I was going to be cool. As cool as an accountant can be, at least.

In my first job out of college, I earned more money than most people my age (more than most Americans in general, in fact) and was financially savvy. That part of my ascent to wealth was right on track. To summarize, I was very financially fit. But I was not financially healthy, nor was I physically, mentally, or socially healthy. My issues in those areas began long before my career, and even before college; but it was during my adult life when they started accelerating faster than a Mario Kart character blasting over a speed boost.

For the majority of my three chaotic years as an auditor, I worked very long hours. When I wasn't working, I was often studying for the CPA exam, including during my paid time off. I liked most of the people I worked with and I liked most of my clients, but I hated my job and I hated the lifestyle. I earned the scheduled promotion to senior associate after two years, but I dreaded work every single day and never felt confident in my abilities. I was surviving, not thriving. I didn't lack desire or aptitude, so why was my career so miserable? I credited burnout and fatigue for my consistent discomfort, and blamed nearly all of my stress on work, but that wasn't totally accurate.

During those years (and years prior), I had mental and social health issues that I simply chose to ignore. I didn't want to admit that I was influenced by anxiety and depression, because it felt silly to do so when I had an objectively quality life. I was as insecure as a mountain snowdrift in the spring — in other words, I was an impending avalanche. I pretended my challenges were just the daily weather as opposed to the climate. Plus, I wanted to feel unbreakable, so I decided to forge ahead. I was going to be so great and successful, and it was going to fix my life. Well, it didn't work. I lost sight of my health, and my quality of life suffered as a result.

People are often surprised when I share that I've had long-standing issues with anxiety and depression (mental health) and self-esteem (social health). I've been told that I "present" well, speak confidently, and am generally lighthearted and positive in social settings. That doesn't sound like the classic face of depression, but it's there just the same. In fact, I think positivity and connecting with people are great ways to cope.

Back in high school I had an abundance of ways to distract from my mental and social health challenges. I could combat my depression with fulfillment from sports, socialization, and student leadership activities. My anxiety was subdued by the hours I spent on physical activities: football, basketball, lifting weights, going for long walks, running in the woods until I threw up, etc. I received enough external validation that I rarely reached for self-esteem when I needed to summon confidence. The problem is, energy from external validation is like fossil fuel; you use it, and then it's gone. To summarize, I subconsciously used my physical and social *fitness* to combat my mental and social *health* issues, and in some ways that was a positive thing. But I was treating the symptoms, not the disease, and my challenges were neither stymied nor isolated.

When your coping mechanisms involve fun and movement, a traditional classroom can be a challenging venue. My anxiety made sitting in class a serious chore, so I did a lot of wandering, socializing, and joking around when I was supposed to be studying. Honestly, that part was pretty enjoyable for me. Depression made it hard to focus and find motivation, possibly because I couldn't seem to connect my schoolwork to any meaningful external reward. I have zero memory of doing homework in high school. I simply stopped challenging my brain, and funneled my mental energy solely into things that made me feel my best in the moment. I was mostly able to skate through high school without much effort, but not always. I failed a class, got a few "D"s, and on multiple occasions had to raise my GPA to stay eligible for sports. My lack of focus and effort wasn't just limited to the classroom, either. I was eager and willing to physically work hard in practice and games, but I was not very coachable. In hindsight, maybe my lack of mental effort was a way to feel some control, or maybe my mind was so cloudy that I wasn't going to learn much even when I tried. Maybe I was too insecure to go out of my comfort zone, for risk of failing and not recovering. No matter the reasons at the time, I stifled my previously curious and ambitious brain.

Despite all that drama, my high school experience was often a blast. I had amazing friends and made memories I still greatly enjoy. But when it was suddenly time to graduate, I realized my study habits needed to improve so I could achieve my dreams of being wealthy and "successful." I enrolled in the local community college for a variety of reasons: I needed to learn *how* to learn; I wanted to limit distractions; I was horrified at the cost of university tuition; and my grades limited my four-year options anyway. I subconsciously decided that it was time to make up for my lack of scholarly achievement, and began to prioritize the pursuit of wealth over all else. I started college with the intent of becoming a workhorse.

I began college at an athletic 195 pounds, and began my adult life in great shape from the active lifestyle of my youth. But it wasn't long until I discovered hoppy beer and started eating so much microwaveable food that I should have worn a radiation suit. I lost sight of my prior fulfillment and coping activities, and tried to replace them with school and employment (neither of which I found fulfilling at the time). I kept lifting weights but was very sedentary otherwise. I opted to manage my ever-growing stress with lots of pot pies, processed foods, and beverages. As you may have guessed, this plan was not favorable for my physical, mental, or social health (or financial, for that matter). Some folks gain the "Freshman 15," but I quadrupled down and went for the "Sophomore 60." I gained nearly 60 pounds in two years, topping out at over 250 pounds at a height of 5 feet, 11 inches (fine, 5 feet, 10 1/2 inches). Whoops!

After realizing I was so out of shape that I literally couldn't run a mile without winding up hurt, I decided to lose the weight. After 14 months of restrictive eating, I was down to 205 pounds. This was just before college graduation, and I was in the best shape I had ever been in. I was typically the strongest and most muscular person in a given room (trust me, I always had to check). My physical confidence bounced between delusional extremes like a tennis ball in a match between self-absorption and self-doubt. Being the kind soul that I am, I happily shared my insecurity with the public by flexing in pictures and taking my shirt off at inappropriate times. To be fair, I loved taking my shirt off when I was obese as well, but in more of a football gameday comedic manner.

As I mentioned previously, my college coursework went well and I quickly found lucrative employment, so I thought I had it made once I was back in shape. At age 22, I developed a vision of my future self being great at everything for the rest of my life, along with the expectation that I'd do anything I could in order to achieve it. I was going to doggedly climb the corporate ladder, keep off the duffel bag of fat I'd just lost, and have unmitigated success in every phase of life. My friends, I'll remind you that I was going to be *so* cool. Probably so cool that the Red Hot Chili Peppers would invite me out to dinner, Oprah would pronounce my bench press as one of her favorite things, and people would look up to me. Maybe the first two are an exaggeration, but I really did want to be someone that other people would want to be (spoiler alert, big mistake!). I'd buy a giant waterfront house that was fancier than Dijon mustard. I'd do cool things like write 5-foot-long novelty checks to save the community center, and in the feel-good news articles that chronicled the deed, I'd only have one chin in the photos. I expected to be rich and fit for the rest of time, and I was certain I'd achieve that. It was going to be enough for me to finally feel OK. For the first time in my life, I was going to be good enough for myself, and good enough for everyone else. I just knew it.

Well, to wrap up that thought, my plan of being fit, rich, and jubilant did *not* happen the way I thought it was going to. My first mistake in evaluating my (then) present and future selves was that I confused health with fitness, in both my physical ideals and my financial ideals. On top of that, I refused to acknowledge my challenges with mental and social health, except when I was using them as excuses for poor behavior. Really, I wouldn't even acknowledge they were a real thing, let alone my struggle with them. I am a guy, after all. I never gave any thought to what might bring me fulfillment. I was very physically fit when I started my career, and had the ability to do things that most people couldn't; but I was *not* necessarily physically healthy. Plus, the fitness didn't last anyway.

Even though my cardiovascular strength was good enough to perform intense exercise, I had horrible blood pressure, as was confirmed at each doctor's visit. I learned that stress, alcohol, caffeine, and salt are the big drivers of blood pressure, and let's just say I went four-for-four on that checklist. By 23, my blood pressure was off the charts, and I was prescribed medication in hopes of mitigating subtle inconveniences such as a heart attack. My doctor read my charts, looked me in the eyes, and said, in these exact words: "Dude, your blood pressure *sucks*." I didn't fill the prescription, because I knew I needed better habits more than I needed pills (it took a while, but I eventually got there). I never had my organs tested, but I also suspect I had poor kidney and liver function. Even though I was generally happy with my relationships, physically fit, financially strong, and others told me I was "successful," I was not a prototype for total wellness.

My feelings of invincibility did not last long, and my career started consuming my life. I continued to self-medicate my anxiety and depression with alcohol, which of course led to more anxiety and depression. It only took two years to gain back 40 pounds, despite muscle loss from a restricted exercise schedule. My face was so puffy that it looked like "Fit Dan" had been stung by a bee. As much as I loved joking about it then (and still love it now), I was insecure about my weight gain. But my physical appearance had very little to do with my eventual decision to get back in shape (more on this in a moment). I felt like crap, I slept like it too, and my best self was hiding in some other dimension. Maybe hardest of all was that I felt like I had instantly failed to achieve the "perfect" vision I had seen for myself.

My intense work schedule sometimes required me to choose between exercise, sleep, or seeing my people. I mostly chose to see my people, and I don't regret that choice; but I struggled to make time to exercise, and I lost most of the physical fitness I had worked so hard to achieve (not to mention exacerbating my other physical health struggles). My social health suffered because I was constantly spending time working and traveling for work, and my daily discomfort affected my relationships. My mental and emotional health struggled due to the impacts of stress; insufficient coping strategies demonstrated suboptimal *abilities* to properly address my issues. So, bad health and bad fitness.

I was financially fit, and was earning and investing in ways that have since brought even more favorable results than I had anticipated. But my desire for money led me to stay in a job that wasn't right for me. I hated it. I was once so overwhelmed that I thought I had the flu. But after taking half the day off, I realized the real reason I had to run out of the conference room to throw up was my stress level. Doing things that you hate simply because you want more money is not financially healthy, even if your wealth is growing.

I don't blame my job for my poor health in that era; instead, I accept that poor health was merely a by-product of my choices. I could have pursued a less demanding job, I could have sought mental health counseling, I could have done 10-minute home workouts, I could have drunk less, and I could have asked my loved ones how I made them feel. There was a lot within my control that I let float by. Some people fail and make excuses;

others fail and make progress. I'm thankful every day that I eventually chose to become a person who turns challenges into strengths. I left the CPA firm on good terms, and found a more sustainable career path that I feel successful in. I've figured out my favorite ways to find fulfillment (move; create; learn; give) and allow myself ample opportunities to pursue those things. It took several years of hard work to get my health to where it is now, but every ounce of effort has been worth it. I now have sharp coping strategies for mental and emotional challenges, I have good relationships, and I'm in the best physical shape of my life — even better than that idealistic college senior who desperately wanted to be better than everyone.

Mental health counseling has taught me that I really don't care as much about what other people think, and that I'd been using the opinions of others to buoy my own self-esteem. I still work very hard professionally and recreationally, but I've learned not to care as much about "results" as much as I do about "experience." I can be mindful, grateful, and present, and I can use tools like journaling to keep myself consistent in those manners. I no longer strain so hard for weightlifting personal bests that I need medical attention year-round. I enjoy limiting delicious treats to special occasions, rather than consistently bingeing them on weekends. I no longer set my career goals based solely on pay. Never again will I run a half-marathon so recklessly hard that I pass out 1,000 yards short of the finish line. (OK, time for our first *Dangent* [Dan tangent]. So what happened was, I saw the finish line, and I started sprinting so I could blow past "red shorts guy," who had recently passed me and ignited a burning fury rivaled only by the smoke-filled heat wave we happened to be racing in. Then I realized the finish line was a mirage. According to the nurses I had suffered from heat exhaustion and kidney failure, which is why I continued sprinting right up until I woke up in an ambulance. That night I vacationed in a hospital bed with an IV in each arm. I call it *"the Half-Marathon that Cost Me $5k."* True story). No, it's been much different for me the more I've learned about myself and my health. After I ran my first full marathon in June 2021, the sorest part of my body was my jaw — because I literally smiled throughout the entire race, making sure to say a genuine "thank you" to every volunteer. Even at the top of each foothill along that course in the Olympic Mountains, when I was sucking air and my knees wanted to punch me in the face — pure joy and gratitude. I was happier than a dog chasing a tennis ball. I lift weights with good form because I can finally accept that someone may be stronger than me. My brain has enough energy to actually finish this book, after years in the making. I'm finally comfortable enough with who I am that I can write in my own voice, rather than pretending to be artificially impressive. And while I hope the book takes off and becomes part of a lucrative brand, I know it's worth my time even if it doesn't — simply because I am enjoying writing it. I can admit that I'm not perfect, and that I'm not better than anyone, and it feels good.

I don't regret my choice to become a CPA and auditor, but rather, I wish I'd had the knowledge and perspectives to approach it differently. In chapter 18 we'll discuss that financial health requires you to "get good at something," and I'm still reaping the rewards of that early career experience, both financially and professionally. But the real reason for my success — I've been evaluated highly each year, doubled my initial salary in six years, and have a better life now — is that I have energy to take care of myself. My brain is now free to reach its full potential. I'm no smarter than I was in my early 20s (in fact, I've even had a concussion since then!) but I'm a better worker because I take better care of myself.

Wellness is about balance, function, and sustainability, and I did not have any of those things early in my adult life. It was my own fault, and that was great news — because that meant I also got to be the one to fix it. I experienced the contradiction that while I pursued money and accolades thinking I'd improve my quality of life, my fixation on them was actively *reducing* my quality of life. This is why *Healthy Dough* isn't about getting rich, it's about being financially healthy.

For some reason, I was content to let my ambition for money and career "success" undermine who I really am at heart, which is just a nice guy who likes to laugh and play outside. I thought that intensity and rigidity would make me good enough in other people's eyes, and good enough for myself. In hindsight, this "ideal" image I had for myself kind of sounds like a, well — it rhymes with whoosh tag. I was always sure that money was going to finally make me feel OK. *A new promotion and then I'll be fine. A new house and then I'll be fine. More money and I'll be fine.* But that's not how it goes.

I am still very driven and can be intense about my goals, but I've lost some of the rigidity. I can go with the flow, and know that *nothing* will ever make me as happy as being myself, and being well. I still deal with anxiety and depression, but I manage it with skill and effort, and don't let it obscure the wonderful realities of my life. I know that what I really want is health, not wealth or external validation. The nifty thing about that revelation is that by sticking to being myself, and prioritizing my health first, I'm actually having *more* success physically, mentally, socially, and financially.

Total health takeaways

Reading *Healthy Dough* may not make earning money less stressful (although it might!), but my hope is that it helps make *keeping* money less stressful. This book can't cure health problems, but it can help you be financially prepared to pay for treatment. It may not make it easier for you and your romantic partner to navigate multifamily holiday logistics, but it could help your relationship by preventing strain from financial woes. It won't make you cool, but it can make you savvy. I want to empower you to understand the impact of your financial decisions so that you can make choices to support your life goals. You deserve the knowledge base and perspectives to help achieve wallet wellness and a comfortable financial life that will benefit your well-being as a whole.

The Five Truths of Financial Health

Now that we've discussed how all areas of health interact with each other, it's time to look at the realities of how daily behaviors can translate into financial results. The vast majority of the time, behaviors and habits are a choice. Staying informed on any given subject matter is imperative to forming quality habits on that subject. For example, it's tough to eat well with no knowledge of nutrition, and it's tough to save money with no knowledge of finance. The relationship between money and behaviors is undeniable, which is why I've come up with the *Five Truths of Financial Health*. As you read this book, keep in mind that these truths are the basis of everything from cover to cover. Remember these five principles when you think about how you want to conduct your daily life:

1: It's easier to prevent health problems than it is to fix them

In all components of health, prevention is better than cure. This truth is easy to see in physical, social, and mental health. For example, it's much harder to lose 60 pounds of fat than it is to practice portion control (trust me). It's much easier to set clear expectations for respect and kindness than it is to repair, or end, a toxic relationship. It's easier to say no to tobacco than it is to kick an addiction. It's much easier to address small things one-by-one than it is to resolve a pent-up mental breakdown.

The same principles are true in financial health. It's easier to live within your means than it is to get out of debt. For most, it's easier to invest in career development early in life, rather than later, when life tends to get busier and more complicated. If you start saving for retirement at age 40, you'll have 18 fewer years to save compared to having started at 22. Don't trash your finances with excessive debt, unhealthy spending, inadequate earnings, and compressed savings timelines. Whether young, middle-aged, or older, taking care of your financial health *right now* is always going to be easier than fixing unhealthy finances later.

2: Healthy people get more value from their money

Healthy people get more value out of their hard-earned money. Their wages go on to support things that benefit to their lives, which leaves them much more satisfied with how their money is spent. Being able to save, invest, and occasionally treat yourself are some of the many signs of balanced health. Conversely, health challenges can lead to increased in-the-moment spending and well beyond.

Physical, mental, and social health difficulties can result in higher expenses, poor spending habits, and even hinder the ability to earn money through employment. The state of being unhealthy is expensive, and so are the habits that lead to it. Some health problems are completely unpreventable, but that's not what I'm referring to. The issue at hand is spending valuable resources on habits that cause preventable health problems. Excessive nonessential spending on things such as junk food, drugs, alcohol, tobacco, and unnecessary luxuries can be highly correlated with physical, mental, and social health problems down the road. Trying to solve such problems by spending money is very expensive, both in the near term and long term, and usually works out as well as a trashy dating show relationship.

No one wakes up in the morning, puts their work pants on, takes a sip of their coffee, makes that obnoxious "Ahhh" sound that seems required in every beverage commercial, and smiles while thinking, "I sure hope I have to use part of today's paycheck to pay for blood pressure medication next month." People want their money to add value and security to their lives. They don't want to be forced to use their wages to fix preventable problems or buy things that don't actually mean anything to them. It's much more satisfying to save, give, and fund their fulfillment buckets.

3: Discipline is an exhaustible resource, and healthy financial habits take discipline

Studies on endurance training have shown that when an individual is strained from non-physical activities, their physical endurance decreases and their rate of perceived exertion increases[v]. In a "time to exhaustion" cycling test, researchers found that comparable individuals had much less physical endurance after they played a repetitive computer game that was not physically demanding, but required a high degree of focus. Picture it as a monotonous task in which you're afraid to blink in case you miss something; edge-of-your-seat excitement, but not in a fun way. One can assume that these activities relate to strain on the central nervous system, caused by stress of the computer task. The nervous system strain decreases energy, motivation, and discipline.

Anecdotes from my own life came into focus when I read about the study referenced above, since I've personally experienced similar results. In the past, when a disproportionate amount of my discipline went to a specific aspect of my life — like during times of severe stress, anxiety, or depression — the discipline in other areas of my life suffered. I experienced significant decreases in self-control, motivation, and abilities; I was more likely to eat too much, exercise less, communicate poorly with my loved ones, and ignore mental health. In addition to harming my physical, mental, and social health, I tended to spend way more money if my energy felt totally tapped.

I've had instances in which my self-control was drained significantly by merely showing up to my job and not quitting on the spot. That caliber of strain has never failed to interfere with my energy for other activities. I typically run for an hour or two on Saturdays, and it's usually my favorite time of the week. I run through beautiful parks, enjoy the fresh air, and am thankful for the use of my body. Sometimes I coast, and sometimes I really push it, and both are equally as enjoyable for me. It's ridiculously fun, and absolutely liberating. After all, there was a time when I couldn't run a mile without acquiring a week's worth of shin splints and tendinitis. However, I've observed that I'm materially slower, struggle to achieve distance, and feel more fatigued during my run if I've had a bad work week or other personal stress. In those times, the run can actually be miserable, even though it is usually my favorite thing to do. A stressful week doesn't actually fatigue my legs or lower my lung capacity, so why can't I perform up to my normal abilities? I believe this is because my central nervous system is fatigued from maintaining discipline in those other situations. It takes energy to slog through a bad work week or keep my cool in tough social situations — the type of stuff that I don't feel like doing, but believe doing them is better than not. My brain is responding to its own diagnostic tests, telling me to stop powering through, take a rest, and let my nervous system recharge. It's putting me in the conservatory "low power mode," like a phone or a laptop does when its battery gets low.

In addition to the example above, I've found that staying disciplined and using energy in nonwork areas affects my work. I'm more likely to miss review steps, half-heartedly address emails, or care less about my work product if I'm feeling drained by other factors that require strict effort. This comes up for a variety of reasons, ranging from marathon training to depression to intense dieting to relationship issues.

Discipline is an exhaustible resource, and it can be drained by disproportionate energy used to stay disciplined in a given area. That said, you can — and should — work to develop your self-discipline battery capacity. You can increase the capacity of your discipline battery through personal growth and development, but it's still a just a battery. It gets used daily and needs to recharge. Elite members of the military, monks, and other extraordinary people may have exceptional discipline, but no human will ever have infinite endurance.

People are less likely to maintain financial discipline if their discipline battery is getting zapped by other areas of life. Self-control and quality decision-making take energy. If all of a person's energy is consumed by physical, mental, or social stress, they won't have much to give to their financial health. They'll be more likely to try to solve their other problems by spending money. They may not keep the money they earn if they use work stress as an excuse to validate unnecessary spending. Ever heard someone say that they deserve to buy what they want, since they deal with so much crap? "I deal with so much, so I deserve blank;" or, "I don't have energy to cook tonight, let's get pizza." Treating yourself sometimes is actually quite healthy, but the key word is "sometimes." And if your personal life is so exhausting that it negatively impacts your work, it may hinder your ability to grow in your career, let alone maintain employment.

Financial health requires self-control and discipline, and that requires energy. Later in the book we'll discuss how to get the most out of your batteries so that you can have consistent quality and success.

4: Healthy people pay attention

It's hard to know where your health stands if you don't pay attention, and it's hard to stay healthy when you don't know where you stand. People with strong physical, mental, and social health are aware of how things are going, what's working, and what isn't. Simply put, they pay attention. As a result, they're better informed. They're educated on wellness, but willing to learn and adapt when necessary.

They can *feel* when things are fine and when they're not. They can identify when they're not eating enough, or when they're eating too much. They'll recognize unhealthy social patterns before things get ugly. They know when they need a mental health day or a lifestyle change. They know how hard they can push themselves without getting hurt. They understand their strengths and challenges, and admit when they need to improve.

Financial health also requires you to pay attention. A person with financial health can recognize patterns and identify spending triggers. They can feel when their pursuit of money becomes toxic. They have well-informed goals. They monitor their finances and have an eye for opportunity.

Paying attention to your health is always a good thing, as long as you reach the proper conclusions based on what you notice. All the attention and analysis in the world won't do any good if the result is an unrealistic, unhealthy, or incorrect assessment such as, "I'm ugly, poor, and lonely because I'm a no-good loser." On the other hand, productive observations might include admitting a lack of control, or just as importantly, accepting areas where you *do* have control. Sometimes they might enable you to recognize unhealthy patterns. Sometimes a proper conclusion is that you have a weakness. And, there may also be times in which bad luck really did drive an unwanted outcome, and there's not much to learn or adjust. Just remember: the first step on the journey to personal mastery is the implied admission that you don't have it yet.

5: Health is better than wealth

People think they want to be wealthy, but they really just want freedom. Wealth can *support* freedom, but freedom and wealth aren't the same thing. Wealth can allow you to break loose from a nine-to-five job, add a sense of security, and provide opportunities to make a difference in things you care about. But wealth is just part of the picture of modern freedom. Wealth doesn't fix anxiety, social pressure, toxic relationships, or physical ailments. Wealth is a measure of financial assets, not quality of life. No, wealth isn't freedom; health is freedom.

Health is freedom of mind, body, and spirit. As someone who's wandered all over the wellness spectrum, I can say with certainty that feeling consistently healthy is *liberating*. Balanced health makes a difference in the potential greatness of every single day. It's the freedom of being able to use your mind and body as a highly functioning human, which feels amazing. It comes with more choice, opportunity, and clarity. When a person is physically, mentally, socially, and financially prepared, life simply feels freer.

The opposite of feeling free is feeling trapped or imprisoned. Things like anxiety and depression (mental), unsafe or unhealthy relationships (social), and ailments, both preventable and unpreventable (physical) are common examples of health problems that lead people to feel trapped. These are all things that can't be solved by the luxuries of wealth alone. They can only be treated with self-care, and professional assistance when necessary. Physical, mental, and social wellness cross over regularly to financial *health*, but they exist completely independently of wealth.

The reason financial health is better than wealth is because it is — by definition — a net positive in life, and works effectively with other health factors. For finances to be a net positive in someone's life, and therefore healthy, they need to leave other aspects of life unharmed. For example, a financially healthy person is able to pay for medical visits and counseling if necessary; they pay attention to their finances, but money doesn't control their life; they have enough financial stability that they can sometimes treat themselves to add a little extra joy. They might have the flexibility to choose a career with a work schedule that allows them to exercise and spend time with their family; or a financially healthy person can leave a bad relationship, if necessary, without fearing how they'll pay the bills. Wealth can help with these things too, but it's not interdependent and supportive in the same way that financial health is.

If you were to ask 100 random people if they wanted to be wealthy and why (or why not), you'd get mixed reviews. Some would desperately want wealth no matter what, some wouldn't want it because they think the pursuit of wealth is unethical, some wouldn't care either way, and some would want to know more details to see if it's actually worth it to them. However, if you were to ask those same people if they wanted financial health (and they knew how to define it), they'd all say yes. Financial wellness requires a certain level of satisfaction and acknowledgement of success, whereas wealth may or may not. It's possible to be both wealthy and healthy, but wealth is nonessential; health is essential.

Being rich only provides two truly meaningful things to a person's life: freedom, and resources to help others. And while wealth *can* provide or enhance freedom, the dreams of liberation may not materialize if not accompanied by balanced health. Wealth without health isn't true freedom. Financial health will always correlate directly with quality of life, but the same can't be said for wealth.

All the money, jewelry, vacations, and mansions in the world don't mean much if you're a miserable and unhealthy person. As 1990s rap legend the Notorious B.I.G. said, "Mo Money Mo Problems." That isn't always true, but it certainly can be. There are plenty of wealthy people with poor physical, mental, or social health, who think that their wealth gives them purpose or value. The glitter of wealth is so alluring to some people that it entices them to ignore their values, stop taking care of themselves, or even marry someone they don't love. You may be able to observe this in the media, or even in your own community or social groups. Money isn't their problem, and it's not their solution either.

As I've mentioned, I intend to be wealthy someday, but only because I want the freedom and philanthropic opportunities that being wealthy will provide. In the meantime, I'm happy to focus on prioritizing financial health rather than obsessing over early retirement and a vacation home. It's not up to me to say how people should live their lives, but I do know this — pursuing wealth at the expense of health is counterproductive in the pursuit of freedom. A healthy person knows that financial wellness is essential, and wealth is merely a bonus. Health is freedom, and therefore health is better than wealth.

Chapter 4: Introduction to Healthy Dough

Healthy Dough is a financial philosophy focused on wellness. Think of it as the basic ingredients in a recipe for financial success. The *Healthy Dough* philosophy relies on basic financial knowledge and thoughtful decision-making based on conceptual framework. Chefs and bakers know how to balance spice, acidity, sweetness, texture, and more in order to make all components of their creation play well together. Designing a financial plan is similar; each person's favorite recipe is a likely a little bit different, depending on what they're trying to make and their own personal tastes. Once you conceptually grasp how to make *Healthy Dough* you'll be able to create your own recipes for success.

Healthy Dough is about empowerment, education, and choice. I believe that everyone can define and achieve financial health in their own way. We can all do it; *you* can do it. You can create a balanced, healthy financial life that is a positive in your overall existence. Sure, I'll give you some specific recipes along the way. But my real goal is to teach you how to make *Healthy Dough* on your own.

Ingredients for Healthy Dough

Have you ever been to one of those urban markets with all the different varieties of food from across the globe? If you haven't, you're oppressing your taste buds. In a single grid of goodness, you may find freshly baked bread, pizza, cookies, dumplings, calzones, bao, empanadas, pasta, pastries, tamales, pretzels, and more. They could practically mop the floor with my drool. A fact that's not quite as delicious as the food, but equally amazing, is that all of these international cuisines share a common origin. Different as each flavor and filling may be, many of the world's most delightful foods start with dough.

Recipes for dough always use two primary ingredients: liquid and flour. A recipe may call for water or another liquid, and ask that it be paired with wheat flour, corn flour, cake flour, or any other kind of flour. When the liquid and flour are combined, they create dough. Regions all over the world have mastered this delicious chemical reaction and promoted it to be pillars of culture. A piroshki from Eastern Europe is actually quite similar to an Argentinian empanada, if you think of it as meat wrapped in dough; however, each shines independently with its own unique flavors. To differentiate their creations people use spices, oils, sugars, sprinkles, and other flavors and textures. But no matter what gets pulled out of the oven, it started off with simple liquid and flour.

Similar to edible dough, financial health has a couple of required ingredients. The first ingredient is basic knowledge of financial terms and concepts — this is your flour, or your base. The second ingredient is the ability to earn, save, and grow your money — this is your liquid. If you don't have both the financial knowledge *and* the ability to take action — sorry, you're not going to produce any dough. Financial health also calls for a financial strategy to suit personal preferences and goals — this is your flavor. To summarize, *Healthy Dough* consists of knowledge (flour), skill (liquid), and strategy (flavor). As long as you have your flour and liquid, you can make dough and add whatever flavor you're looking for. As long as you have financial knowledge and the ability to earn and save, you can add your own flavor and reach your financial goals. *Healthy Dough* is the nutritional staple that fuels success.

Knowledge (flour)

The base, or "flour," of your financial success is a basic understanding of financial terms and concepts. You need to be educated on these things so that you can understand what you see and hear. We'll cover some basic terminology and financial concepts to build a solid foundation for you. This isn't the most fun part of financial education, but I've observed that it can be very satisfying for people when they start recognizing words and basic concepts. Would you enjoy being lost in a foreign country, needing help to find your destination, with limited currency in your tourist fanny pack, and unable to comprehend the things you see and hear? Probably not — because being helpless isn't fun. Don't get into a similar situation with your financial health. The first step in taking control of your finances is learning to speak the language. Knowing basic terminology can save you from misunderstanding conversations, which can be very expensive. Need proof? Story time!

I was once on a vacation in Maui, and having a carefree chat with an older couple as we sat in the hot tub. It came up in conversation that I was a CPA, and they asked me if I had any tips for when they'd be ready to retire. One of the points I made was that they should not carry any debt into retirement if at all possible, and that one good indicator that someone is ready to retire is that they own a home and have no mortgage. They responded, sharply: "Why in the world wouldn't you keep your mortgage in retirement?" They immediately diagnosed me as a curly-headed fraud, and changed the subject. I realized after they left that they thought a mortgage was a synonym for home ownership. A mortgage is actually a *loan* used to purchase a home, so inherently, anyone who *has* a mortgage doesn't own their home outright. They literally had the term backward. Their confusion led them to shift the conversation instead of continuing to receive free financial advice from someone who wasn't trying to sell them anything. Knowing basic terminology and concepts will allow you to comprehend more as you read, research, discuss, and otherwise explore financial literacy. I'm excited to help you build a solid base as part of your financial education, even if you and I both think the section is sort of boring.

Skill (liquid)

Financial health can't be achieved solely through theoretical knowledge and textbook memorization; *Healthy Dough* requires liquid in addition to the base. You need certain skills in order to consistently earn and save. The most brilliant investor in the world can't build wealth if they have nothing to invest.

Most of us have to work in order to survive. We work to acquire money to pay for our basic needs such as food, water, and shelter. We also need to set some extra money aside in case we need it at a later time, especially a time when we're not working (such as retirement). Knowledge of financial concepts isn't enough to achieve financial success — action is needed, and that action is working to earn money, and saving some of that money. Earning and saving can be simplified into basic math, but it's more fun to look at it as a game. We will explore some practical tips and strategies for earning and saving as part of the Section 3 of this book, "Building a Winning Game Plan."

Strategy (flavor)

Designing a financial strategy to match your goals is crucial in creating your own perfect recipe for financial success. Your own version of *Healthy Dough* can be whatever you want it to be, and it's up to you to figure out. I'll suggest some of my favorite recipes and flavors, but I can't make specific recommendations for you. Just like I don't know your favorite foods or your allergies, I don't know you, your goals, career prospects, starting point, strengths, or challenges — so how could I tell you definitively what you want your financial health to look like? We will look into some strategies, best practices, and how to pick the right mix of flavors to suit your unique tastes.

Participating in personal finance

Most people are able to accept the need to earn money. They are often more intimidated by the need to build the knowledge base required to effectively manage and grow it. I understand that not everyone is fascinated by the nuts and bolts of finance. Some may even find the idea scary, boring, or both. Well, plane rides can be scary, boring, or both, but I hope that wouldn't keep you from vacation.

I don't know what your personal level of financial knowledge is at this point, but let's just pretend it's very minimal (for now). Imagine yourself as a preschooler in your first month of swim lessons. Do you want to be the kid who wails and snivels, clinging to mom's leg as soon as the goggles go on? Or do you want to be the kid loving every minute, even if you still need some practice before you get to use the diving board? Get in the pool, you magnificent dolphin, and enjoy the process!

Don't be intimidated by the financial world around you. Too many people are too scared or embarrassed to try something new, whether it's swimming, dancing, or financial education. But I know that's not you, because you're here! This is going to sound patronizing, but I really do admire you for being here and participating. Some people just won't try, and that makes me sad for more reasons than lost book sales.

There are three levels of participation with any given activity: absentee, participator, and creator. Absentees won't try, and they miss all of the benefits as a result. Participators know the basics, but aren't masters of the craft (yet). Creators are thoroughly versed in their craft, enough that they can consistently create their own work without assistance.

Consider the three levels of participation for musicians: absentees never pick up an instrument; participators know the basics, and can play songs using sheet music or tabs; creators can make their own music and develop their own style. Cooking is similar: absentees won't try, and live off of cereal, microwave fare, and takeout; participators can cook, but typically rely on a recipe; and creators know how to cook, can make things the way they want to, and don't need a recipe. This same method could be used to categorize mastery of any craft, including financial management. In finance, absentees remain ignorant of finance, and pay the price; participators understand financial concepts, and rely on templates and outside advice; and creators are informed and clever enough to take full control of their financial life.

This book is designed to get you to the "participator" level, which may be as far as you need to go to reach your goals. Just like you don't have to go to Parisian culinary school to bake cookies at home, you don't *really* need to be a world-class financial expert to have *Healthy Dough*. The lion's share of the wealthy may never reach the "creator" level, and there are entire industries that rely on that fact. You probably don't need the financial acumen of a multimillionaire tax attorney to reach your goals. Together we can start with the basics, and then you can take it as far as you want from there.

Section 2: Financial Essentials (Flour)

Chapter 5: Overview

Learning the language of finance is vital to success. You need to be able to understand what you see and hear in order to make informed decisions. At some point we've all struggled through a discussion that we couldn't follow, since we didn't know enough about the subject or terminology. There may be negative consequences for getting lost in any given situation, but the consequences of not being able to communicate about money can be severe.

I bet we've all placed a regrettable restaurant order because we didn't know or understand what the options were — or the risks. Someone, somewhere, has nearly fainted from eating ghost pepper chicken wings, mistaking one of the world's hottest peppers for a cutesy Halloween special. Some clueless kid has taken his crush to the local burger joint, not realizing that ordering extra onions on his burger guaranteed that his date would end with a handshake instead of a smooch. I know someone who used to frequently order biscuits and gravy, not realizing that both the biscuits *and* the gravy were poor choices for their severe dairy allergy (OK, that was me).

Your knowledge base — the flour of *Healthy Dough* — is an essential ingredient in your recipe for financial freedom. I hope you enjoy it, but if you get bored in this section, just remember that this is the least flavorful part of financial education. Have you ever eaten a tablespoon of flour by itself? As someone who falls prey to classic dare tactics, I'm sure I've done that at some point. And flour, by nature, is really, really dry. That's why this section is only one component of the book. Without the other ingredients, it's not worth much. So while building your base knowledge may feel like dry reading, just remember, it's going to be combined with other things later — to create what you're really after.

I've provided many additional key terms in the Appendix at the end of the book. If at any point you come across an important looking term that you're not familiar with, check the Appendix to see if it's covered. If not, I recommend looking it up on your own to ensure comprehension.

Chapter 6: Income

Active Income

The most basic form of income is active income, which is essentially income earned by working. Salaries and wages earned for work performed at a job qualify as active income. An employee provides a service on behalf of an employer, and the employer pays the employee. For example, I provide accounting services and my employer pays me for it. A small business owner provides customers with a good or service, and the customers pay for it.

Gross pay

Gross pay is income earned before any deductions. An employee with a stated annual salary of $60,000 per year would have gross pay of $60,000 per year. An hourly employee with a pay rate of $25 per hour would have gross pay of $1,000 if they worked 40 hours ($25 per hour times 40 hours).

Net pay

Net pay is the cash received in a given paycheck, and is the remainder after deductions are subtracted from gross pay. In other words, due to legally required payroll taxes and other voluntary or discretionary deductions, the amount of cash deposited into your bank account will be less than the gross pay. An oversimplified equation for net pay might be as follows:

Net pay = Gross pay – federal income taxes – payroll taxes – voluntary deductions. Graphic 2-1 illustrates the same idea:

Figure 2-1
Calculating Net Pay
Gross pay
- Taxes & deductions
Net pay

In the real world, voluntary deductions may affect federal income taxes, so the amounts are sometimes contingent on one another. Federal income taxes and other payroll taxes are nonnegotiable, and each will be discussed briefly in the taxes section. Voluntary deductions include deductions for benefits such as health insurance, voluntary life insurance, other forms of insurance and contributions to tax-advantaged programs such as a retirement plan, Health Savings Account (HSA), or Flexible Spending Account (FSA).

Passive Income

Passive income is income earned from sources other than "active" employment — hence the term "passive." Think of passive income as positive cash flows from owning assets. Examples of passive income are investment earnings, rental income, and income from royalties or book sales. Many forms of passive income aren't completely effortless, such as managing and maintaining a rental property, but the idea is that the assets do the work for you, and you can sit back and relax.

The Dream

The Dream is to generate enough passive income from assets that you don't have to rely on active income. The key to independent wealth — or at least being able to retire someday — is to earn and save active income, and invest it into assets that provide reliable passive income streams. Achieving *The Dream* doesn't mean you have to stop working, it just means you *can*. That's organically grown, red-hot freedom, baby. The. Dream.

Chapter 7: Expense

Expenses can generally be defined as money out the door (with money spent investing being the lone exception). They aren't inherently bad, but less is certainly better, and not all expenses are created equally. Let's take a look at different expense categories.

Essential vs. Nonessential

Essential spending looks a little different for everyone, but in general, the costs of supporting your health are the only things that qualify as essential expenses. It starts with food, water, and housing. All humans need some form of nutrition and shelter to maintain physical health. But outside of those basic needs, what qualifies as valid costs of supporting health are unique to each individual. Your own individual essential expenses support *your Four Circles of Health*. A gym membership might support physical, mental, *and* social health. A home internet connection might support financial and social health. Nutritional supplements or medicine may be essential for physical and mental health. It really just depends. You will have choices in how much you spend on each essential cost in your life, but consider it essential if cutting it out would negatively affect your health.

Nonessential expenses don't serve a purpose other than enjoyment or convenience. Don't worry though — nonessential is not synonymous with evil or irresponsible. Folks, you can get rich even if you pay for cable. Heck, I bet you can still meet your savings goals if you rent a movie once a month. GASP! Nonessential costs may or may not be value-added, but they are the areas in which you have the absolute most control of your money. On a sinking ship, these would be the first things to throw overboard. Paying for luxuries such as TV, movies, concerts, music, art shows, sporting events, dining out, travel — I know, everything fun — may not be necessary in order to take care of your health. If essential expenses support your health, nonessentials can color your life. And if you find that you're spending money on nonessential expenses that aren't adding value to your life, congratulations! You just found an easy way to have more money next month.

Sometimes essentiality isn't easy to determine, such as healthy hobbies and recreation. Are favorite pastimes essential or nonessential? In my mind, it really doesn't matter, as long as those activities make it into the financial plan *somewhere*.

Recurring vs. Nonrecurring

A recurring expense is an expense that must be paid at some interval (monthly, weekly, annually, etc.). Examples of recurring expenses may include monthly rent or mortgage, groceries, car insurance payments, student loan payments, and many more. A nonrecurring expense is basically a "one time" thing. Examples may include less frequent or single instance spending such as a purchase of a new computer, unscheduled car maintenance, or tickets to a concert.

Fixed vs. Variable

Fixed expenses typically arise as part of a contract. Once the contract is entered into, the payment amount does not change. Common examples of fixed expenses are rent (per rental agreement), health insurance premiums (per health insurance election), and monthly debt payments (per borrowing agreement). Variable expenses are flexible and can be adjusted according to need or preference. You generally have more autonomy to adjust variable spending on a routine basis, because for the most part, variable spending is not related to a contract. Common examples include groceries, entertainment, utilities, and shopping in general. You may not control broader factors like prices of groceries or utilities, but you have choices in purchasing and usage.

To throw a wrench into these basic definitions, it's possible to have a variable rate borrowing agreement, where you may have variable interest expense but no control over the variability. My general recommendation is that variable rate agreements are not for you, because you're probably not a masterful macroeconomics speculator (even if you passed econ in school), and would rather skip the risk and hassle of not knowing an interest rate.

Debt payments vs. other expenses

Debt payments are not optional, nor are they flexible. If you're running low on funds, you can adjust other spending habits to lower expenses, but debt payments are often about as flexible as a boulder. The only time debt *could* be flexible is if you qualify for debt restructure or debt forgiveness — but if you follow the basic personal finance principles in this book, it's unlikely that you'd ever need those.

Fixed essentials

Fixed essentials are costs that support health and are fixed (static) in nature, meaning that the amount is known and does not change. As noted previously, a "fixed" cost is likely identifiable within a contract. My standard definition of fixed essentials includes housing, other loan payments if applicable (student loan, auto loan, etc.), health insurance, car insurance, cellphone service, and internet service. Housing, or at least some form of shelter, is widely accepted as a basic need. Other debt payments are also essential because you are contractually (thus, legally) required to make payments. There are some programs available that may help negotiate debt balances down, but this is not a guarantee — once you sign the contract, you have to pay, and that means it's a fixed essential. More examples of fixed essentials: I require home internet, since I work at home, so my home internet contract is a fixed essential in my budget. For a professional bodybuilder, a gym membership may be "essential" since the gym is their iron office. For someone required to take prescription medications for an underlying medical condition, their prescription costs may be a fixed essential. Your essentials, whether fixed or variable, can be anything that meets the criteria of being a contractual payment for an essential cost.

I want to point out that fixed essentials may be "required," but that doesn't mean you are entirely without choice in what you pay for or how much you pay. You do require a home for shelter, but you have at least *some* choices in which home you pay to live in. You also have some control over what you choose to pay for schooling, your vehicle, your internet package, your cellphone package, and any other fixed essentials — just know you may not get many chances to change your choices, if at all.

Variable essentials

Variable essentials are costs of necessary purchases for which the amount may fluctuate. Think of things like groceries, utilities, fuel, and other things that vary with usage or routine decisions. Essentials, by nature, are required to meet your basic needs: food, water, shelter, health, safety, and your ability to earn money. You do not have a contract for grocery shopping, and your grocery bills fluctuate, even when you purchase the exact same items each time. Similarly, utility costs fluctuate with usage and rate changes.

Fixed nonessentials

Fixed nonessentials are fixed costs that are not absolutely necessary to include in your life. Think TV, streaming services, wine-of-the-month club dues, a membership to the only spray tan salon that doesn't turn you into a carrot with eyes, and so on. Basically, any contract that is not legally required to be paid and is not essential to health and survival is a fixed nonessential. For some people, the cost of a gym membership would be a fixed nonessential, if they have alternatives for physical activity. "Wait, what!? Didn't that dude just say the gym was essential a minute ago? I need to get a sick pump!" Remember, what constitutes essentiality isn't identical from person to person. Taking care of physical, mental, social, and financial health is essential, and if someone doesn't need the gym for any of those things — maybe they'd rather walk outside and do bodyweight workouts — then a gym membership would be nonessential for that person.

Variable nonessentials

When you think of variable nonessentials, think of things that aren't necessary for survival, and also aren't likely to be recurring as part of a normal "bill." This could be concert tickets, dining out, vacations, new furniture, gifts, and other forms of recreation. Oftentimes, variable nonessentials are synonymous with fun. Be careful not to allocate too much of your money into variable nonessentials, but when you do, make sure you're enjoying yourself!

Sunk costs

In personal finance, I define sunk costs as those that have been, or will be, incurred, and are not recoverable, nor are they cancelable. Most economic definitions associate sunk costs solely with a historical (prior) cost, but my accountant brain also views noncancelable future obligations to pay as a sunk cost. Sunk costs are about a lack of control in the present state — you can't change the cost you've incurred. For example, imagine you've signed up for a membership to a big box store, and paid a nonrefundable up-front fee for the 12-month membership. The nonrefundable fee is a historical sunk cost. It doesn't matter if you actually shop at the store or not — the money is gone and unrecoverable, thus it is sunk.

This term typically refers to financial resources, but can also refer to resources such as time. For example, have you ever spent an hour waiting in line to get into a restaurant? That hour is gone, whether you ate at the restaurant or not, and you can't recoup it. Thus, the hour spent waiting is a sunk cost.

Opportunity cost (Financial FOMO)

The loss of value when choosing among alternatives is called opportunity cost. It is the reason my generation constantly has "FOMO," or fear of missing out, and generally doesn't like having to make big decisions. If choosing between option A and option B, the opportunity cost of selecting option A is the value of option B; that's because you can't reap the rewards of option B if you select option A. Opportunity cost exists in every decision, not just financial decisions. But it is important to understand opportunity cost in personal finance, because you need to accept that you may experience *Financial FOMO*.

Opportunity cost, or *Financial FOMO*, is why making decisions is difficult. It is the "What it?"; it is the "What will I miss out on?" The choice to complete a four-year college degree is an excellent example of how tough opportunity cost decisions can be. Firstly, it likely comes with the opportunity cost of lost income compared with starting a full-time job. If your aptitudes are more suited for manual work than for book learning and a desk job, you might be forgoing new opportunities in a career that better matches your hands-on skills and interests. The significant cost of a college education could instead be saved or invested. Plus, there are so many schools, programs, and majors to choose from that picking one means you're missing out on the benefits of the others. What if you have other opportunities you'd prefer, but your parents met in college, and you'd always hoped you'd meet your person the same way? Do you accept the opportunity cost of going to college for fear of becoming a lonely recluse that not even a dog could love?

On the other side, there is plenty of opportunity cost associated with *not* going to college: the general costs of experience and expanded education; not having a degree is a barrier to a significant amount of career opportunities; and studies have shown that college graduates earn more over their lifetimes, so not going could result in lost earning potential.

Am I suggesting you begin an infinite maniacal mental monologue, hop around, and pull your hair out because you can't ever win and life is rigged against you? No. Having choices is actually pretty cool, but you need to get comfortable making tough choices at the expenses of other opportunities. Sometimes these choices can be financial, or health related, or even social — you may have to tend to personal responsibilities instead of hang out with friends. While that can sometimes be frustrating, often you have to choose between alternatives, and just hope you've chosen the most valuable option.

You will never bat a thousand in your decision-making. At worst, you'll be dissatisfied with every move you make, and constantly undermine your own choices. At best, you'll calmly accept that it's impossible to know whether the "What if?" would have been better if you made a different choice. This is true in finance, and it's true in every other decision-making scenario.

Always, *always*, consider opportunity cost when you make decisions, because it's extremely important. But don't be afraid of choosing, and don't beat yourself up, or weigh yourself down, with *Financial FOMO*. Even if you could have timed the market better, spent less on traveling in your 20s, spent *more* time traveling in your 20s, gone on that blind date, or picked a different career — you'll never know if it would *actually* have made your overall life better than it is right now. The power you do have is to learn from everything and be grateful for what you *did* get out of a given decision.

Chapter 8: Flexible income

Flexible income is calculated as net pay minus essential expenses.

Figure 2-2
Calculating Flexible Income
Net pay
- Essential expenses
Flexible income

We use net pay in this calculation because it's the actual cash available for spending. It already factors in amounts withheld to pay for taxes and tax-advantaged investing. Then, any cash left over, after essential expenses are paid, is flexible income available for nonessential spending and other saving and investing opportunities. Consistent flexible income is a requirement for those seeking financial health. It allows the freedom to treat yourself and enjoy things that add joy and value to life. In my opinion, this flexibility leads to healthier, happier lives more often than maximizing margins does.

Your financial goals may ask you to adjust flexible income up or down, depending on the desired mix of cash savings and tax-advantaged investing. If cash is in a good place, it may be prudent to contribute more to retirement, thus reducing net pay and flexible income, albeit for good reasons. Conversely, there may be times when stacking cash is the goal, and it makes sense to increase net pay in favor of the need. Of course, reducing essential expenses can also increase flexible income without impacting retirement contributions.

You may have already heard the term "disposable income," which is a phrase that I enjoy as much as I enjoy saltwater taffy (FYI, I *hate* saltwater taffy). The term "disposable" implies a green light to dispose of your money. Having flexible income is fun and rewarding, because you can do what you want with it. You work hard for your money, so make it work for you. *Don't throw your cash in the trash.*

Chapter 9: Net margin

Net margin is calculated as net pay minus total expenses.

```
Figure 2-3
        Calculating Net Margin

        Net pay
      - Total expenses
        Net margin
```

It's basically what you were paid in cash minus what you spent in cash, regardless of what you spent it on. You can also think of net margin as what you were able to save, in addition to tax-advantaged investment contributions deducted from your paycheck. Any cash that isn't spent can be saved or invested (remember, total expenses means that nonessential spending is already included). Net margin is the proverbial "bottom line." You can have excellent flexible income, but spend it on nonessential overload and end up with low or negative net margin. That's not great. Consistently generating quality net margin is critical to earning sustainable financial freedom. If you don't consistently create net margin, your bank account will be emptier than the men's room at a women's retreat.

Chapter 10: Investing

An investment is something that can improve or protect your cash flows, and investing is exchanging a resource to acquire a resource of greater benefit (hopefully, at least!). This could be exchanging cash to invest in a retirement account; exchanging cash and time to invest in career development (i.e., college, trade school, certifications); exchanging cash and acquiring debt in order to purchase a primary residence; exchanging time to create and review a household budget; or exchanging cash to pay down debt and save on total interest costs.

Understanding the basics of investing is a required ingredient for making *Healthy Dough* and achieving *The Dream*. It's hard to gain financial health without learning how to acquire assets and make them work for you. You need to be able to characterize what activities actually count as investing and what just counts as spending money. You may want to sit down for what comes next, because you're about to feel as shocked and overwhelmed as a mountain hermit at a Van Halen concert. OK, here it is: investing is the act of acquiring investments. BOOM. Guitar solo.

That was a pretty weak definition, right? But it's a good rule of thumb when trying to determine what counts as investing and what doesn't. Spending money on things that aren't investments can't be classified as investing. You can't invest in a $400 Easter ham, because delicious meat and glaze don't improve or protect your cash flows. Since an investment is something that can improve or protect your cash flows, and investing is the act of acquiring investments, let's remix the definition as follows: investing is the act of acquiring something that can improve or protect your cash flows. Investing in a retirement account such as a 401(k), IRA, or 403(b) can protect and improve your cash flows. Making a responsible home purchase can protect your cash flows in the long term, and is an example of an investment in a tangible asset. Earning a college degree may improve your ability to produce cash flows from active income, and thus qualifies as an investment in intangible assets.

In summary, you're not investing if you're not improving or protecting cash flows. So unless you're charging your friends and neighbors a resort fee every time they visit your back patio, there's no such thing as "investing" in a hot tub.

Chapter 11: Hierarchy of control

My favorite healthy activity is to simply walk as much as I can. I mostly venture out by myself as part of my own daily routine, which means no one cares whether I actually get outside or not. Since I'm walking year-round in the Pacific Northwest, the majority of my walks are cold, rainy, or both. That may not sound pleasant to you, but I love my walks and they give me life. Getting out for my stroll — rain, shine, or snow — is a choice I make for myself every day. The joy of prioritizing myself and being outside is worth the occasional numb hands and soggy feet. But it took me a bit to learn that my daily walks provide the most value when I focus on what I can control, and mitigate some of the things I can't. For example, I can control my effort, which I demonstrate by simply choosing to lace up and go. I can choose my route and duration. I can influence my comfort by wearing the appropriate gear for that day's weather conditions. But I have no control over the weather in any way, so I forge ahead and try not to worry about it too much. In perfect conditions, I focus on how lucky I am to have a beautiful day. If it's extra hot, I appreciate the sunshine. If it's dumping rain, I soak it up and give thanks for all the life and nature that couldn't survive without it. I try to get out as much as possible, but I allow myself to skip my outing if dangers like lightning or gale-force winds make being outside a bad choice.

In summary, I have total control of certain components of my walking experience, but I can't control the weather. I can be thoughtful about how I prepare for the weather, but I have no influence over it. All I can do is check the forecast, dress accordingly, and most importantly, not be bothered by something I can't control.

You can take the same lessons I've learned on my walks and apply them to finance (and life in general): focus on what you can control. It's also a good idea to stay informed on things you can't control, so that you can actively respond or mitigate negative effects; but at the end of the day, you'll never be able to stop the rain.

Life is full of situations in which you have control, situations in which you have influence, and situations that you can't control at all. An exhaustive list of categories in which this holds true invariably includes health and finance. For example, you have control over your diet and exercise habits, and you can influence your metabolism, but you can't control your genetics. You can't control your emotions, but you can control the way you respond to them, and you can sometimes influence your emotional environment. You can't control the way others treat you, but you often have a choice in who you associate with, and you can control the way *you* choose to treat others. Your effort will always be most effective if you focus on the areas in which you do have choices, rather than fixating on things that are completely immovable.

I like to help myself prioritize my effort by using what I call the "hierarchy of control" to guide choices about where to focus my financial energy.

Full control

You have full control over discretionary nonessential purchasing. Identifying and taking charge of nonessential spending is the most reliable way to improve your margins.

Variable nonessential expenses

Variable nonessential expenses, by nature, are not required and not a contractual obligation. If you're trying to save more money, the easiest place to start is to rein in your variable nonessential spending. You don't even have to cancel anything — you can just abstain from making additional purchases.

Fixed nonessential expenses

You probably have full control over fixed nonessentials. While these may take the form of a contract, you should usually have an option to cancel, lapse, or never sign up in the first place. For example, if you realize you don't *really* need a dozen streaming services, you can cancel the ones you use the least.

Some influence

Some influence means that you can control your own decisions and behaviors, but other factors exist outside of your control. Developing areas in which you have some influence will improve your odds of success.

Active income

You have some influence over the active income you earn. You can choose your career path, and should be able to choose between various employers. You can control your work habits and productivity, which can improve your chances of getting a raise or pay bump by way of high evaluations or promotions. But, although you may be able to influence your employer's hiring or promoting decisions, at the end of the day, someone else makes that decision. You have *zero* influence over the broader wage market. Work hard and work smart, and you'll have some influence over your salary.

Fixed essential expenses

You can have some influence over fixed essential expenses, because you can control your behaviors and choose between alternatives. You can generally choose where you live, which vehicle you purchase, which insurance policies to carry, which college to attend, and so on. However, you have no control over the housing market, auto market, insurance industry, or tuition rates. You can influence your chances of success by making thoughtful decisions about fixed essential spending, but you'll always be somewhat at the mercy of the markets.

Variable essential expenses

You can influence your variable essential spending, because you can control your behaviors and choose between alternatives. Most of your purchasing decisions offer you some choice, but the cost is not fully within your control due to external factors. For example, you can lower your utility bills through reduced usage; however, you have no influence over utility rates. You can make budget-conscious grocery shopping decisions, but you can't control broader costs of food. You can try to limit health care costs by taking good care of yourself, but sometimes health issues happen anyway — and you *definitely* don't control health care charges.

No control

Investment performance

Historical data, financial experts, and personal speculation can help you guess how investment securities and other assets might perform. But don't put too much energy into trying to predict the future, because you have no control. You can't control stock values, dividend decisions, interest rates, or rental rates. A stock issuer could always tank and a debt issuer could always go bankrupt. You can place some reliance on investments performing a certain way, but your energy is better spent on things you can control or influence. Try to stay informed so that you can make educated, thoughtful decisions related to your investments, but don't obsess over trying to predict the market. Choose reliable investments and monitor their performance occasionally, but do your best to let them ride while your energy goes toward things you can influence or control.

Chapter 12: Assets

Defining financial assets

As we've covered, the general term "asset" refers to something of use or value. An asset is a positive on your personal balance sheet. There a variety of things that can provide you use or value, but do each of them count toward your financial profile? Toilet paper, a trusty pair of pliers, a beloved macaroni picture from a niece or nephew — these are all things that provide use or value to your life. But in personal finance, not all things of use or value count as an asset. When determining if a personal possession is an asset for financial purposes, it's all about the money, baby. Unless that niece or nephew becomes famous, good luck fetching any cash for that macaroni picture.

You can determine if something is a financial asset by subjecting it to a couple of tests: the cash value test and the cash flow test. If one or both of these tests are passed, you've got an asset.

Cash value test

Cash value in an outside market, which could also be called "market value," differentiates between a true asset and other things of nonmarketable use or value. Consider a "market" or "outside market" to be the collection of buyers and sellers of a given product. There is a housing market, stock market, bond market, vehicle market, labor market, market for used instruments, a celebrity-endorsed clothing market, and more. In the modern world, a market isn't necessarily an actual location, like a supermarket; however, there are still certain markets with a physical presence, such as car dealerships or the New York Stock Exchange on Wall Street.

Cash value means that the outside market would be willing to exchange cash to acquire your product. There are various ways that assets are valued in financial accounting and actuarial measures, but in personal finance the cash value test can be performed by answering a question: "Who would buy this, and for how much?" If there is a real chance you could sell the item for a material amount, consider that your item has received a passing grade for the cash value asset test.

Cash value is only realized if an item is actually exchanged or sold. The market value may increase over time, such as with a primary residence, or decrease over time, such as with a personal vehicle. But if it has cash value, it is an asset.

Cash flow test

The other asset test is the cash flow test, which evaluates the item's ability to generate cash inflows or reduce cash outflows via expense reduction. The purpose of acquiring assets is to maintain or improve cash flows. Some items such as investment securities may routinely produce income, and other investments such as energy efficient home renovations may reduce expenses.

In summary, the cash value test and cash flow test can help you determine what counts as an asset versus merely being useful or valuable. The standard measurable asset classes in personal finance are cash, investment securities, real estate, and personal property (other marketable assets). These categories are generic and aren't intended to perfectly match specific tax code definitions, since laws may change over time. Let's review why they pass at least one of the two asset tests.

Cash Assets

Cash savings, such as those deposited in a savings account, qualify as an asset because they pass the cash value test — they already *are* money. Cash assets may include your deposit balances (such as deposits in checking or savings accounts) and any other stash of cash you may have. Cash that is deposited with a financial institution such as a bank or credit union is likely to earn a negligible amount of interest, so for our purposes we will consider deposits to be simple cash and not investments. Cash assets that are *not* deposited with a financial institution do not earn any investment income.

Investment securities

Investment securities generally pass the cash value test, although values can change rapidly and are not guaranteed. They can be acquired with cash assets, and are intended to eventually be converted back into cash assets upon sale. They also pass the cash flow test — or are at least intended to — because they are expected to generate interest, dividends, or appreciation.

Real estate

Real estate may be held for personal use (a primary residence) or for passive income (a rental property). We will look at each kind individually.

Owning a primary residence

Ownership of a primary residence (personal use) passes the cash value asset test nearly one hundred percent of the time. Since real estate markets are active — especially now, in the era of real estate apps — the home likely has material cash value, and is therefore an asset. The cash value of a responsible home purchase will likely appreciate over the long term, as long as it is maintained. However, it is important to remember that not all investments are good investments. Overpaying, buying in a decaying region, or trashing the house will make it awfully hard to enjoy appreciation in cash value.

In addition to providing cash value, the ownership of a primary residence can pass the cash flow asset test in a couple of other ways. Buying a home — and staying there in the long term — is likely to have a positive impact on cash flows. It won't increase money coming in, but it can reduce money going *out*. If you obtain a fixed mortgage, your price is locked in for the life of the loan. With what we know about inflation, I'm sure you can see how that's a very good thing. If you stay in the home after it's completely paid off, your only housing costs will be maintenance, property taxes, and insurance. Just keep in mind that home maintenance costs can be very expensive, so owning comes with plenty of cash outflows as well. Overall, a personal residence is an excellent asset to acquire once you are financially prepared to do so.

A primary residence may also pass the cash flow test if the owner is renting out space for money. This is a great way to make your assets work for you if you can find roommates who don't drive you bonkers.

Owning a rental property

A rental property will almost always pass both the cash value and cash flow asset tests. Similar to a primary residence, the home likely has some amount of cash resale value. A rental property can also provide strong passive cash inflows, as long as rents are consistently higher than costs of ownership. Again, the costs of ownership can be quite high for homeowners, so investing in real estate properties is only a savvy move for those who are financially prepared for the risk. If you can't consistently and easily afford the cost of all of your mortgages — primary and investment — in any given month, it probably isn't the right time to invest in rental property. People who try to build wealth by taking on massive debt to acquire rental properties tend to advise against it in later years, because it requires an investor to be good *and* lucky. Lecture aside, an investment rental property can be an amazing asset to own if you're insulated against the risks.

Personal property (other marketable assets)

Personal property, or personal use property, is a term that describes most other miscellaneous possessions, only some of which are actually marketable assets. Some common examples may include vehicles, major appliances, quality instruments, memorabilia, or intangible items such as intellectual property. Remember that "marketable" means that there has to be a market with willing buyers. If you can sell it, it has cash value and qualifies as an asset; if you can't expect to sell it, there's no cash value, and it's not an asset. If you own a piece of art created by an artist whose works are actively traded, do you have an asset? Yes, because there's a "market" for works by that artist, and people will pay cash for it. But don't try to quantify the value of your latest paint 'n' sip masterpiece — no one wants to buy it from you.

Personal use property can sometimes, *sometimes*, help protect cash flows. For example, if you buy a personal use vehicle and are able to use it exclusively for 20 years, that would probably result in better vehicle cash flows compared to buying more frequently. You'll be stretched to find many examples other than that.

In summary, anything you own that you can likely sell for a material amount of money can be counted as an asset, under the cash value test. The cash flow test will usually be a stretch for other personal property, unless you buy something essential that saves a material amount of money in the long run.

Investment Avenue – home to investment products

You may stumble across an overwhelming buffet of investment options in your lifetime. Just like looking at row upon row of food at an all-you-can-eat restaurant and knowing you can't feasibly try *everything*, it may seem hard to choose. Well, you will find various account types and security types, each with different perks and different purposes, but your objective should be retirement planning. Most people define their "retirement savings" as their stockpile (lol, pun) of investment securities. While there are many different ways to invest, the most universally accessible option tends to be investing in the securities market. Opening an investment account may require little or no money at all, and in the modern world of funds and partial shares, it doesn't take much cash to get into the game and start acquiring securities. As such, you're going to want to know your options and which ones are most advantageous for your circumstances.

Tax-advantaged investing

Tax-advantaged investing is the number one choice for most investors because it saves on costly taxes. Those with extremely high income may not be eligible to participate in certain tax-advantaged accounts, but most folks can. Tax-advantaged investment accounts come with restrictions on withdrawals and uses, as well as annual contribution limits, but don't be fooled — they're the cat's meow.

Tax-advantaged accounts – Employer-sponsored plans

An employer-sponsored plan is a type of benefit plan offered to employees of an organization at zero or relatively low cost, and could refer to a variety of benefits such as retirement plan options available to employees. Some common employer-sponsored retirement plans include 401(k), 403(b), and 457(b). Since most employers offer a 401(k) as opposed to the other plans, I'll refer to all employer-sponsored plans simply as "401(k)."

A 401(k) is likely to come with extra perks in addition to the tax benefits. Account fees and transaction fees tend to be materially lower than they would be with individual accounts. Additionally, these plans are likely to offer employer contributions, which, in layman's terms, means *free money!* If you know what it sounds like when Homer Simpson says "Woo-hoo!" feel free to make that sound in your head.

A common form of employer contribution is the employer match. Your employer may make "matching" contributions to your employee accounts based on what you contribute. For example, your employer might match 50% of employee contributions up to 6% of eligible income, or match employee contributions dollar for dollar up to 4% of eligible income. And some are even better than that. Employer match programs are likely discretionary, which means that the contributions are planned but not guaranteed. Since you are in control of the amount you contribute, this will likely be your preferred employer contribution option because employees who can contribute a lot on their own can maximize the matching contribution from the employer. Maxing out matching contributions is a classic strategy and should always be considered, unless doing so would prevent other higher-priority uses of cash. If your employer will match your 401(k) contributions dollar for dollar up to 3% of wages, make sure you contribute at least 3% so you earn the full match. If you only contribute 2%, they'll only contribute 2% as well. If the employer matches 50% of contributions up to 3% of wages, make sure you contribute at least 6%. Consider it an optional 3% raise, with tax advantages — and take the option. *Woo-hoo!* Utilizing a quality employer match can make a gigantic difference in total compensation and retirement savings.

Another popular form of employer contribution is the profit-sharing program. Unlike employee match, a profit-sharing contribution amount isn't determined by what you, the employee, contributes, but rather by what the employer determines will be contributed. These amounts are discretionary and are not guaranteed to be paid. Profit-sharing programs tend to be preferred by employees who wouldn't be able to contribute enough to maximize an employer match.

Some employers can't offer a true "profit-sharing" program, because they are entities that are not organized to seek profit; but they can still offer nonmatching discretionary employer contributions to a separate 401(a) account. Nonprofit, governmental, and educational entities tend to use a discretionary 401(a) contribution in lieu of profit-sharing.

Tax-advantaged accounts – Individual Retirement Account (IRA)

Not everyone has access to a 401(k) or similar employer-sponsored program. Maybe your employer doesn't offer it, or maybe you are not eligible to participate because you're too young or you work part-time. Fortunately, you folks may find comparable value from investing in an Individual Retirement Account (IRA). IRA contributions are tax-advantaged, and may come with more flexibility than an employer-sponsored plan. Having an individual account allows the investor to choose their provider, and possibly pick from a broader range of investment options. The downsides of an IRA are that contribution limits are lower than in employer-sponsored plans, fees are likely higher, and employers won't "match" contributions. Overall, an IRA is still a fantastic option deserving of a standing ovation and hearty applause.

Traditional (pre-tax) accounts

"Traditional" 401ks and IRAs allow you to defer federal income taxes until withdrawal, at which point you pay income taxes on the contributions and investment earnings. Another way to say this is that traditional account contributions are made pre-tax, which means that amounts contributed reduce your taxable income.

For example, assume you that you contribute $6,000 to a traditional account in year one. In this scenario, your $6,000 pre-tax contribution will reduce your income that's subject to income taxes by $6,000. If your marginal tax rate is 20%, the $6,000 contribution will lower your tax bill for the year by $1,200. You won't actually pay income taxes on the amount contributed until withdrawn in retirement. If you later retire after 42 years of work and make your first withdrawal in year 43, the withdrawal is fully taxed at whatever your tax rate is in year 43. The tax rate may be higher, lower, or exactly the same as it was when contributed in year one.

Roth (after-tax) accounts

Contributions to a Roth account are made with after-tax dollars, and eligible withdrawals are never taxed. Compared with a traditional pre-tax account, which lowers federal income tax burdens up front, a Roth account lowers tax burdens later. By paying income taxes up front, a Roth account helps mitigate the risk of higher tax rates when money is withdrawn in retirement. And even better than that, the earnings are *never* taxed. That means decades of tax-free investment growth for those who start early. If you're learning about this arrangement for the first time, your jaw may be dropping as if your dog just looked up at you and said, in perfect English, "Goodnight, best buddy."

Withdrawal rules vary between Roth IRAs and employer-sponsored Roth plans (i.e., Roth 401[k]s), but in general, withdrawals from Roth IRAs are never subject to penalties, while certain employer-sponsored Roth plans may have certain penalties for early withdrawal. For up-to-date information on withdrawal rules, contribution limits and other specific parameters for Roth and other deferred compensation plans, check out the IRS website. Please also keep up with *Healthy Dough* online so you can access easy-to-use references and guides when available.

Picking a plan

In my experience, employers are most likely to offer pre-tax options, though more and more are offering a Roth option as well. Since opening an IRA is entirely up to your discretion, you should be able to easily find providers that offer traditional accounts, Roth accounts, or both. So, if you are fortunate enough to have options, which should you choose?

Most folks who can choose between Roth or traditional plans make their choice according to what they think their income and income taxes will be like in retirement. We can make educated guesses, but no one can really predict what the tax environment will be like throughout their retirement. For all we know, the government might drastically change the availability and options for tax-advantaged accounts. But there are some general guidelines to follow. If you expect taxes to increase over time in general, Roth may be for you. Also, Roth is a great option for young people, since people tend to earn more over time, thus increasing their tax rates in a progressive tax structure. So if tax brackets stay similar over time, you'll likely pay a lower rate when you're starting out, *plus* earnings can grow tax-free for a longer period of time for young investors. On the other hand, high earners may greatly benefit from reducing taxable income while in higher tax brackets. I do know quite a few people who are very pro-Roth, but are fortunate to earn so much that contributing to a traditional account makes more sense for each of their situations.

There are also some other factors to consider in the current financial environment, though they may not be relevant to all. Since traditional accounts are untaxed until withdrawal, the withdrawals will need to cover both bills and income taxes in your retirement. This is the known trade-off between traditional and Roth accounts, and one potential lurking consequence is that higher taxable income from retirement savings could bump your Social Security benefit taxes up to a higher tax bracket. This could also potentially increase the cost of Medicare Part B premiums during your retirement. That said, this does *not* mean traditional is an unfavorable option. It's extremely favorable, and if you have so much to withdraw in retirement that you pay extra taxes, good for you.

Open market investing

Investing on the open market means investing in securities outside of a tax-advantaged retirement account. Securities are purchased with after-tax dollars, since no special tax deferral treatment is utilized (you get your paycheck, net of income taxes, and you go and buy an investment product using after-tax dollars). Then you're taxed again on the income from those investments (at least in the current U.S. tax environment). You can generally buy and sell without restriction. The best advantage of regular market investing is the freedom and flexibility: you can buy whatever, whenever, and there are no restrictions on how much you can invest. The downside is, of course, that it doesn't come with preferential tax treatment or benefits like employer contributions.

Other tax-advantaged accounts

Health Savings Accounts (HSA)

A Health Savings Account (HSA) is a tax-advantaged savings account available to those enrolled in a high-deductible health plan (HDHP). Participants receive tax benefits as a reward for contributing funds to an account that can only be used to cover eligible health care costs. While an HDHP isn't right for everyone, anyone enrolled in one should consider utilizing the tax benefits of contributing to an HSA. The money deposited into the HSA is not subject to federal income tax at the time the deposit is made. Employers may also make elective contributions to HSA plans, and those contributions are tax-free benefits to the employee. More free money! Woo-hoo! Additionally, HSA funds will accumulate year-to-year if the money is not spent, and earnings are generally not taxable.

Consider this simple example: you have a tax rate of 20% and expect out-of-pocket health care costs to be $500 during the year; by putting $500 into your HSA, you reduce your taxable income by $500, meaning you'll save $100 on your federal income taxes ($500 contribution times 20% tax savings).

Flexible Spending Accounts (FSA)

A Flexible Spending Account (FSA) is an employer-sponsored benefit plan. Employers can offer an FSA with other benefits as part of a cafeteria plan. Similar to an HSA, participants receive tax benefits as a reward for contributing funds to an account that can only be used to cover eligible health care costs. Contributions from the beneficiary reduce taxable income, and employer contributions are tax-free benefits to the employee. Funds can be used for qualified medical expenses, but unlike an HSA, the funds expire and are not recoverable. The money is "use-it-or-lose-it," which means that anything unused at the end of the plan year is forfeited and does not roll forward; however, some plans allow funds to be used for an additional 2.5 months following the plan year, to help employees reduce the risk of forfeiture. The key to making the best use of an FSA is accurate estimation of medical expenses for the year. FSA contributions must be determined before the beginning of the plan year, so there's no option to manipulate contribution amounts according to actual expenses. The risk of underestimating is the opportunity cost of the lost tax savings, and the risk of overestimating is forfeiture of funds. As long as the contribution amount is reasonably close to actual spending, the tax benefits can make this a great option.

Qualified tuition programs (529 savings plans)

Qualified tuition programs — also referred to as 529 savings plans — are designed to help with the costs of higher education. The idea is to incentivize parents, guardians, and other supporters to help dependent children save for school, thus reducing future debt burdens for the child. The "529" comes from the section of the IRS codification that discusses the rules and options for these plans. Plans are operated by a state or educational institution, with tax advantages and potentially other incentives to make it easier to save for college or post-secondary training, or even for tuition at a K-12 school. Account earnings are not subject to federal tax and generally not subject to state tax when used for qualified education expenses of the designated beneficiary. These expenses may include tuition, fees, books, or room and board at an eligible educational institution. Similar to Roth accounts, contributions are not tax-deductible, but earnings are never taxed as long as funds are used for a qualified purpose.

I won't dive too deep into the rules and options, but want to make sure you're aware of the opportunity. Some may find that investing in a 529 savings plan is a good fit for their family, especially if others in the support network like to contribute, and if they get started early in life to maximize time in the market. I'll admit, I am the boring uncle who contributes to college savings plans in lieu of birthday presents (but don't worry, I wouldn't dare do that for Christmas). Anyway, I recommend looking into taking advantage of the tax-free earnings that a 529 plan can offer.

Chapter 13: Debt deep dive

Debt is a bet. Taking on debt is a gamble in which you wager that you're going to have more money at some later date. When thinking about whether a debt decision is productive or toxic, think about how your planned use of the money affects the odds of your gamble, and place your bets carefully.

When you borrow money, you're taking the stance that having cash now will provide more favorable opportunities compared to waiting and saving. That may be true sometimes, and other times it's so false that it's silly. We will review some scenarios in which debt can support financial health, and take a brisk look at when it's a bad idea. Some transactions can help you thrive, and others can leave you as broke as a sunken cellphone.

Productive Debt vs. Detrimental Debt

All humans are created equal, but debt is not. Some forms of debt, such as a mortgage, can make a lot of sense for most people. But even with debt that's generally productive, it's not hard to find someone willing to give you a bad deal. If you have decent credit, you're likely to be offered terrifyingly high credit limits in the form of credit cards, personal loans, or collateralized loans for things you don't need. I bet if I were to go into a music gear chain store right now, it would take me four minutes to secure a loan to buy a $10,000 vintage guitar with zero dollars down. But that doesn't mean it's a good idea. Just like deciding whether or not I'm going to eat an entire chicken pot pie by myself, "can" and "should" in this situation are very different things.

Guidelines such as "debt is for essentials only" can help set boundary flags for borrowing decisions. But I also like the idea of reviewing debt for productivity using a *HOP analysis*. No, I'm not talking about putting on a giant bunny costume and jumping around while you weigh your options. And no, I'm not talking about taste-testing delicious hoppy beer while you think it over. *HOP* is just an acronym that I came up with in hopes that it will be easy to remember. Since the "H" is for "honesty," I figured you should know.

HOP analysis

Honesty: Be realistic, objective, and honest with yourself when considering the reasonableness of the amount, structure, and purpose for considering new debt. Answer yourself honestly: Is this productive?

Opportunity cost: Consider the opportunity cost of new debt, and ask yourself questions accordingly: What are the benefits of my other options, and how do those compare to the benefits that borrowing money would provide? On the other hand, what is the opportunity cost of waiting and saving?

Plan: Draft a plan for how you'll be able to pay off the debt. Ask yourself: Will I be able to pay this back according to the debt agreement? How will this affect my other personal and financial decisions, and what levers might I need to pull in order to make it work?

Breaking down debt scenarios

Let's review a few common debt situations and check them for productivity using a *HOP analysis*.

Housing debt

General rule: housing debt can be productive

Gone are the days of wandering west, chopping down a few trees by hand, and building a family homestead without applying for permits. As our populations continue to soar and the last remaining inhabitable spaces are developed, property is becoming more scarce. And like all things, from water to diamonds to baseball cards, scarcity and rarity lead to higher prices. Unfortunately, this means acquiring property is much more financially challenging now than it was for prior generations, and requires most people to take on debt. It sucks, but it's reality.

In modern finance, housing debt typically comes in the form of a mortgage loan. As I just mentioned, the increased demands for housing (and other factors) have made it so that most people can't afford to buy a house using their own cash. Additionally, even those who *could* build their own house independently would still have a hard time paying cash for all the materials, permits, and other costs of a new build. So while some financial philosophies say to never take on debt for any reason — even a house — I, sadly, don't think that's realistic anymore. Maybe it was reasonable to acquire a home with little or no debt 30, 40, or 100 years ago, but I don't think we'll ever get back to that in the United States. Now imagine a mustachioed man in a top hat, using his ridiculous roaring twenties accent to rapidly chirp out, "You think you need debt for a home? Is this some kind of goof? Malarkey! Debt-free living is the cat's pajamas. Everything's jake when you don't owe nothin' to no one. Now if I could just stop betting the ponies …" Sorry Gatsby, but times have changed. It may be ironic, but the American dream of property ownership is usually financed. Here's the first scenario in our review of different debt situations, which will focus on how to make housing debt work for you: "A Mortgage Story."

A Mortgage Story

James is a 32-year-old social worker who is quite adept at keeping his hard-earned money. He expects that he and his girlfriend will soon be married and starting a family, and decides it's time to buy a home to support that dream. He has saved plenty of cash for a quality down payment toward a home purchase, but will require a mortgage loan to pay for the rest. His liquidity and strong credit make it so he can qualify for any mortgage option he wants, and he does his homework to determine the best deals out there. He looks at the standard products available through his credit union and other lenders, and also researches homebuyer support programs that offer great deals to first-time homebuyers, racial minorities, and social workers. He chooses a product that fits his goals and his budget, and gets ready to take the next steps.

James then gets a preapproval letter from his lender and finds the right house. His offer to purchase the home is accepted. He uses his savings to put down a responsible down payment, and his lender pays the rest of the sale price so that the seller can be paid in full. The lender and James agree on a 30-year fixed mortgage, in which James has 30 years of fixed monthly payments to pay back to the lender for the amount the lender paid the seller (the amount James has borrowed).

James and his family will keep the house forever, long after the 30-year loan is paid off. Decades will pass by, trends and hairstyles will change, his kids will visit their childhood home with grandkids in tow, and the Seattle Mariners will probably only make it to the playoffs once or twice. James will retire at age 65, and own the house until he dies at age 90, having owned the house 58 years. The American dream, well-lived.

So, was shelling out most of his savings and borrowing lots of money to buy a home a smart move by James? Was it a responsible investment? Let's add some more details and review.

Housing is an essential expense, so in that regard, James was somewhat validated for using debt to purchase a house. But was it more than just cost of living and a place to raise his family? Could it have even been a smart investment? When determining if the home was an investment, let's first evaluate this scenario as it relates to investing in offense, in other words, an investment that will generate positive cash flows. Did the purchase of the home generate any income? The answer is, it did not. No one paid him to live there, and because he and his wife never sold it, he would not necessarily benefit from any appreciation of housing market values (though his taxes and insurance may have increased along with the market). So the purchase of a home in this case did not generate any offense, and was instead cash out the door. A primary residence can only generate offense as an investment when it is sold (unless renting out space), and depending on the timing of the sale, that's not even guaranteed. In general, buying a house isn't a reliable offensive investment because it doesn't produce cash flows unless sold or rented out.

Now let's evaluate this as a defensive investment: did the home *protect* his cash flows? In the 58 years after he bought the home, the economy was consistently impacted by inflation, and both home sale prices and rental prices increased over time. Since he and his family were responsible homeowners, owning the home and keeping it likely protected their cash flows over time. The 30-year loan was bearing interest at a fixed rate of a certain percentage agreed upon in the contract, and James was responsible to pay back the principal and interest each month. Because this was a 30-year fixed loan, his monthly payments of principal and interest were the same until the loan was paid off (note that property taxes and insurance on the home likely increased over time, but the actual mortgage payments never changed). That means that for the 30 years between age 32 and age 62, James' cost of housing did not increase. Meanwhile, in that same period, the purchase price of homes *and* cost of renting increased with inflation — meaning that other people's monthly payments for housing went up while his stayed the same. Therefore, his home served as a defensive investment by controlling his cash outflows.

By age 62 James and his wife had paid off the home entirely, and continued to live there for 28 years beyond payoff. That means that for 28 years (most of which he was retired) he didn't have any payments on the home, and only paid taxes, insurance, and home maintenance. Having a minimal cost of housing in retirement is much more comfortable than having costs that increase annually as retirement balances simultaneously get smaller. If James had *not* owned a home and was renting, rental rates for similar dwellings would have been much more expensive due to inflation; he would have had increasing housing costs that were compounded with decreased purchasing power as retirement assets were liquidated. Owning the home certainly helped protect his cash flows in that manner; and by not having to draw as much on his retirement, he was able to continue to generate more "offense" by keeping his retirement assets in the market for longer.

To recap, James made a quality investment in a home that protected his family's cash flows. The mortgage debt was used to turn an essential expense into an investment, so it was a great option for him. But there are some drawbacks of home ownership to remember as well. One drawback is that owners are solely responsible for maintaining their home. This means that when you own a home and need a new roof, new furnace, or monthly maintenance, you are responsible for the costs. If climate change turns your once-comfortable house into a sweat lodge, you're the one who needs to pay for air-conditioning. If you make a responsible home purchase, and are a responsible homeowner who takes care of their investment, this should never be severely more expensive than renting. And besides — I think it's safe to assume that long-term costs of maintenance and repair, as well as costs of taxes and insurance, are at least partially built into the rental rates charged by landlords.

Housing HOP analysis

All said, a responsible home purchase is essential and can be a great defensive investment, in addition to providing a place to grow and thrive.

Housing is an essential cost because it supports your health and safety. Most folks prefer to live in a house or apartment rather than a van or tent, so I think it's safe to say that most everyone will need to make a decision about housing debt at some point in their lives.

The partially completed *HOP analysis* below can help you get started asking the right questions related to mortgage decisions.

Honesty: When it comes to considering debt for a home purchase, the most important honesty moment is to ask yourself: Is this productive? Am I *really* ready for this? Will I be prepared for all the add-on costs and maintenance responsibilities of owning a home? Am I willing to sacrifice current flexibility in favor of long-term benefit? What changes may be ahead that could affect my ability to afford the house? How long until I sell and give 6% to the realtors?

The answers to those types of questions are highly individual. In the meantime I can help you understand whether you're financially mature enough to start considering a home purchase. You may "qualify" for a mortgage at a bank, but in my opinion, you're not truly "qualified" to buy until you've had success with the following four things: One: creating an accurate budget; Two: producing consistent net margins; Three: accumulating emergency savings; and Four: saving for a meaningful down payment.

1) *Creating an accurate budget:* In order to know what a safe and reasonable monthly mortgage payment might look like within your financial picture, you need to really understand what your other costs are and how to manage them. I recommend a very absolute *minimum* of one full year of living within an established and accurate budget before considering taking on debt for a home purchase. I don't care if your salary starts at $300,000 per year right out of college — that's not the same as being able to *manage* your money. So build experience and confidence by operating off of a budget and reviewing financial results.

2) *Producing consistent net margins:* If you're adhering to a budget, you should be consistently producing positive margins each month, meaning that you have money to save. I'm talking about meaningful cash savings, net of any recurring contributions to a tax-advantaged retirement account.

3) *Accumulating emergency savings:* Don't even think about buying a house unless you currently have three to six months' worth of living expenses in cash emergency savings. And don't consider buying anything that would bleed your cash reserves down below three months of emergency savings under the *new* monthly expense amounts including that potential mortgage.

4) *Saving for a meaningful down payment:* If you've been sticking to a budget, producing consistent margins, and have adequate emergency savings, excess cash can be used to save for a meaningful down payment. In general, lacking a sizable down payment, in addition to lacking budgeting experience and sufficient emergency savings, may be indications that it's just not time to buy yet. There's nothing wrong with accepting where you are and making decisions accordingly. Sure, a lot of people have done just fine with no money down, and some have even benefitted from getting into the market earlier than if they'd waited. But in my opinion, that's like a backpacker trying to save pack weight by leaving all their warm clothes at home — it could pay off if conditions are perfect, but the plan isn't well-insulated against risk.

Opportunity cost: Consider the opportunity cost of new debt to purchase a home, and ask yourself questions accordingly. What are the opportunity costs associated with taking on debt for a home purchase? A down payment and monthly mortgage payment both require material financial resources that could produce benefits elsewhere, and both the up-front cost and contractual nature of a mortgage reduce flexibility as well. On the other hand, there are also opportunity costs to *not* buying a home once you're "qualified" and the time is right.

Plan: Draft a plan for how you'll pay off the debt. Make sure you understand the costs and risks of home ownership, and have a plan for how to mitigate those risks. Think through how purchasing a home could conflict with other plans, financial and nonfinancial alike. Housing is an essential expense, so you'll need to pay for housing whether you rent or own. If and when you do buy, just try to make sure the monthly payment feels achievable in the near and long term.

If you can complete a *HOP analysis* and find that you're prepared to take on a mortgage to buy a home, that's fantastic. I "qualified" and bought my first home at age 24, and feel grateful to have been given the opportunity to do so. I'm also glad that I made sure I was ready first. Owning a home is one of the great American freedoms, and is essential for financial health. As such, taking on mortgage debt to own a home is generally a decent idea if you can't pay cash. When you get your first set of keys, I hope you're proud and grateful.

All that said, remember that more of a good thing doesn't necessarily mean better. Olive oil can be a nutritional staple of a healthy diet, but that doesn't mean you should chug it from the bottle. While some housing debt can be productive, you'll obviously want to avoid excessively large loans, even if the interest rates are low. And also know that assuming there is urgency to buy a house *immediately* can be misguided, even if prices will continue to rise. A home loan is still debt, and debt payments can't be cancelled. The real estate crash and congruent recession that began in the late 2000s is great evidence that both lenders and consumers can end up getting burned by greed. That, combined with some level of inadequate planning and plenty of ignorance, led to a housing crisis in which citizens owed more on their homes than they could sell them for, and banks and businesses failed. In the end, existing tax dollars were channeled to the unbudgeted government bailout, meaning that the taxpayers had to pay the bill. A person's individual politics and beliefs may influence whom they view as the villains and victims in the 2000s mortgage crisis, but the circumstances and bailout are historical fact — and the magnitude may have been mitigated by more responsible home purchases. I hope this helps us avoid the "next" crisis. Thus concludes the "Debt *Dangent*: Housing Edition."

Student loan debt

General rule: student loan debt can be productive

While school tuition may not be essential for all, investing in oneself is essential, and I believe that pursuing meaningful career advancement counts as investing. In general, people pursue education of some kind for improved employability.

At the time of writing, the political climate holds polarized and passionate discussions on the future of student loan debt, so I won't bother too much with specifics that may change at some point. But one reason student loan debt is ridiculously common is because college degrees are in high demand, which (among other reasons) has greatly increased the cost of tuition. The glory days of paying their own fare through school are gone for most students at this point, even for those who are employed and get good grades. So your grandma paid for her own college tuition using the tips from her job as a roller skating waitress at the local drive-up burger joint? That's awesome, but it's been a while since that was feasible. And sure, some kids get their educations paid for by relatives, scholarships, or even financial aid, but most don't. Most undergraduate and graduate students will need to make financial decisions related to schools, programs, and student loans.

Factors such as cost of tuition, loan forgiveness programs, employment prospects, and others should play into making a responsible student loan decision. Let's start asking some questions about student loans as part of an example *HOP analysis*.

Student loan HOP analysis

Honesty: Is taking on student loan debt productive? The answer is: maybe. If you make the most of your schooling and are placed into a career in which you can easily afford your student loan payments, then it's probably a good idea. However, taking on $100,000 in debt to earn a degree with poor job placement and low industry salaries might not be a good decision. Sometimes the honest truth might be that the university you'd prefer to attend isn't a good financial fit. That's tough, but not as tough as making a dumb debt decision. Be honest with yourself about what your aptitudes are, what you're wanting to get out of your schooling, and which schools are the best fit for you. Your best fit might be a giant, prestigious public university with a legendary alumni network. Or, your best option might be starting at a community college, just like it was for me. You might be disappointed to find that the top program for your major is at a school with no football team (or even worse, a *terrible* football team). Be honest about your wants versus needs for college. You *need* to learn to improve your employability. Your wants are important too, but shouldn't dominate debt decisions.

Opportunity cost: Consider the opportunity cost of new debt to pay for school, and ask yourself questions accordingly. What are the benefits of your other options, and how do those compare to the option that requires debt? Well, some people may find in their "honesty" questions that college really just isn't the right fit for them. If that's you, then I have good news. A four-year education has been forced so heavily on the population that we have a shortage in skilled trade workers such as electricians and plumbers. And from what I've observed among friends and family, those jobs pay pretty dang well these days. A low supply of workers combined with consistent demand for skilled labor means higher wages for those workers.

That said, there are certainly opportunity costs of *not* pursuing a college education. Those who find that their desired career path requires a four-year degree may just have to swallow the opportunity costs of borrowing money to get a job. It's like the fact that elephant seals rate their potential mates' attractiveness by nose size — silly, but true.

One common way to avoid student loan debt is to enlist in the military and subsequently pay for school using military benefits. This may not seem feasible to all, but there are certainly some who emerge from the experience stronger and debt-free. Another less intense option can be a tuition program through an employer. Large corporate employers, especially those in retail and fast food, are famous for providing academic assistance to workers who want to pursue the management track.

I want to clarify that I'm not against the traditional plan of attending a four-year university right after high school; I just don't think it's the right fit for everyone. I do think it's unfair that nearly all office jobs seem to arbitrarily require a degree, and believe this is causing our nation some serious financial trouble. Some of the most highly evaluated white-collar workers I know do not have a college degree, and were able to work their way up from the bottom sheerly based on talent and effort. Some of my top accounting colleagues, who earned their way up through hard work and on-the-job training, were only able to do so because they'd started before degrees were required. Otherwise they wouldn't have gotten the opportunity, and the organization wouldn't have gotten the benefit. I think college is great, and I'm glad I went. My accounting degree has certainly paid off for me. But I think the current climate of trying to force everyone to attend college — regardless of aptitude and cost — isn't really working out. Thus concludes "Debt *Dangent*: Student Loan Edition."

Plan: How might you plan to pay off student loan debt, and how does that impact your other plans? Well, picking the right combination of career field and affordability will help ensure that you'll be able to make your monthly debt payments. After all, the idea is that pursuing education opens up opportunities to earn money. If you find that it's hard to imagine paying back a particular student loan scenario, it may be time to consider other options. Additionally, be sure to research opportunities for loan forgiveness, such as those available to teachers and social workers. Make sure you understand that if you do take on a large debt burden, it will affect your other financial plans for years to come. This might mean forgoing other financial opportunities, or being stuck working in whichever job pays most, even if it's a bad fit.

Auto loan debt

General rule: nonproductive, but fine in moderation

Taking on debt when you absolutely need a vehicle, but don't have cash for it, can be fine, but in moderation. It can also be healthy to take on a small auto loan as part of a broader cash usage strategy, but that right is reserved for experienced financiers. Let's *HOP* to the analysis.

Auto loan HOP analysis

Honesty: Is taking on debt to pay for a car productive? Answering this question comes down to wants versus needs. Let's say you need a commuter car to travel to work and run errands. Pretty common, pretty reasonable in my view. However, if you have just enough set aside to buy a reliable used car for cash, but would prefer a luxury model that costs twice as much, it'd be hard to sell me on the validity of an auto loan for the luxury car. You wouldn't be able to look at yourself in the mirror and honestly say, "It was smart to finance that car I couldn't afford, because the comfort of resting my buttocks on luxury seat warmers is *definitely* worth my financial freedom." Be. Honest.

Opportunity cost: Ask yourself questions about the opportunity cost of new debt. What are the benefits of your other options, and how does that compare to taking on an auto loan? Well, the possibilities are endless here. If you can avoid an auto loan by buying something you can afford with cash, the difference in cost could easily be invested or saved. If you can avoid buying a car by walking or taking public transit, you could save a *lot* of money.

Plan: How could you plan to pay back an auto loan? Well, a vehicle provides utility to get to work and run essential errands, but it's not likely to earn or save you money unless you're a rideshare or delivery driver. If you decide to take on an auto loan, make sure it's one that you can easily afford.

Other Consumer debt

General rule: bad idea

Let's take a quick look at a *HOP analysis* for other consumer debt.

Honesty: No one ever got rich buying crap they couldn't afford. Thus concludes "Debt *Dangent*: Consumer Crap Edition."

Opportunity cost: See "Honesty."

Plan: See "Honesty."

Chapter 14: Net worth

Your personal net worth is equal to your total assets minus total liabilities. This is the measure of your financial position at a given point in time.

Figure 2-4
Calculating Net Worth
Total assets
- Total liabilities
Net worth

While your net worth may start off negative when you're younger — for example, you have $10,000 in savings and $20,000 in student loan debt — you should reach a point of breaking even and never *ever* look back. I like to think of net worth as the amount that would be left over if you decided to sell off everything you own, pay off any existing debts, and "walk away" to start a new life from scratch. If you had more debt than assets, the proceeds from the sale of your assets wouldn't be enough to pay off your debt, and you couldn't "walk away" if you wanted to (or needed to). If you had more assets than debt, you'd be able to sell everything you own, pay off your debts, and start anew. You could take a train to the big city and change your name, like in *The Waterboy* when Bobby Boucher's dad moved to New Orleans and started calling himself "Roberto." OK fine, he was broke and leaving his life behind, so maybe that's a bad example. My point is, all things being equal, people with net worth have a more flexible life than people who don't. In the pursuit of financial health and financial freedom, net worth is king.

A word of caution: remember to never confuse net worth with *self*-worth. Your net worth is a measurement of your financial position, not your value as a person.

Chapter 15: Taxes

Love 'em or hate 'em, taxes are part of the financial picture for any citizen who lives in a place where government exists. Taxes are like flies; they're annoying and no one wants to be swarmed by an overwhelming amount, but they serve a purpose in the broader ecosystem. Individual taxpayers in the United States may be subjected to taxes imposed by the federal government and state and local governments in order to support governmental functions, and they are inherently a topic of political debate and negotiation. Anything that is open to the public is funded by taxes: public schools, public parks, public roads, and so on.

Quick tax tangent: Taxes are one of the reasons it's more advantageous to spend $1 less than it is to earn $1 more. "But Dan, a dollar is equal to a dollar, right? A pound of feathers weighs the same as a pound of rocks!" Nope, earning an extra dollar doesn't equate to keeping an extra dollar, even if you don't spend it, because of taxes. If you earn $1 more at work, you'll pay income taxes and payroll taxes on that dollar, resulting in an actual cash flow of less than $1 (sometimes significantly less, depending on the relevant tax structure). But if you lower a bill by \$1, your cash flow is 100% of that dollar. Defense is better than offense!

Tax laws change constantly, and I will not be providing specific information such as active rates because that would inevitably become outdated, likely even before this book hits shelves. Tax purposes, methods, populations, and rates are always subject to change. I encourage you to stay educated on taxation as part of your overall financial education and civic duty.

The sections below provide general terminology on taxation relevant to personal finance.

Tax rate

Tax rate is the percentage of tax to be charged. This may be a fixed or variable rate, depending on the law.

Tax base

The tax base is the subject of taxation. There are a variety of tax bases, with common examples being income, retail purchases, and property. With income taxation, the tax base is an individual's total taxable income. In retail (sales) taxation, the tax base is the sale price of the good or service being purchased. In property taxation, the tax base is the assessed value of the property.

Income tax

Income taxes are imposed on taxable earnings, such as wages earned by working, or certain passive income earnings. U.S. citizens are subject to federal income taxes (with rare exceptions), and may also be subject to income taxes within state and local jurisdictions, depending on the tax laws where they live.

Payroll tax

Payroll taxes are typically based on a percentage of salaries and are deducted from an individual's paycheck. The employer and employee may each be obligated to pay certain payroll taxes on the employee's earnings.

Payroll taxes can exist at federal, state, and local levels.

Capped vs. uncapped

Certain taxes may have a fixed maximum, or "cap," and some may be unlimited. For example, payroll taxes might have a cap, in which case a tax is levied at the determined percentage, but only up until reaching a specified fixed dollar amount. For example, let's imagine a rate of 1% on total taxable wages, with up to a maximum annual amount of $500. That would mean that someone with taxable wages of $40,000 would pay $400 ($40,000 x 1% = $400, which is under the cap), but anyone with taxable wages over $50,000 would pay the $500 maximum ($50,000 x 1% = 500).

Sales tax

Sales taxes are transactional taxes charged by state and local governments. A percentage of sales tax is applied to certain purchases, most commonly finished goods such as retail products. Not all governments levy a sales tax.

Property tax

This tax is levied on certain property, such as real estate. The tax base is the value assessed by the applicable taxing authority.

Tax withholding

A tax withholding is an amount withheld from an employee's paycheck and sent to the applicable taxing authority by the employer, in the employee's name. The withholding is based on an estimate of what total taxes will be for the period of taxation (i.e., calendar year). If the employee withheld less than their actual tax bill, they "owe" taxes. If they withheld more than necessary, they get a tax refund. If they withheld *way* less than their actual bill, they may be charged a fine (it's happened to me!).

The total amount of taxes imposed for the period does not change regardless of whether you withhold more or less, and as long as it's close, you won't be fined. Some people treat withholding as a quasi savings account, and knowingly withhold too much so that they aren't tempted to spend the cash. Others withhold as little as possible, so that they can take advantage of the benefits of having cash available to invest or pay down debt. There is no "wrong" method, as long as you ensure you're withholding based on a reasonable estimate. That said, I tend to prefer not lend out my money interest-free, and prefer to owe a little each year rather than get a big refund. When I set up my withholding, I tend to repeat the famous Marshawn Lynch quote in my head: "I'm just here so I won't get fined."

Tax avoidance vs. tax evasion

Tax avoidance is the use of existing laws and programs to minimize taxes, and it is totally legal. Tax avoidance is critical in maximizing net worth. Businesses and individuals tend to want to pay as little tax as possible, which is why there are CPAs, tax attorneys, wealth management professionals, tax preparers, and other everyday experts who are hired to minimize taxes. That's how important it is — people *pay money* for help in avoiding unnecessary tax consequences. There is nothing unethical about tax avoidance, and no one will ever go to jail for it.

Tax avoidance is one of the most beautiful, fundamental money management strategies available. Simply think of taxes as any other bill — and wouldn't you try to minimize or delay your bills whenever possible? "Excuse me sir, this shirt costs $15, correct? Could I please pay $60 instead?" Don't be silly, and don't overpay the government — they expect us to try to minimize taxes. One of the *greatest* incentives governments use to drive citizens' behaviors is manipulation of tax. For example, tax-advantaged investing, such as through a 401(k) or IRA, was designed to incentivize taxpayers to invest on their own rather than rely solely on governmental programs like Social Security. There are also extra taxes for behavior they'd like to discourage. Invest in your retirement, and you get to pay less; wreck the environment, and you get to pay more. Just be honest, play within the lines, and utilize quality tax strategies. The classic routes will get you a long way; those who eventually do become very wealthy can hire a clever pro to help with advanced planning once the need arises.

Tax *evasion* is lying, and it is illegal. It is breaking the law through false tax reporting, or a simple refusal to pay. When you see a celebrity (often a total jerk) in the news headlines for tax fraud, they are guilty of tax evasion. They may not have the money anymore because they've already spent it, and I sure don't feel bad for them. Folks who deliberately choose to defraud their government are making a choice — evasion requires intent.

But not all people who don't pay their taxes are jerks. Remember when *Happy Gilmore*'s grandma had her house repossessed, right before Happy realized he could hit the long ball? She hadn't been paying her taxes. And she would have paid, but she was old and just didn't have any money. The sweetest lady in the world just couldn't pay, because (I'm speculating here) she was living off of Social Security in her old age, and couldn't make ends meet. That's not really tax evasion, it's not having enough money to pay bills.

In summary, tax avoidance is good, tax evasion is bad, and some people get in trouble for not paying taxes because they truly can't afford it. Your taxes are just another bill, and there's no reason not to try to lower your bill. If you ever want to further support something that is otherwise funded by taxes, public parks for example, just donate on your own whim instead — it may even get you a tax deduction.

Progressive tax structure

A progressive tax structure means that tax rates vary depending on earnings, with higher earnings resulting in higher tax rates. The United States federal income tax currently uses a progressive tax structure, which attempts to charge a higher effective tax rate on those with higher taxable wages. This structure establishes "tax brackets," which set different tax rates for different income levels.

A simplistic two-bracket progressive tax model is shown in Figure 2-5 below:

Figure 2-5

Simplistic Progressive Tax Model

Taxable Income	Tax Rate
$0-40,000	10%
$40,001 or more	$4,000 + 20% of the amount over $40,000

Taxable wages of $0 to $40,000 are taxed at 10%, and wages $40,001 or more are taxed at 20%. This means that anyone earning $40,000 or less would pay $4,000 or less in taxes ($40,000 x 10% = $4,000). Anyone earning over $40,000 would pay $4,000 in taxes on their first $40,000 of taxable wages, and then 20% of every dollar earned over $40,000. So if they have taxable wages of $50,000, their taxes due would be calculated as shown Figure 2-6 below:

Figure 2-6

Example Tax Calculation Steps

Steps	Earnings	Tax Rate	Tax
Step 1	$40,000	10%	$4,000
Step 2	$10,000	20%	$2,000
Total	$50,000		$6,000

This is a good time to hash out some key terms. For the individual making $50,000 in the scenario above, their "marginal tax rate" — the tax rate for the next dollar earned — is 20%. That is because their "tax bracket" calls for a 20% tax rate on each dollar earned over the prior threshold of $40,000. Their "effective tax rate" — the average tax rate in a progressive tax system — is 12%, which is calculated as their total tax of $6,000 divided by their total tax base of $50,000.

Flat tax structure (fixed tax structure)

People refer to a "flat tax" in two different ways: a flat (or fixed) dollar amount, or a flat (or fixed) percentage. In a fixed dollar tax structure, everyone pays the same total dollar amount, regardless of income or other factors. This means that the *effective* tax rate would fluctuate depending on the value of their tax base value (if applicable), but the *marginal* tax rate doesn't really apply, since the dollar amount doesn't change. In a fixed percentage tax structure, the marginal rate and effective rate are identical, because the tax rate doesn't change for any reason.

FICA Payroll taxes

The Federal Insurance Contributions Act (FICA) requires that employees and employers pay into two key governmental programs: Social Security and Medicare. The rates for any given year are easy to track down, either by looking at your paycheck or by using your favorite search engine. Below is a quick overview of what FICA taxes support, and why.

Social Security

Social Security is a governmental program that was established to provide partial income replacement for qualified retired adults and individuals with disabilities, as well as for their spouses, children, and survivors. According to their website, Social Security replaces a percentage of pre-retirement income based on lifetime earnings. The portion of your pre-retirement wages that Social Security replaces varies, based on your highest 35 years of earnings and when you choose to start benefits.

If you've ever wondered why you have to provide employers with your Social Security card, now you know. It's so they can withhold Social Security taxes from your paycheck and make payments into the program on your behalf. It's worth noting that no one has an "account" with Social Security; they're merely entitled to benefits. The money you put in while you're working actually goes toward paying benefits for currently qualified individuals, and the hope is that when you're eligible, the next generation will be paying for yours. So don't call the White House hoping to get someone to provide you with your account balance. That's just not how it works.

At the time of writing this book, most people, especially those nearing retirement, consider Social Security as part of their retirement income replacement plans. A variety of factors may alter the way Social Security looks in the future though, such as changes to the imposed tax rates, benefit eligibility, and benefit calculations. Challenges such as increased cost of living and increased life span will put significant pressure on the program, but the hope is that anyone who pays into it will get a fair shake when it's their turn to benefit. Fingers crossed.

Medicare

According to their website, Medicare is the federal health insurance program for people who are 65 or older, certain younger people with disabilities, and others with certain diseases. Similar to Social Security, Medicare taxes are withheld from employee paychecks in order to fund benefits for those currently eligible. Unlike Social Security, however, Medicare also receives funding from other sources. The intent behind Medicare is to provide health insurance in retirement, since retirees typically lose their employer-sponsored medical insurance when they stop working.

The future of Medicare will be interesting to watch unfold. Since its introduction in the 1960s it has been a very visible debate topic in political campaigns, with opinions offering more variety than a supermarket. But in its present state, Medicare is the primary insurance program for the elderly and disabled.

Chapter 16: Insurance

Insurance is a critical piece of any complete financial strategy. Insurance is designed to protect against the financial consequences of bad outcomes. Purchasing an insurance policy is the exchange of cash now for help mitigating a financial disaster later. Health insurance is there to cover excessive health care costs, if they arise. Homeowners insurance is available to cover the potential cost of your home being damaged or destroyed. Actual insurance strategies will be discussed in the "Defense" chapter in Section 3, but for now, here are some basic insurance terms.

Premium: The amount a consumer pays for an insurance policy. Premiums for individual policies, such as for car insurance, are paid directly to the insurance company. Premiums for employer-sponsored plans, such as health insurance, are withheld from the employee's paycheck and paid to the insurance company by the employer.

Insurance claim: A formal request by a policyholder to an insurance company for coverage or compensation for a covered loss or policy event. For example, you may need to file an insurance claim related to car issues, or a medical office may submit an insurance claim to your insurance company on your behalf if you provide them with your insurance information in advance.

Deductible: The amount the insured person is required to pay before the insurance company pays for a claim. For example, a $500 car insurance deductible means you, the policyholder, are responsible for the first $500 of damage, and the insurance company is responsible for amounts beyond that.

Section 3: Building a Winning Game Plan (Liquid and Flavor)

Congratulations! You made it through the plain flour challenge without throwing up (hopefully). Now it's time to start looking at skills and strategies — liquid and flavor — so you can start making *Healthy Dough*. Remember to check the definitions in the Appendix if you see a term you're not positive you understand. Let's go!

Chapter 17: Margin — building a lead and winning

A winning game plan, whether in sports, games, or finance, is designed to create a positive margin. In games and sports, a margin is basically the difference between your score and your opponent's score. If you have five points and your opponent has four, you have a "margin," or lead, of one point. In general, a higher margin is desirable, and a negative margin means a loss.

To win a basketball game, you need to outscore your opponent — simple as that. There are different perspectives regarding how to earn that lead. An offensive-minded approach means your strategy is to win by scoring more points than your opponent. A defensive-minded approach may be that you need to allow fewer points than your opponent to win. Winning a basketball game 127-125 is basically the same outcome as winning 4-2 — you win by two points either way, even though there was a huge disparity in method. Let's use those same scores in a financial context, and pretend each point is worth $1,000. A margin of $2,000 is equal to $2,000 regardless of the numbers that are accumulated in the process. If person A earned $127,000, and spent $125,000, they saved $2,000. Person A built a winning game plan, but spent over 98% of the money they earned. If person B earned only $4,000, but spent only $2,000, they also saved $2,000. Person B spent only half of their earnings and saved the other half. The game plan of person A may benefit from quality offense (earning and scoring) but needs more focus on defense (protecting money). The game plan of person B isn't great either, because it's really hard to win consistently if you're barely scoring. If you want to win consistently, you need to have a good balance of offense and defense.

The basic winning game plan for building financial prosperity is as follows:

1) Offense: Earn money from working
2) Defense: Keep your money
3) Offense: Grow the money that you've kept

The next few topics will provide some practical tips for creating a high financial margin using healthy, productive offensive and defensive strategies. I'll also cover one of the most important, yet undervalued, things in sports and life — the intangibles. Anyway, here's the plan: I'll break down some keys to the game for offense, defense, and the intangibles, and you get out there and go win.

Chapter 18: Offense

Learn how to score

To win a game, you have to be able to score. The same holds true in personal finance — you can't win unless you're able to get some points. For our purposes, consider the "scoring" aspect of offense as your ability to earn money by working (active income). There are an infinite number of ways someone can earn money and score through producing active income, because there are many different types of work throughout the world. Doctors, farmers, artists, chefs, builders, and even accountants can follow the same guiding principles to become a scorer. The best ways I know for developing earning potential are to get good at something, to work hard, and work smart.

Get good at something

There are many reasons I'm not a professional race car driver. I'm not very interested in cars, I don't really like driving very much, and, according to reviews from my most frequent passengers, riding with me feels about as smooth as a porcupine. No one is going to pay me to drive a sponsored race car, because I'm not good at it. I can't provide the sponsors any value by going out and placing last, or crashing their car (or both), while I represent their brands. Since I cannot provide adequate value to a racing team by driving their race car (other than maybe comedic value for fans), no racing team is going to pay me to do so. My point is, you have to be good at something for someone to pay you to do it. I have lots of "dream" careers — professional athlete, freelance chili judge, rock star, beer tester — but my talents in those fields don't provide anyone with enough value for someone to pay me to do it. And even if you *are* really great at something, you'll only get paid if there's demand. You may be great at belching the ABCs, but that probably won't pay the rent.

In order to earn money for your work, you need to get good at something that provides enough value for someone to afford to pay you for it. For most people, their employer pays for their work, while business owners are paid by their own customers. In my opinion, it doesn't matter what you "get good at;" if you provide value and there is demand for your profession, you will be able to earn money. People will pay you for your work if you have the knowledge, skills, or products they require. If you're a skilled electrician, consumers and businesses will pay you for your electrician services. If you're good at managing a retail store, a retailer will pay you to manage a location. If you're learned in bird law, clients will pay for your legal services. If you're a good accountant, a corporation will pay you to produce their financial records, and even pay you a little extra to lie (just kidding, friends).

To be able to consistently earn decent money and generate "offense," you have to find a way to be in demand and provide unique value. I think the continuous controversies around minimum wage rates point to the fact that it's very tough to "win" financially when you're not earning much money. Most entry-level roles that pay minimum wage do not require a particular skill set in order to complete the work, and because of that, there is a much larger candidate pool to choose from. Higher supply means lower prices, so employers pay less for entry-level roles. Conversely, the reason surgeons are paid such high wages is because surgical work requires a specific and complicated skill set, and the work is in high demand. I'm not opining on whether or not it's fair, but it's true, and those are the underlying economic concepts as to why.

I don't know anything about your aptitudes, education level, or skill sets — but I can guarantee that if you want to earn decent money, you will need to offer some sort of unique skill that provides value to meet market demands. Build skills that would be challenging to replace with a robot, such as critical thinking, creative problem solving, social intelligence, skilled labor, and so on. Do that, and you'll improve your odds of success. That said, let's take a quick detour and consider how to define career success in a healthy way.

Defining success

Defining success is very personal and subjective, even though there are sometimes measurables associated with it. Some think it's possible to calculate a person's financial success because certain components are quantifiable, such as salaries. Additionally, most would agree that, all other things being the same, more money is better. But success is not synonymous with high salaries or even high net worth. There can be significant overlap, but not always. Let's look at an illustrative example to add some clarity to this concept.

A registered nurse and a medical doctor work in the same facility and support the same patient populations. They happen to be the exact same age, having just celebrated their 30th birthdays. The doctor's salary is $210,000 per year, and the nurse's salary is $70,000 per year. Who is more financially successful? Who is more successful overall? As with most things, it depends.

The doctor earns more money and has achieved the most advanced standard medical license. They also earn over three times the national median income by themself alone. Is the doctor successful?

The nurse earns more than the national median income by themself alone, and the RN designation is a prestigious title in a critical field. Is the nurse successful?

Conventional American wisdom says that both the nurse and the doctor are successful. It would also tell us that the doctor is more financially successful than the nurse because they earn significantly more money, and the doctor is more successful overall because they have a more advanced license. Would you agree? I'd still be undecided, because occupation and salary are not the sole determinants of financial success, let alone success overall. Success can't be reviewed in a vacuum. Inherent in the determination of success is the presence of an objective or a goal, and so what seems to be a positive outcome to outsiders may not actually be success for the individual. We should each allow one another to define success in our own way.

Career success isn't just about money and prestige. If we ignore the financial aspects of this scenario for now, questions about the success of the doctor and nurse can be focused around career satisfaction and performance. Are they good at their jobs? Do they receive quality evaluations? Do they connect with their patients? Do they like coming in to work? Are they happy with their chosen field, or do they wish they were doing something else? Do they feel they're making appropriate use of their abilities? Is their career a net positive in their life?

There are plenty of examples of people in the alleged "upper class" who meet traditional measures of success, and who also meet my definitions of success. I've been fortunate to observe such examples among coworkers, friends, and family members who stack up remarkable accomplishments in healthy ways. However, there are also plenty of "elite" who do not meet my definitions of general success, *nor* financial success, even though they have prestige and earn lots of money. People with sophisticated careers and high earnings are generally considered successful in American culture, and those with lackluster careers, few achievements, and low earnings are viewed as less successful. I don't think these views are totally meritless, and know I've caught myself basing career decisions around money and status; however, there are rich people who are failing, and still others who remain less fortunate despite overachieving.

Counterexamples to traditional measures of success are going on in the world right this second, as you read this page. Somewhere out there, a middle management team carries the extra weight of an incompetent executive. In a hospital near you, a nurse is making less money than a doctor, but contributing more positively to their shared patients. Your local social worker is making a huge impact on one of your neighbors, even though they don't earn a fortune doing it. A mechanic's shop is the top business in town, despite their parents pushing hard for a four-year university education. A single parent manages multiple entry-level jobs to pay for basic needs, and still finds time to let the kids know they're loved. What was that "thud" sound? Just another bankrupt celebrity hitting rock bottom. Somewhere out there, the world's most incompetent CPA populates random spreadsheet cells with big, sloppy tears.

So now let's talk turkey, and go back to the example of the nurse and the doctor. Who is more financially successful among those two? Who has a higher net worth? Easy answer, because the doctor earns three times what the nurse does — right? *Wrong.* The correct answer is, of course, that we don't have enough information, and it depends.

Debt and lifestyle, not salary, are the greatest determining factors in net worth. Who has more student loan debt? It isn't necessarily the doctor, even though medical school is incredibly expensive. They may have used an inheritance to pay for school, or they may have a few hundred thousand dollars in loan debt. Who has the more expensive house, or drives the more expensive car? Do either of them have a second income at home, or possibly even a financially irresponsible partner? Did they borrow a bunch of money for a huge wedding? The doctor could earn three times what the nurse does, invest it well, and retire early; or they could live beyond their means and be suffocated by debt. The nurse could make one-third of what the doctor does, invest well, and retire early; or they could live beyond their means and be suffocated by debt. Debt and lifestyle can always take net worth below zero, and therefore are way more impactful on financial success than salary. The good news is, you generally have choices regarding lifestyle, and you can make informed decisions regarding debt. Wealth isn't about what you make — it's about what you keep, and how you grow what you keep.

Financial success should be defined individually — not by society. Someone may be tremendously wealthy, yet have *never* achieved their financial goals, and never be satisfied. Someone may set and achieve very average financial goals, and be completely content with that. All too often there's also the heartbreaking combination of someone who is not achieving their financial goals and can't make ends meet; their life is made exponentially worse by poor financial health. I'll say it again — that is heartbreaking. I think it is also something that a person can break out of with the right skills, perspectives, and knowledge.

Finances should be a net positive in your life, so the way you earn money should not drain the life out of you. Develop your willpower and be appreciative of your opportunities. Find balance. The *Five Truths of Financial Health* tell us that people in poor health spend more money, and that discipline is an exhaustible resource. If a high-paying job or career choice is causing excessive strain on mental, social, and maybe even physical health, the extra money may not really translate into enhanced well-being.

So what are your financial goals, and how does your career success support that? What are your career goals, and how does your financial success support that? Being good at managing money allows you to pick a career you can enjoy and feel successful in. And when you're happy and confident, your work will be better, which may end up helping you earn more money anyway.

Work hard and work smart

Working hard and working smart increase your value to the people who pay you. Find efficiencies, gain experience, share ideas, and showcase your ambition. Working hard and working smart will help you get promoted, and getting promoted improves your offense via higher wages. Two of the best ways to work hard and work smart are to thrive on feedback and work on your weaknesses. This will lead to personal growth, and that growth will provide your employer or customer with more value, which should command higher wages. Get better at your job as you gain experience! Hard work, persistence, and escalating value are the underlying ingredients to the scenarios in which someone starts in the mail room and works their way up to being a corporate leader.

Takeaways for learning how to score

Most people generate active income until they reach normal retirement age, either because they have to work to meet their financial needs, or because they are fulfilled by working. The most productive ways to generate active income are by getting good at something that provides unique value to an employer or customer, and consistently growing in order to achieve advancement and higher wages.

Grow your lead by investing responsibly

A good investor is like a good poker player: they usually find a way to win, or at least stay alive, even though they don't control the cards they're dealt (or do they!?). The skills of a good poker player mitigate their risk of being dealt bad cards. They know the game and how to read the room, and they make calculated decisions based on "risk and reward." A bad investor is more likely to be like a slot player, haphazardly tossing money around in hopes of getting rich.

There are varied modes of investing, such as investing in securities, real estate, career advancement, debt paydown, and more. Investing responsibly means making informed decisions that match your goals and circumstances at the time. Taking factors into consideration such as your current financial position, short and long-term goals, and "risk and reward" are critical in making quality choices. Every single cash decision has risk and opportunity cost. Investing involves risk, but so does *not* investing.

The risks of not investing

Why isn't saving enough? Why do I have to save and *then* invest responsibly? The reason we must invest in profitable assets in order to be financially healthy is because of inflation. At a minimum, your overall investment portfolio needs to outpace inflation, or the money you've initially saved won't have the same purchasing power when you use it later.

I learned about the impact of inflation from an investment banker who presented as a guest speaker at my high school. In the auditorium where he presented to us, he held up a $1 bill and said, "In 1950, this $1 bill would have bought me 20 king-size candy bars; today, it would buy me only one. If I kept this dollar bill hidden under my mattress for several decades, it would buy me only one candy bar compared to the 20 it would have bought when I put it under the mattress. The reason for this is inflation."

I never did check his math, but the concept still makes sense. In economics, inflation and deflation refer to changes in the purchasing power of a given currency over time. An approachable way to define inflation is "prices going up," while deflation is "prices going down." The "inflation rate" refers to price fluctuations for a broad mix of consumables, and is used to explain changes in valuation and purchasing power of a given currency. For example, an annual inflation rate of 3% per year means that in general, prices of goods and services have risen approximately 3% per year.

Due to inflation in the U.S. economy, $1 buys much less candy than it did in the 1950s, because $1 was *worth more* in the 1950s. The purchasing power of one U.S. dollar has declined over time. Consider this example involving Liz, a young adult who saves her first dollar.

Just before midnight on Dec. 31, 1976, Liz finds a dollar in her pocket. What a finish to the year! She decides that she's going to keep it in her pillowcase for the rest of time, because it has to be lucky somehow.

The dollar delivers her great luck in 1977, or at least that's what she tells herself. Liz spends her time listening to Fleetwood Mac's brand new album *Rumours* while wearing her bell-bottom jeans. She sees Led Zeppelin in concert on their final North American tour, and is blown away watching *Star Wars* at the drive-in theater. She enjoys 1977 so much that she decides the dollar needs to keep staying tucked in her pillowcase, so it can keep bringing on the groovy vibes.

Fast forward to 2020 when Liz is 65 years old and retiring. After years of work and saving, she decides to give the dollar to her grandchild for safekeeping and good luck. Her grandchild appreciates the gesture, but doesn't understand why grandma feels like finding a dollar is such a big deal; it really isn't worth much these days. Unfortunately, since the dollar was not invested and wasn't producing investment income, it buys about 22% of what it would have when it was hidden in 1977.

To recap, the purchasing power of $1 in 2020 was similar to the purchasing power of $0.22 in 1977. Flipping the equation around, it's also true that $1 in 1977 had the same purchasing power as $4.50 would have in 2020. During the 43 years from 1977 to 2020, the average annual inflation rate was 3.56%, which means that prices increased an average of 3.56% per year during that time period. Since Liz didn't invest her dollar in 1977, it did not earn any income, and its purchasing power decreased significantly. Thank goodness it was at least lucky.

Let's change the fact pattern slightly, and assume that Liz had invested that dollar in a Roth IRA (pretending Roth IRAs existed back then). If her dollar had earned 2% per year tax-free in the Roth account, it would have compounded to be $2.34 in 2020. Thus, the investment earnings for the dollar would have resulted in greater purchasing power than if she had kept it under her pillow. That said, $2.34 in 2020 would be worth about the equivalent of $0.52 in 1977. Even though her investment would have been worth more after the 43 years it was invested, $2.34 in 2020 still wouldn't have the same purchasing power as her $1 did in 1977. This is because her annual investment earnings of 2% were less than the annual inflation rate of 3.56%. Her growth would have been less than the general increase in her costs due to inflation. Earning 2% is much better than earning 0%, but since her investment returns were less than inflation, Liz's $2.34 in 2020 money would still be less valuable than her $1 in 1977, because that $1 from 1977 had the same purchasing power as $4.50 in 2020 dollars. Whoa. Bummer. Far out.

Let's change the fact pattern one more time, and assume that Liz had invested her $1 in a Roth IRA and earned 4% tax-free during the 43 years between 1977 and 2020. Since Liz's investment returns were higher than inflation, she actually would have had *more* purchasing power in 2020 than she did in 1977. Her original dollar would have grown to be $5.40 in 2020, which is equivalent to $1.20 in 1977. By investing in a way that outpaced inflation, Liz would not only have been able to retain the value of her original dollar, but she would have wound up with even *more* purchasing power than she originally had. If Liz's investment returns had been exactly equal to the inflation rate of 3.56% for those 43 years, her money (in general) would have had the exact same value and purchasing power as it did in 1977; but since her earnings were higher than inflation, she would have had 20% more purchasing power in 2020 than she did in 1977. This is where we arrive at our key to the game. Liz could have built a lead by saving a dollar, and in this last scenario, she could have *grown* her lead by investing responsibly and producing earnings higher than inflation.

The table in Figure 3-1 and corresponding line chart in Figure 3-2 show how inflation rates can impact purchasing power over time. Notice how the value erodes over time, and especially quickly as the inflation rates increase. The exponential impact of higher rates can certainly be daunting. So just remember, a single dollar bill in the present will generally buy more than that same bill in the future, because of the impacts of inflation. This is why we have to invest our savings into assets that will generate positive cash flows, or increase in value over time, or preferably both.

Figure 3-1

Future Value of $1 with
Given Inflation Rate (Table)

		Inflation rate			
		1%	**2%**	**3%**	**4%**
	0	1.00	1.00	1.00	1.00
	5	0.95	0.91	0.86	0.82
	10	0.91	0.82	0.74	0.68
Y	15	0.86	0.74	0.64	0.56
e	20	0.82	0.67	0.55	0.46
a	25	0.78	0.61	0.48	0.38
r	30	0.74	0.55	0.41	0.31
s	35	0.71	0.50	0.36	0.25
	40	0.67	0.45	0.31	0.21
	45	0.64	0.41	0.26	0.17
	50	0.61	0.37	0.23	0.14

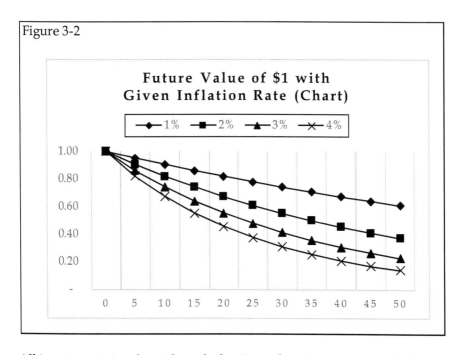

Figure 3-2

All investments involve risk, and oftentimes there is a strong correlation between "risk and reward." Risk is not static. The world is constantly changing, and so are its businesses and investment opportunities. At a minimum, you need to invest in a way that beats inflation. But when you are weighing your appetite for risk, realize that the potential returns of an investment aren't between 0% and infinity; they're actually between *negative* 100% (total loss of investment) and infinity. Some investments, such as debt securities, have a stated return — but even *that* isn't a guarantee. There's still a risk that the borrower won't pay interest payments on time, or won't return principal. Equity investments have a theoretically limitless potential, but of course there are practical ceilings on equity investments, and the stock could always go skydiving.

In my opinion, investing responsibly comes down to patience and risk management. Saving cash is not an investment, unless you're somehow doing that as part of currency hedge strategy, which I promise you, you're not.

Go find some inflation tables online and check them out for yourself.

Investment growth tables: subtitle, math is cool

Before you start imagining inflation as a giant beach ball that keeps inflating until it's too big and you can't seem to find a sharp object to stab it with and you watch in terror as you're smothered by this metaphorical beach ball economy, I have some good news. You can benefit from exponential growth — enough to outpace inflation in the long term — if you invest responsibly. Let's review some tables that show how intensely awesome exponential growth is when it's working *for* you instead of against you.

Figure 3-3 depicts the future values of a $1,000 lump sum investment. Lump sum simply means a onetime, nonrecurring amount. Each cell in the table represents the future value at a given time interval and return rate. You can also determine future values using a "return factor," which would be the numeric factor you can multiply your lump sum by. Figure 3-4 shows the return factors for a given interval and return rate. Suppose you open a Roth IRA when you turn 18, and you retire 45 years later when you're 63. Your initial investment is $1,000, and it reliably earns 6% annually during those 45 years. By multiplying the return factor of approximately 13.76 by the lump sum investment of $1,000, we can calculate that the initial investment of $1,000 will be worth $13,765 at retirement (as shown in the tables). Changing the fact pattern slightly, assume you receive a net bonus payment of $5,000, and invest the lump sum in a Roth IRA. If it earns 8% for 30 years, it will be worth $50,313 (future value factor of 10.06 times $5,000 lump sum). Dang. That's sweeter than sugarcoated cherries.

Figure 3-3

Future Value of Single $1,000 Lump Sum

		Return %				
		2%	4%	6%	8%	10%
Y e a r s	5	1,104	1,217	1,338	1,469	1,611
	10	1,219	1,480	1,791	2,159	2,594
	15	1,346	1,801	2,397	3,172	4,177
	20	1,486	2,191	3,207	4,661	6,727
	25	1,641	2,666	4,292	6,848	10,835
	30	1,811	3,243	5,743	10,063	17,449
	35	2,000	3,946	7,686	14,785	28,102
	40	2,208	4,801	10,286	21,725	45,259
	45	2,438	5,841	13,765	31,920	72,890
	50	2,692	7,107	18,420	46,902	117,391

Figure 3-4

Future Value Factor

		Return %				
		2%	4%	6%	8%	10%
Y e a r s	5	1.10	1.22	1.34	1.47	1.61
	10	1.22	1.48	1.79	2.16	2.59
	15	1.35	1.80	2.40	3.17	4.18
	20	1.49	2.19	3.21	4.66	6.73
	25	1.64	2.67	4.29	6.85	10.83
	30	$1.81	3.24	5.74	10.06	17.45
	35	2.00	3.95	7.69	14.79	28.10
	40	2.21	4.80	10.29	21.72	45.26
	45	2.44	5.84	13.76	31.92	72.89
	50	2.69	7.11	18.42	46.90	117.39

All that said, most people don't invest with lump sums, for reasons we'll discuss later. So what would it look like to invest $100 per month, perhaps as part of a monthly payroll contribution to an employer-sponsored 401(k) plan? See Figure 3-5 below. If you were to work for 40 years, earning 6% annually (compounding monthly), your account would be worth $199,149 upon retirement. That may sound like a lot now, but it's definitely not enough to serve as the sole source of income in a normal retirement. The problem isn't the return percentage as much as the contribution amount. At the time of writing, a total of $100 per month and $1,200 per year (not factoring in employer contributions) simply isn't a very large contribution. When you factor in 40 years of inflation against the balance, it's clearly important to escalate contribution amounts when possible. That said, investing a little is much better than not investing at all.

Figure 3-5

Future Value of $100 Per Month Compounding Monthly

		2%	4%	6%	8%	10%
				Return %		
Y e a r s	5	6,305	6,630	6,977	7,348	7,744
	10	13,272	14,725	16,388	18,295	20,484
	15	20,971	24,609	29,082	34,604	41,447
	20	29,480	36,677	46,204	58,902	75,937
	25	38,882	51,413	69,299	95,103	132,683
	30	49,273	69,405	100,452	149,036	226,049
	35	60,755	91,373	142,471	229,388	379,664
	40	73,444	118,196	199,149	349,101	632,408
	45	87,466	150,947	275,599	527,454	1,048,250
	50	102,961	190,936	378,719	793,173	1,732,439

Keeping the return rate at a modest 6%, Figure 3-6 (below) shows future values for a strategy with higher contribution amounts. If you were to invest $500 per month ($6,000 per year) in an employer-sponsored tax-advantaged retirement plan throughout a 40-year career, the value at retirement would be $995,745. If you had $5,000 or more cash in the bank, you'd be a millionaire! And imagine that you also own your home and have absolutely zero debts — that million-ish could last a decent amount of time – even after inflation takes its toll. If this were a Roth account, the earnings of $755,745 (see Figure 3-7) would never, ever be taxed. That's as cool as an autumn breeze on a motorcycle. Plus, this math below is based on $500 each month without ever escalating contributions or receiving an employer match. Maybe you would have to start off with $100 per month, but be able to increase contribution amounts each year as salaries rise. You could start at $100 and end up at $1,000, or even max out the annual limit each year. The point is, investing early and often, combined with a responsible lifestyle and other key financial factors, will get you where you need to be to retire.

Figure 3-6

Future Value of Investments for Monthly Contributions
Earning 6% Annually, Compounding Monthly

			Contribution amount		
	$100	**$250**	**$500**	**$750**	**$1,000**
5	6,977	17,443	34,885	52,328	69,770
10	16,388	40,970	81,940	122,910	163,879
15	29,082	72,705	145,409	218,114	290,819
20	46,204	115,510	231,020	346,531	462,041
25	69,299	173,248	346,497	519,745	692,994
30	100,452	251,129	502,258	753,386	1,004,515
35	142,471	356,178	712,355	1,068,533	1,424,710
40	199,149	497,873	995,745	1,493,618	1,991,491
45	275,599	688,998	1,377,996	2,066,994	2,755,993
50	378,719	946,798	1,893,596	2,840,393	3,787,191

Y e a r s

Figure 3-7

Earnings Over Time for Monthly Contributions
Earning 6% annually, Compounding Monthly

			Contribution amount		
	$100	**$250**	**$500**	**$750**	**$1,000**
5	977	2,443	4,885	7,328	9,770
10	4,388	10,970	21,940	32,910	43,879
15	11,082	27,705	55,409	83,114	110,819
20	22,204	55,510	111,020	166,531	222,041
25	39,299	98,248	196,497	294,745	392,994
30	64,452	161,129	322,258	483,386	644,515
35	100,471	251,178	502,355	753,533	1,004,710
40	151,149	377,873	755,745	1,133,618	1,511,491
45	221,599	553,998	1,107,996	1,661,994	2,215,993
50	318,719	796,798	1,593,596	2,390,393	3,187,191

Y e a r s

Don't try something bold if something easier will work

Let's say you're out on a hike and you need to cross a river that is deep and wide. You see a bridge, which appears to be stable, unaffected by recent weather, and perfectly passable. You see a group of reasonably ordinary people easily cross the bridge, but it lacks excitement — after seeing how easy their traverse was, you immediately decide the bridge isn't right for you. No, instead, you will do something different; something so rebellious and brave that you'll instantly be two points hotter on a 10-point scale. You will find a fallen log and walk it 100 yards up the river. You'll lie down face-first on the log, and launch into the water facing the opposing bank. You'll then paddle across as if on a boogie board, hoping to arrive at about the same place the bridge would have put you. You'll have found an interesting and unique way to get to your destination, and later people will ooh and aah as you delight them with the tale of your wild journey. Soon that bridge will be obsolete as your boogie-logging technique sweeps the nation — right? No, of course not! Unless you're looking for something interesting to talk about, or want to be perceived as eccentric and adventurous, there's no reason to try something bold when there is a simpler option that yields similar results. Consider basic, fundamentally sound personal finance habits to be a bridge to where you want to go. They may not be cool or sexy, but they're the most reliable way to get across the river. This ridiculous analogy about boogie-logging (a water sport I made up, and honestly want to try for fun now) represents how silly it is to try to reach your goals through gimmicks and pizzazz when the basics can get you pretty dang far.

The Three Keys to Financial Freedom

The best way to turn your active income into improved cash flows and asset appreciation is by taking advantage of classic saving and investing opportunities. There might be something out there that *could* provide greater returns in the near term, but that doesn't necessarily mean they would last. Before you get too crafty, make sure to take advantage of the *Three Keys to Financial Freedom (Three Keys)*.

The *Three Keys* are reliable, sustainable, and simple. They're also all but required if you ever want to enjoy long-term financial health, let alone retire. Ask around, and you'll find that financially healthy folks agree: the *Three Keys* are the bee's knees. Let's check 'em out.

1 – Investing in tax-advantaged accounts

Investing in tax-advantaged accounts is a top-tier investment opportunity for anyone who is eligible — and you're probably eligible. For decades, countless citizens have achieved staggering rewards for taking advantage of this strategy — especially those who started early.

Regardless of whether you choose Roth or traditional, employer-sponsored or IRA, investing in your tax-advantaged retirement account is a quality investing choice. If you have an employer matching contribution, make sure to contribute enough to maximize the match, since it's "free" money. *Woo-hoo!*

Additionally, contributing to a tax-friendly Health Savings Account or Flexible Spending Account can be a huge help to cash flows.

2 – Responsible home purchase

Owning a home is a staple in the pursuit of financial freedom. A responsible purchase should mitigate costs of inflation, provide equity in a marketable asset, and appreciate in cash value over time. Plus, being a homeowner can provide more *Pride and Joy* than a Stevie Ray Vaughan tune (lol, wordplay). That's a *home* run investment, as long as you buy within your means and needs (lol, pun).

3 – Ditching debt

Paying off interest-bearing debt early is a guaranteed way to reduce scheduled future cash outflows, and provides flexibility and freedom. Ditching that debt as soon as possible will save on interest costs and free up cash flows, which can then be saved, invested, or used to pay down other loans. In general, the first priorities should be to pay off debt with higher net costs, factoring in interest expense, fees, and potential tax impacts (such as certain interest cost deductions for federal income taxes). All of us should make an initial goal to be debt-free except for a primary residence mortgage. That means no consumer debt, no auto loans, no student loans — nothing else. Then, if you have three to six months of emergency savings, you're investing large sums in your tax-advantaged retirement account, and you own a home, I love the idea of throwing any excess cash at that mortgage until your home is owned free and clear. In addition to providing savings on future interest payments, completely removing debt from your personal balance sheet means your monthly expenses will decrease, which could mean more freedom of choice. It could allow more flexibility in career and retirement decisions, and may provide extra margins to support fulfillment, philanthropy, or even advanced investing opportunities, if desired.

While we're here, I hope you have a minute for a quick rant. Credit card debt is a dangerous infection, and may be the single greatest threat to financial health. It's tough to be healthy with a system loaded with toxins.

Trying to achieve prosperity while credit card interest eats away at your net worth is like trying to run a marathon with pneumonia. Cure the disease first, then start building your strength again. And don't count on your investments outperforming the bank's investments. And *don't* get suckered into the validity of credit card debt just because a lot of people have it. A lot of people don't ever floss their teeth, but that doesn't make it a favorable choice. It's OK to use credit cards to earn cash back and assorted points, but never *ever* carry a balance unless it's truly your only way to pay for basic needs at a given point in time. Thus concludes "*Dangent*: Credit Card Edition."

Which Key is best for me?

Each of the *Three Keys* is equally important for different reasons, and should be prioritized based on individual circumstances. In the early stages of financial maturity, it might make sense to focus on investing in tax-advantaged accounts and eliminating nonmortgage debt before starting on the path to homeownership. Others may be in a place where they should focus on purchasing a home by investing just enough to max out their employer match and saving all other cash toward a down payment. In a high interest rate environment, debt paydown can be extra favorable; but even in low-rate environments, the nonmathematical factors can still make it a preferred choice. For example, the long-term cash savings of accelerated debt paydown are known and guaranteed, which may be more attractive to those who stress about investment performance. Look at your own financial and nonfinancial goals and use the *Three Keys* to achieve them.

You can get a long way toward your financial goals if you take the path of least resistance. No need to search for a fallen tree and boogie-log across the river toward financial independence; just walk across the bridge that's right in front of you. I genuinely believe that most people can retire comfortably and on schedule if they've consistently contributed enough to their retirement plan, own a home, and have no debt of any kind. The *Three Keys* can lead to health and wealth without ever having to think about rental property, venture capital, stock picking, or any new wave that comes along.

Finding your balance

Chemistry is the key to good music. Groups like the Red Hot Chili Peppers and Grateful Dead (later Dead & Company) put together incredible live shows because they work so amazingly well together. Vocals, guitar, drums, and bass all feed off of one another. Individually detectible, yet perfectly blending together. The composite vocal sound of groups such as the Beatles, the Eagles, and Brandi Carlile's bands are excellent in a way that goes well beyond the stunning individual vocal talents. Even electronic music created by one person using a synthesizer needs to have chemistry. It needs both the bass and the melody. If it were only bass, it would sound like a horrible three-note tuba recital.

Musicians and musical styles can be exceptional on their own, but not fit well with other exceptional things. I absolutely love the early music of Black Sabbath, and I also love the music of Elton John. But can you imagine Ozzy singing *Crocodile Rock*? Can you picture Sir Elton singing *War Pigs*? Actually, that could be pretty awesome, but he'd need a band around him that could absolutely rip. My point is, chemistry and balance are the most important things in music. Chemistry is also incredibly important in building a financial portfolio.

Everyone's goals, circumstances, and aptitudes are different, which means their financial portfolios will be slightly different as well. Age, financial position, housing situation, career trajectory, family arrangement, investment opportunities, market conditions, retirement goals, and other factors all play a role in what makes a quality mix for a financial portfolio. Your investments don't exist in a vacuum; they are one part of your financial portfolio.

A diversified investment portfolio has variety and balance similar to a great song. It's built around a sturdy foundation, like Alicia Keys' piano, Jimi Hendrix's guitar, or any given pop star's vocals. But there's more than just the foundation. There are other sounds to complement and balance the dominant force. Similarly, investors can pick a main avenue and find supporting features to nicely round out a complete portfolio.

The next section will break down some basic investment strategies. Some are general concepts and others are designed with a well-balanced and diversified portfolio in mind.

Basic investment strategy

Invest early and invest often

I recently learned a Chinese proverb about taking action: "The best time to plant a tree was 20 years ago. The second best time is now." Investing early and often is a classic investment strategy — because it works. Knowing what you know about compounding interest, passive income, and appreciable assets, you're correct to presume that the longer a quality investment is held, the better. Therefore there are two basic applications of the "invest early and often" principle: time in the market (invest early) and dollar cost averaging (invest often).

Time in the market vs. timing the market (invest early)

Time may be the greatest intangible asset of all. Getting into the market early is key for quality growth, and is especially effective with vehicles that allow tax-free growth such as Roth accounts. Starting to make responsible investments as early in life as possible is a good idea, even if it starts with small amounts. Think back to those investment growth tables from Figure 3-3 through Figure 3-7.

I've refrained from listing "buy low, sell high" as an investment strategy, because individuals don't have a high degree of control on market prices, which are also challenging to predict. Buying assets at low prices and selling them at higher prices is a mathematically sound strategy, but it's a lot harder than it sounds. If it were that easy, everyone would do it. It's nearly impossible to time the market in lucrative ways, even for sophisticated professional investors (without foul play, anyway). Most sophisticated investors will tell you that people are more likely to lose money trying to time the market than they are buying at a less-than-optimal time. Don't rely on guessing when stocks will be on sale or when it's the best time to sell. Focus on what's in your control, which is getting into the market sooner rather than later.

Dollar cost averaging (invest often)

The complement to getting into the market sooner rather than later is the concept of dollar cost averaging. The idea behind dollar cost averaging is that investing frequently will help reduce the volatility of securities prices. Sometimes you may buy high, sometimes you may buy low, but it balances out over time because you're riding the wave throughout. We can review a simplistic example of a 12-week period (approximately three months) of a security's pricing to demonstrate how this works.

Figure 3-8

Dollar Cost Averaging: Example Security
Over 12 Weeks with a $1,200 Investment

Week	Price	Purchase Amount (Dollars)				
		Weekly	Biweekly	Monthly	Quarterly	Perfect
Week 1	60	100	-	-	-	-
Week 2	54	100	200	-	-	-
Week 3	61	100	-	-	-	-
Week 4	64	100	200	400	-	-
Week 5	62	100	-	-	-	-
Week 6	58	100	200	-	-	-
Week 7	48	100	-	-	-	1,200
Week 8	56	100	200	400	-	-
Week 9	66	100	-	-	-	-
Week 10	62	100	200	-	-	-
Week 11	57	100	-	-	-	-
Week 12	65	100	200	400	1,200	-
	Total	$ 1,200	$ 1,200	$ 1,200	$ 1,200	$ 1,200

Week	Price	Purchase Amount (Shares)				
		Weekly	Biweekly	Monthly	Quarterly	Perfect
Week 1	60	1.67	-	-	-	-
Week 2	54	1.85	3.70	-	-	-
Week 3	61	1.64	-	-	-	-
Week 4	64	1.56	3.13	6.25	-	-
Week 5	62	1.61	-	-	-	-
Week 6	58	1.72	3.45	-	-	-
Week 7	48	2.08	-	-	-	25.00
Week 8	56	1.79	3.57	7.14	-	-
Week 9	66	1.52	-	-	-	-
Week 10	62	1.61	3.23	-	-	-
Week 11	57	1.75	-	-	-	-
Week 12	65	1.54	3.08	6.15	18.46	-
	Total	20.35	20.15	19.55	18.46	25.00

		Weekly	Biweekly	Monthly	Quarterly	Perfect
Week 12 Account Value		1,323	$ 1,310	$ 1,271	$ 1,200	$ 1,625

The chart shown in Figure 3-8 depicts a security that has gone through a volatile 12-week stretch, with prices rising and falling regularly. The price increased from $60 to $65 over the 12-week stretch, with a low price in week seven of $48 and a high price in week nine of $66. These scenarios are shown to compare investing a total of $1,200 during the 12-week period at different frequencies: weekly, biweekly, monthly, quarterly, and optimal ("perfect") investment timing. As you can see, the perfect time to buy the security was in week seven, since the price was lowest. It was on sale! The $1,200 bought 25 shares at $48, and at the end of week 12 those 25 shares were worth $1,625 (25 shares times $65). Hot *dog!* What a pro. But it's not reasonable to plan on guessing the best time to buy. Instead, build your strategy around things you can control, such as purchase frequency. The weekly pattern acquired the second-most shares with 20.35, resulting in an ending week 12 value of $1,323. A different price was paid each week, including the highest price and lowest price. But overall, the average price paid was $59.42. This was much better than the quarterly purchase scenario, in which the $1,200 was only able to acquire 18.46 shares during that same time period.

This example is a short duration, and simplistic, and it could be modified to show a pattern in which coincidences produce better results with less frequent purchases. But generally, the market prices go up over time, which means that getting in early and using dollar cost averaging to smooth out price volatility is a reliable strategy.

Diversify

Picking a few stocks and calling them a financial portfolio is like planting a few privacy trees along your property line and calling them a forest. A quality portfolio is broad and diversified, and while some features may be dominant, like trees in a forest, all other life-forms between the roots and the canopy have a role in healthy sustainability. A balanced portfolio with a good mix of risk, reward, and variety will survive through your lifetime of spring blooms and winter storms. Just like there are many types of forests that thrive in their own unique environments, there are ways to diversify your financial portfolio and align it with your personal goals. You can diversify with a balance of stocks and bonds, a variety of stocks in different sectors, investment real estate with less risky securities to complement it, aggressive stock holdings paired with accelerated mortgage paydown instead of bonds, and other options as well. Don't plan your future around a random stand of homogenous trees; seek the bounty of a thriving forest.

Buy and hold

Buying and holding investments is a quality strategy, and is better for most people than active trading. Any sale of an investment — whether securities, real estate, or otherwise — is likely to come with taxes and transaction fees. Those can really eat into margins. Buying and holding —

while monitoring to make sure everything still fits in the portfolio — is a classic strategy for a reason.

"Set it and forget it"

At the beginning of the COVID-19 pandemic, there was a surge of hunkering down humans buying houseplants, in hopes that some greenery would keep them sane during quarantine. Most people placed the plants randomly in their homes and completely forgot about them until they realized the plants were dead. They shared photos and laughs over the internet, and it became a thing. Well, that's not what I'm referring to when I say "set it and forget it."

When it comes to investing, the "set it and forget it" strategy is in the same spirit as "buy and hold." The idea is to pick a strategy and stick with it, without worrying about making microcorrections along the way. Just leave it be and let it do its *thang*. It's OK to monitor performance and alignment with goals as they change, but most people who adjust too frequently are more likely to make errors than money.

Max out your employer match

Whenever possible, maximize employer contributions to retirement accounts. I know I'm repeating myself like a creepy talking doll, but at least I'm right. Go ahead, you know what to say. *Say it:* "It's free money! *Woo-hoo!*". Employer match programs vary, but it's likely always a good idea to max out employer matching somehow, unless doing so would result in your inability to pay for basic needs (and therefore forcing you to choose between basic needs and debt). Sometimes it may take as little as 3% contribution to earn a full employer match, and sometimes they may match up to a higher percentage. If you invest $100 and your employer matches that $100, your investment has already earned a tax-free return of 100%. Good luck finding that in the open market. Do whatever you can to maximize your free money.

Reallocate as needed

This is about as "active" as most folks should be in their investing. This principle is similar to dollar cost averaging in that it aims to smooth out volatility, and attempts to "buy low and sell high." Consider the example of a 401(k) retirement account that allows regular reallocation within a portfolio, and pretend that your preferred mix of securities is 80% equity and 20% debt. You start off with $50,000 at your desired mix, meaning you have $40,000 in equity funds and $10,000 in debt funds (see Figure 3-9A). With consistent contributions to the account and an exceptional year of earnings for stocks, your portfolio at the end of year one is now worth $75,000, with $64,000 in equity funds and $11,000 in debt funds (see Figure 3-9B). This new mix is 85.3% equities and 14.7% debt, which is off target from your preferred mix. A choice to reallocate back to the preferred 80-20 mix between equity and debt would redistribute the $75,000 to consist of $60,000 in equities and $15,000 in debt securities (see Figure 3-9C). Simply put, it would be reallocating $4,000 of equity funds into debt funds. It would work the same way if the equities market took a big dive and became cheaper during the year; a reallocation would buy up the securities at lower prices.

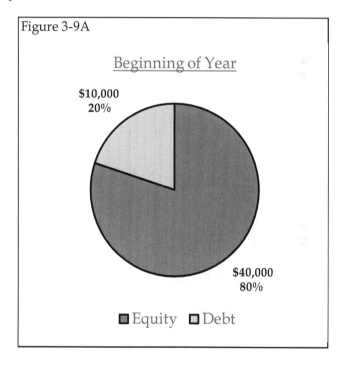

Figure 3-9A

Beginning of Year

$10,000
20%

$40,000
80%

■ Equity □ Debt

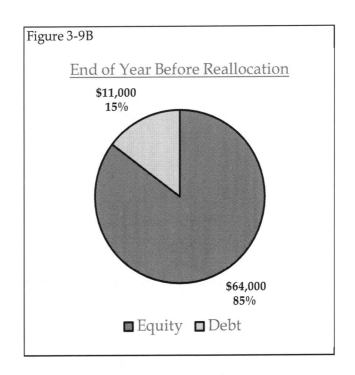

Figure 3-9B

End of Year Before Reallocation

$11,000
15%

$64,000
85%

Equity   Debt

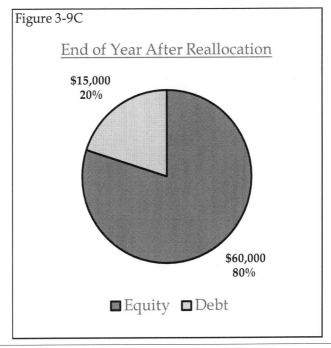

Figure 3-9C

End of Year After Reallocation

$15,000
20%

$60,000
80%

Equity   Debt

The reason this can be so effective is that it sells off funds that have appreciated significantly, and buys those that haven't been doing as well. This is best applied to time-tested index funds, especially those that track a major market index. It's not as scary to buy index funds when prices are declining, because the funds themselves are frequently adjusted to track the best performers in that index. It's less risky than latching on to one particular stock, in which case the company might be supplanted by a competitor. An index fund may merely drop the old stock and pick up the new one, which means there's less cause for alarm if the market starts selling the funds for cheap.

I've reallocated a couple of times, and it was very simple. I requested my transactions using a cellphone app while sitting in my recliner, and I doubt I even had socks on. It's a pretty easy strategy to maintain, and can work great for those who want to be a little more involved than the "set it and forget it" method suggests. That said, I've only ever done this when my account balances deviated significantly from my desired target mix, or if my desired target mix materially changed. Don't let the ease of reallocation tempt you into adjusting too frequently or responding to market frenzies.

Weighing "risk and reward"

Measurements of "risk and reward" are subjective, but "risk" and "reward" tend to be strongly correlated. Well, that's at least true for things that people actually pursue. Things that don't have a positive correlation between "risk" and "reward" don't often materialize for long. Would you attempt to brush an alligator's teeth if your friend said they'd give you a dollar to do it? You wouldn't take that dare — because you're not a jerk to animals and you don't want to lose an arm — in other words, the risk doesn't match the reward. Conversely, the market rarely offers up huge rewards with minimal risk. Anyone who promises you risk-free riches is probably not a friend. Let's take a look at some practical "risk and reward" matchups that you may come across in the personal finance world. Remember, these are my personal opinions on "risk and reward," and not professional investment advice.

Moderate risk, high reward

Tax-advantaged retirement

Tax-advantaged retirement investing comes with tax benefits that make otherwise high-risk investing a comfortably moderate risk. Everyone should invest in a tax-advantaged retirement account, especially if it has an employer match that can be maximized.

Responsible home purchase

For a home purchase to be responsible, you need to be quite certain that you can consistently afford the cost of the home, even as circumstances change over time. This is why it's so important to make sure you're "qualified" before you buy (think back to the Housing *HOP Analysis* we discussed previously).

The reason a responsible home purchase is moderately risky is because even an average-priced house likely requires a significant amount of debt to secure the purchase. Homeownership is also expensive due to home maintenance. However, homeownership is a basic requirement of sustainable financial security, because it mitigates increases in cost of living over time. Plus, it's one of the few investments that directly supplies nonfinancial benefits as well. Owning a home may result in extra joy, freedom, and comfort in addition to the financial rewards.

Employee stock purchase plan (ESPP)

An employee stock purchase plan (ESPP) allows employees of an organization to purchase company stock at a discounted price. There may or may not be rules on vesting and options to sell, so the actual risk varies. However, since the prices are inherently at a discount, the normally high risk of stock picking is reduced to moderate. Some plans allow immediate sale, and in that case, it's probably a no-brainer. Imagine that you participate in an ESPP with immediate vesting and no sale restrictions, and an employee discount of 10%. You pay $90 for $100 worth of stock, and immediately sell for the market value of $100. Your $90 investment just made $10, or about 11%. That $10 can go right into savings or be reinvested. That's a good gig.

Stock purchased in an ESPP can also be held for the long term in hopes of even higher reward, but it's less secure than taking the margin and running with it.

Debt payoff

Debt payoff can be an incredibly effective use of cash, especially if interest rates on the borrowed money are higher than what's available in the open market. Aggressively paying down debt isn't always the best use of cash, depending on interest rates and other goals. However, it is an excellent way to receive a guaranteed reward that likely outweighs the risk. If given the choice between buying securities or paying down a credit card with a high interest rate, the debt paydown is the way to go. The interest expense paid out will nearly always exceed the potential opportunities in the open market. An aggressive payoff of a mortgage can lead to tens or even hundreds of thousands in savings on interest over time, even when factoring in the tax implications. The risk of debt paydown is nearly nonexistent — it's really only about opportunity cost. And it can save lots of money and lead to more financial security, which gives you more flexibility for career choices and investment strategies down the line. The reward outweighs the risk, so this is a great strategy. I particularly like the idea of debt paydown when paired with adequate savings reserves and an aggressive equity-focused approach in a Roth account. Debt paydown can be used as an alternative to bonds, especially when an individual's existing borrowing rates are higher than market bond rates.

Low risk, low reward

Savings accounts, savings bonds, Certificates of Deposit

Having savings reserves is important in order to be prepared for emergencies and insulate yourself against debt. But they will only generate a negligible amount of income, and will be eroded by inflation in the long term. Consider these to be simple cash assets opposed to investments. If you can find a reputable option with a return that materially exceeds inflation, it may qualify as low risk, moderate reward.

Most debt securities

Debt securities don't often pay much. They offer small returns but are generally pretty safe. If you can find a reputable debt security with a return that materially exceeds inflation, it may qualify as low risk, moderate reward.

High risk, high reward

Stock picking

Stock picking is very risky but can generate great returns. It takes both luck and skill, and should only be completed with money that you can afford to lose.

Debentures

High risk debt securities — also known as debentures — are securities from institutions with bad or unproven credit. They pay more because they are more risky, simple as that. Like stock, they should only be purchased with money that you can afford to lose.

Investment real estate and alternative investments

Investment real estate and alternative investments, such as venture capital, should be reserved solely for sophisticated investors, or those who can afford for the investment to go south. They should only be pursued by those with a strong financial foundation in place to support routine costs or any other subsequent financial burdens the investment may bring. For example, a real estate investor should only invest in properties that they can consistently afford even when unoccupied. Some folks get rich taking on significant debt to pursue risky endeavors, but that is the pursuit of wealth rather than health. All that said, this type of investing is one of the most lucrative avenues in the world for people who have a good combination of skill, luck, and resources.

Chapter 19: Defense

Imagine that you're standing by a whiteboard in the front of a classroom, looking out at 20 mildly enthusiastic high school seniors. A friend of yours is the teacher responsible for educating this pack of future voters, and has invited you to be a guest presenter. Knowing that you've become a financial aficionado, your friend thinks you can help the kids get interested in their financial health as they enter adulthood. You introduce yourself, explain why you're here, and then kick things off with a contest.

"We're going to conduct an experiment in the form of a game. The game has two rounds."

You hold up a $10 bill, and announce the rules of the first round: "The first person to complete the task will win 10 dollars. You may begin the task as soon as I announce it. Are you ready to play? OK, the task is: raise your hand."

In your imagination, do all 20 hands go up? I wonder if your friend's hand is even raised. Once you determine who has raised their hand first, you hand them the $10 bill (it's OK, you have plenty to share at this point). The winner is beaming and laughing, another kid is griping that they raised their hand first, another demands participation trophies and $20s for all, other general buzz and banter. Things settle down after a few moments, and you explain round two: "The rules and prize are slightly different. This time, I will announce the prize, and then if you want to claim it, be the first to raise your hand after I clap my hands. Ready? Here we go. The first person to raise their hand gets to *give me* one dollar."

You wait a one second count to ensure the kids have a moment to think, and then clap. In your imagination, does even one hand go up? Maybe only the spoiled kid who wants to show off their allowance puts their hand up, but chances are no one has. Why would they?

You make a joke about the kids being greedy, and then explain the point of the exercise: "You can always find someone willing to take your money, but it's a lot harder to find someone to give you money." That, my friends, is the reason it's important to play defense.

Spend responsibly

Create a budget

Budget basics

In order to protect your money, you have to spend responsibly. Maybe you already know how, but for many people it's something they have to learn. I can provide a conceptual framework, but it's up to *you* to define what responsible spending means to you. Make sure your definition is aligned with your circumstances, options, and values. Interpretations may change as your life changes, and that's normal. So how do you decide what responsible spending means? You write it out and think about it.

I believe that creating a household budget is the key to spending responsibly. A budget is a tool used to estimate, plan, and monitor income and expenses. It also sets a baseline for spending decisions and can be used as a benchmark for accountability. Budgeting for businesses and governments can be very complex, but budgeting for personal finance doesn't have to be. Household budgets can simply estimate and plan cash inflows and cash outflows in whatever format makes sense to the individual.

Ever heard the phrase "out of sight, out of mind"? Well, a lot of folks don't review their finances because they don't have anything — such as a budget — that's easy to look at. It's pretty easy to avoid something you can't see. Like when people hide clean laundry in the guest bathtub, because they just don't want to deal with it right now (of course, *I've* never done that). But while hidden laundry piles aren't great, they're not overly problematic. Invisible finances are a big, *big* problem. You don't have to tape your budget to your vanity, but it needs to be accessible and familiar. Oh yeah, and it needs to actually exist. Comparing actual inflows and outflows to budgeted inflows and outflows helps clarify spending patterns and lead to informed decisions going forward. Thinking about finances periodically can prevent financial issues that dominate life later.

Create your monthly budget based on what you think is reasonable and realistic. All goals need to be reasonable in order to be meaningful, and setting a budget is no different. You need to select a budget-setting method that makes sense to you, and build it out based on realistic savings goals. Sure, you can track and analyze your spending without a budget, but setting a budget adds significant accountability and clarity compared with approaching it willy-nilly.

Budget templates

There are several common budget styles, all with varying complexity. Do whatever makes sense to your brain. Some folks use spreadsheet tools on a computer, and some find that they have better recall if written by hand. My preferred method is a variation on the *essential margin method* (explained below), built out and automated in Microsoft Excel, but I am a legitimate personal finance nerd (and Excel nerd, and maybe just a nerd). I know other financially successful people who use the simplest of simple budget methods, and it serves them just fine.

It doesn't matter how you set up your budget, so long as it includes the following three components:

1) your expected net pay (cash in)
2) your expected "expenses" (cash out)
3) your "net margin" (cash savings)

I've provided several suggested templates below to help you get started designing a budget that makes sense to you. The templates don't show examples of specific expense details, but in practice it helps to list out individual expense categories when calculating your totals. Some examples might include rent, groceries, loan payments, utilities, or even the name of a specific vendor (especially for vendors that provide multiple services).

Basic

Aggregate method

Net pay – total expenses = net margin

	Net pay
Minus:	Total expenses
Equals:	Net margin

Intermediate

Expense character method

Net pay – fixed expenses – variable expenses = net margin

	Net pay
Minus:	Fixed expenses
Minus:	Variable expenses
Equals:	Net margin

Essential focus method

Net pay – essential expenses – nonessential expenses = net margin

	Net pay
Minus:	Essential expenses
Minus:	Nonessential expenses
Equals:	Net margin

Advanced

Essential margin method

Net pay – fixed essential expenses – variable essential expenses = essential margin; Essential margin – fixed nonessentials – variable nonessentials = net margin

	Net pay
Minus:	Fixed essential expenses
Minus:	Variable essential expenses
Equals:	Essential margin
Minus:	Fixed nonessential expenses
Minus:	Variable nonessential expenses
Equals:	Net margin

Fixed margin method

Net pay – fixed essential expenses – fixed nonessential expenses = fixed margin; Fixed margin – variable essentials – variable nonessentials = net margin

	Net pay
Minus:	Fixed essential expenses
Minus:	Fixed nonessential expenses
Equals:	Fixed margin
Minus:	Variable essential expenses
Minus:	Variable nonessential expenses
Equals:	Net margin

Budgeting tips

The section below provides some basic budgeting tips to help you make yours meaningful and reliable.

Go with the (cash) flow

Stick to monitoring cash only. It's not necessary to track investments nor changes in asset value as part of your household budget. Start with net pay — the cash you actually expect to receive for the period — and treat that as your income. Then deduct cash expenses using whichever method you prefer.

Pick the right cycle

A monthly budget interval is useful for most people, because most pay and billing cycles are approximately four weeks or monthly. It's not really necessary to budget by cycle to incorporate seasonality or one-off charges. It's good enough to estimate material nonrecurring expenses and spread them over the smaller periods.

Choose the correct net pay

Base your net pay on the *minimum* amount you feel guaranteed to receive during the budget period. I like to treat discretionary bonuses, modest commissions, and unscheduled overtime as, well, bonuses. The global economy has seen times in which bonuses haven't been paid, commissions have tanked, and workers have lost their overtime opportunities. If your pay is entirely or substantially based on commissions, base your budget off of the lowest monthly pay you deem possible. If you're paid in a cycle that doesn't align perfectly with your budget cycle, choose the periods with the least number of paychecks. For example, if you're paid 26 times per year (biweekly), 10 months of the year provide two paychecks, but two months will have three paychecks. In that case, base the budget off of two payments per month, and then pump those extra paychecks right into cash savings, retirement, or lump sum debt paydown. The same strategy works great with bonuses as well.

Start with essentials

A bare-bones budget is merely net pay minus essential expenses. Don't bother budgeting for boxing lessons if it could mean choosing between debt or basic needs. If essential expenses are dangerously close to net pay, you don't really have room for nonessential spending. To use a cliché, there's not enough room in the budget. Start with essentials to see how much room you have for fun and fulfillment, and don't forget to take opportunities to lower essential expenses when they come up.

Pick a margin, and fill in nonessentials from there

Don't let nonessential spending dictate your estimated savings target. Figure out what your savings goal is, and then feel free to plan for nonessential spending and make room for fun and games.

Factor in big purchases

Make sure to factor in room for sporadic major cash outflows such as health care costs, car maintenance, home maintenance and the like. And if those budgeted expenses aren't actually incurred, that's great news! There's value in building in the nonrecurring, but common, expenses that *do* come up sometimes.

<u>Don't get too picky</u>

It's OK to use broad estimates for variable costs like groceries or nonrecurring costs like travel. Your budget isn't a self-indulgent Hollywood suspense thriller — you don't get bonus bucks for making it intense and complicated. Just do what you can to make the budget useful for your decision-making.

<u>Budget for Passion, Fulfillment, and Empowerment (PFE) activities</u>

What are you currently doing to fill your life with passion, fulfillment, and empowerment (*PFE*)? Do some of these activities cost money? While it's important to have at least a few staple hobbies that are free, it's pretty common for people to spend regularly on *PFE* activities. Pursuing *PFE* is very healthy, and can make life more enjoyable in the process — as long as it doesn't leave you broke. Make sure to build the costs of supporting *PFE* activities into your budget. It doesn't matter if they fall in essential or nonessential expenses, so long as they're part of your financial plan.

Some *PFE* activities, such as volunteering, can be completely free, and finding cost-friendly *PFE* activities will help your wallet and your wellness. But most of us — myself included — end up paying for unique experiences that we think add value to our lives. For me, live concerts and live sports are a passion. Visiting national parks provides me with fulfillment. I feel empowered when I test my physical capabilities in assorted endurance events. Those are three of my *PFE* activities that I build into my financial plan, but what are yours? Travel? Hosting gatherings? Giving to charity? Camping? Woodworking? Give it some thought, and find ways to afford those experiences.

Redefine your wants and needs

Your list of needs is much shorter than you may think. You don't *need* internet-compatible sunglasses that change tint to alert you that your cellphone battery is low. You don't *need* to cover every inch of wall space in your home with decorations, as if the bare paint was offensive graffiti spray-painted on the side of an elementary school. You don't *need* your voice-activated virtual assistant to wipe for you after you use the bathroom, and if it offers to do so, *run*. Your only true needs are those that support your health.

No one really wants or needs a specific product; they want or need *value*.

You don't buy dish soap because you have a biological need to own the same blue goo that allegedly saves animals after oil spills. No, you buy dish soap because clean dishes help keep you from getting sick. So while dish soap may be a need, it's only a need because it provides value by supporting your health.

If you think hard enough, you might realize that even your "wants" may not be what you previously thought they were. Oftentimes we think we want something just because we want it, but we're subconsciously trying to serve another purpose. Learning what that purpose really is can help prevent unnecessary spending.

Spending money to provide value is one thing, but spending money to *feel* valuable is different — and a little dangerous. I'll share an example I bet we can all relate to: spending money on our appearance. Most of us want to look our best and be considered pleasant-looking in whatever way we define that to be, right? Well, I don't actually think that's the whole story, especially if we try harder to understand why we even care. We really just want to *feel valuable,* and we think our appearance can help us get there. Maybe we think a certain look could convince coworkers and clients that we're more "professional," or we think a certain stylistic attitude is preferred by a partner. So while we may see physical presentation as a means to creating value, we're actually craving the self-esteem that's critical for both mental health and social health. There's got to be something like that going on, because people spend a *lot* of time and money trying to look a certain way, and I don't think many actually get much out of it — I don't care if the mirror tells you you're the fairest of them all, or if it shatters while you brush your teeth. Spending on appearance is just one example of people using money in hopes of making themselves feel valuable. And maybe that's kind of OK sometimes, so long as it's in moderation, with an understanding of what the underlying urge really relates to. Just remember that wearing a suit doesn't give you powerful ideas, but feeling confident *does.* Try to think of some other examples of times when you or others have spent money to try to feel valuable (you can also think back to Stan from Chapter 2). Remember to stop and ask yourself: "What do I *really* want?" Finding more meaningful ways to acquire value and feel valuable can improve even the most enviable lives.

Go green: save the world, save more money

Pump up your defense and save the world by going "green." When you waste less, you keep more money. When you waste less, you hurt the environment less. Creationists and evolutionists alike can agree that we shouldn't knowingly wreck the amazing planet we've inherited. Going green helps conserve our natural resources, increase gratitude, and save money on household bills and tax bills. That's a pretty darn good combination. The standard method to go green is to use the three Rs: Reduce, Reuse, and Recycle. Learn to love all three, because they can all save you money. Let's look at some practical applications of how doing this can help your finances:

Reduce

Reducing your consumption of goods will translate directly into cost savings. Pretty simple, right? Buy less, spend less. You can buy less by realizing you need less; realizing you don't need a fast car or a giant house bursting with nonessential junk. For things you *do* need — such as food and water — you can try to reduce waste (more on that later).

Reuse

Reusing things that you do buy is an incredible way to save money. Maybe that means buying a quality pair of jeans and wearing them for 10 years, rather than buying new jeans every single year. Buy sustainable products like reusable water bottles. Borrow things from friends, family members, and neighbors, and return the favor when you have something you can loan. Don't be ashamed of hand-me-downs and used gifts, and be proud instead! I've been wearing hand-me-downs from my older brothers my entire life. Literally just the day before writing this sentence, my brother gave me a jacket that he couldn't use any more. He had gotten it from a family friend. I am going to be a millionaire and still be wearing my older brother's clothes that shrunk in the dryer. Chances are, I'm wearing one of his shirts *right now.* Anyway, the combination of reducing consumption and reusing things could save you hundreds or thousands per year, and prevent an unbelievable amount of waste.

Recycle

Recycling doesn't directly or immediately result in savings, but it will at some point. Landfills aren't free, and they're going to keep getting more and more expensive. Between 1970 and 2020, the world population approximately doubled. In those same years, we've amplified our consumption rates. This means that we have way less space and way more junk. The more things you can recycle, the less you'll pay in garbage costs.

And that will become more and more impactful over time.

The brutal reality of waste

Brace yourselves, because this section is going to be a bummer. Like, flat-tire-in-a-blizzard bummer. We're talking, finding-out-your-favorite-musician-is-a-phony bummer. Like, finding-out-that-Santa isn't-real-on-the-same-day-you-get-your-first-zit bummer. Just know that I'm not yelling at you or accusing you of being reckless or murdering the planet. I just really think that facing the realities of waste will help you financially and otherwise. Buckle up, buttercup.

I don't care whether you believe that human activity impacts climate change or not. If you want to argue that erratic weather patterns existed long before carbon emissions — the "ice age" for example — I'd agree with you. But I hope we can at least agree that waste is bad for our household budgets, and that our behaviors are causing real problems on earth. We are living longer and exponentially increasing the population every year. To accommodate the spatial needs of our huge population, we are cutting down forests and destroying wildlife. Plants are oxygen producers, and we're getting rid of them while simultaneously replacing them with oxygen consumers (humans). Without oxygen producers, we'd all die.

On top of our decrease in oxygen producers and increase in oxygen consumers, current modern lifestyles only make things scarier — we can be so incredibly wasteful that it's sickening. This is especially true in the United States, where we've become sedentary consumption machines. We waste a full range of resources, most notably food, water, and petroleum (in the form of plastic). Go online and look up the statistics on food and water waste, furnished by the U.S. Environmental Protection Agency (EPA) and United States Department of Agriculture (USDA). It's brutal.

At the time of writing, the USDA estimates that over one-third of all available food goes uneaten through loss or waste.[vi] Meanwhile, one in 10 households in the country suffers with food insecurity, and the percentage is even higher for households with children.[vii] You may have been part of that one in 10 before; even the most insulated oil heir knows someone who has. Let that reality slap you in the face for a minute, and let it sting. As we continue to overpopulate and lose natural resources and farmland, it's very possible that those statistics will continue to get worse. Our mitigation of these concerns starts with knowledge, but requires action.

Now that we've discussed waste of essentials like food and water, let's think about waste of nonessential purchases. We can *all* relate to the compounding waste of buying something we don't need, and then paying trash fees when we inevitably throw it away. Think about the amount of plastic you alone have thrown away in the past year. I get pretty upset when I think about the volume of my own plastic trash, which feels too high even though I work hard at the three Rs.

As a society, we are such dependable junk addicts that manufacturers are able to validate making cheap, flimsy things that will quickly wind up in a landfill. Some even intentionally make things that aren't designed to last, so that they can sell to you a second time (yes, there is a business strategy called "planned obsolescence").

When I recently moved, I had to take an appalling amount of crap to the local landfill, also known as "the dump." It felt horrible. It felt like I had just run over a reindeer. I wanted to donate or sell all the stuff, but there was no market for either. Some of it was still usable, but I didn't have the space or use for it, and I literally couldn't give it away. The worst part was seeing the line of 40 trucks and trailers in front of me on the same errand — dumping plastic junk that was likely made in a high-pollution factory with poor working conditions. That day, I swore that I would never *ever* allow myself to accumulate possessions the same way again. I hope you'll join me.

Now, go watch a nature documentary, cry like you just won a beauty pageant, and get ready for some ideas on how to save money while you save the planet.

Save your money, save your planet

Here comes a montage of simple ways you can save resources, increase gratitude, and help the world while you keep your money.

Learn to love simpler food. Taste buds change, and you can teach them to be more low-maintenance. You'll waste less. Invest in quality food storage options like reusable containers and high-efficiency deep freezers. Buy (or grow) foods that are naturally slow to perish. Research food sustainability and figure out which sustainable foods sound tastiest. Develop a healthier relationship with food to eat less in general. Stop throwing food away simply because you don't like the taste or you've had it for too many days in a row — get tougher.

Invest in energy-efficient appliances. Cook ahead and in bulk, so that you can use less water and energy compared with cooking more frequently (you'll have more time, too). Turn off the faucet when not actively using it (brushing your teeth, washing dishes, maybe even showering). Take shorter showers. Only run the dishwasher when it's full. Fill your property with plant life that doesn't require significant watering.

Research tax credits for environmentally friendly purchases or activities. *Stop buying so many damn nonessentials.* When you do spend on nonessentials, spend on experiences rather than things. Wear shoes and clothing as long as possible, even if they're out of style. Borrow things rather than buy (and lend when it's your turn). Teach manufacturers to be responsible by only purchasing durable, recyclable, or reusable products. Take care of the possessions you do have, so that they last. Donate anything you don't need — there may even be a tax benefit for you. Shop local to support Main Street and reduce the impacts of (and needs for) transport fuel and factories.

I'm not suggesting you stop taking warm showers or only eat peanuts, but even minor changes can really add up. Just remember the three Rs, and that you need less than you think. If you recognize how much of your spending is nonessential, or even wasteful, good fortune will follow. You'll waste less and you'll be even more grateful for the luxuries you do have. Go green. Save money, save the world.

Debt is for essentials only

Debt is neither good nor bad. It can be part of a healthy financial strategy, and it can be also be deadly poisonous. *The Difference Between Medicine and Poison is in the Dose* (great song by Circa Survive, by the way). Certain forms of debt can provide opportunities to acquire sound investments. On the other hand, toxic debt can limit freedom, cause bankruptcy, or even convince people to stay in unhealthy relationships for fear of paying the bills.

Debt should only be used to support essentials. Think back to what essentials are: things that support your total health and well-being. Sometimes people get into a pinch and need to borrow money to pay for essential expenses, such as living expenses or medical bills. This is *not* an acceptable financial plan — this is an emergency response. This means that the only time it's practical to carry a credit card balance is if it comes down to choosing between that and going without basic needs.

Investing is essential, and certain investments like housing and education may require some initial seed money to get in the door. Using debt to invest isn't always a good idea, but it can *sometimes* be part of a quality investment plan. The general rule is that money should only be borrowed if absolutely necessary *and* you're sure the benefits of borrowing exceed the costs.

Borrowing money to pay for nonessentials is a very, very bad idea. It's like rigging dynamite to a balloon, and placing the balloon on the floor in a room with 30 cats. This isn't judgment, it's truth. I'll be honest — I borrowed money for nonessentials a few times in my early and mid-20s. The amounts were immaterial, and the decisions were part of an otherwise successful financial strategy, but I still wish I'd have done it differently. I'd have preferred to eliminate or reduce the cost of those nonessentials rather than living outside my means, even though it didn't cause me much grief. I've also done other foolish things and survived, but that doesn't mean they were good choices.

Understand what you're buying

To have financial success, you need to be able to make informed purchase decisions. If you don't, your hard-earned money will sprint out the door like a kid on the last day of school. Being able to consider the value that you're seeking and compare it with the value provided by a given purchase is a fundamental skill required for responsible spending. You may already do it subconsciously to an extent, but it's better to be deliberate about it. It's especially important to be thoughtful when investing or entering into contracts, but still worth taking a few seconds to contemplate day-to-day purchases. Making a bad purchase of something inexpensive and unimportant is easy enough to bounce back from — like the time I decided to make my girlfriend homemade chocolate chip cookies for Valentine's Day, and bought granulated sugar assuming it's a reasonable substitute for the brown sugar I couldn't find in the store (those cookies were terrible, by the way). Bouncing back from buying a useless item like the wrong baking ingredients or a bad haircut doesn't take long; but it's not quite as easy to bounce back from a misguided investment decision or an unfavorable contract. Let's look at another cautionary tale in order to explore the consequences of not understanding what you're buying.

Kate and Darren go coat shopping

Kate and Darren are friends who just moved to a city with a wet, rainy climate. They both like to spend their free time outdoors, and prefer walking to driving. While trekking to a restaurant to meet up with some friends, they get caught in a heavy rain shower. They stop and look into each other's eyes, each secretly waiting for the inspirational romantic comedy music to play, wondering if they're about to realize that they're in love with their best friend. But instead of that, they just get drenched, and by the time they make it to the restaurant they have to wring out their clothes before the hostess lets them in. They realize that they each need to purchase more reliable raincoats.

Darren goes to a department store and tells the salesperson that he wants a coat. The salesperson directs him to the coat section, and suggests that he would look amazing running through the city in a red windbreaker jacket; he'd be certain to turn some heads cruising along. Darren agrees that he would look great in a red windbreaker, and happily buys the jacket for $60. That same week, Kate goes to the same department store where Darren bought his windbreaker, and tells the same salesperson that she is looking for a waterproof raincoat that she can wear walking, hiking, and running. The salesperson takes Kate to the coat section and suggests that she would look amazing in a light blue windbreaker. Kate checks the tags on the windbreaker and notices that it says "water-resistant," which means it isn't the "waterproof" type of coat that she needs. Kate points this out to the salesperson, who laughs and apologizes, having not realized that the coat isn't actually waterproof. The salesperson explains that the store doesn't have any additional stock of coats, so they apparently don't have the type of raincoat Kate is looking for. Kate makes her way to a sporting goods store and explains to the sales staff what she needs in a coat (waterproofness). They're able to show her several different waterproof raincoat options. One is $110, and one is $150. She prefers the more expensive one, but assesses that the less expensive one is the most practical because it meets all her needs, and even some of her wants, such as color. All she really needs is to stay dry, so she buys the one that costs $110.

The next weekend Darren and Kate go on a run together in the local park. Both of them wear their new coats in case it rains. They run long enough that it inevitably starts raining. Kate is able to stay dry in her raincoat, because she had asked the right questions and made sure that she bought what she had intended to. Her phone even stayed dry in the waterproof pockets. Darren was glad to have his coat on, but it didn't keep him or his phone completely dry — water-resistant and waterproof sound similar, but they're not the same. Now he's worried that his phone is broken, and realizes that he needs to buy another coat. Kate recommends the same model that she just bought, and Darren buys it for $110. He tries to return his red windbreaker, but seeing as he's already gotten it sweaty and then shrank it in the dryer, the store won't take it back. Darren ends up having spent $60 on a coat that he didn't need, because he didn't understand what he was buying.

The consequences of not understanding what you're buying

In the Kate and Darren story, it's easy to imagine that Darren was kicking himself for not thinking to double-check that he was buying what he had intended to. Fortunately, it was only a $60 mistake, but it was unnecessary and easily preventable. Buying the wrong jacket is irritating and expensive, but not likely life-changing. Have you ever done something similar? I've certainly made ignorant mistakes before by not asking enough questions, buying the wrong product, getting talked into something I didn't need, and falling prey to aggressive marketing. I've been lucky enough to be able to endure my errors without much drama, but unfortunately, not all purchases are immaterial or inconsequential.

Be thoughtful and mindful about all purchases, but especially so for the big ones, which I will explain on the following pages. If you show up to these decisions uninformed and unplanned, there's a good chance it will bite you. A bad contract is like a forest critter that bites your behind and won't let go. You can spin around trying to toss it off, but its teeth are sunk in and you can't seem to get a hand on it.

Remember that even someone who genuinely believes in what they're selling wants to sell to you whether it makes sense for you to buy or not. Think about advertisements: while you are just watching a show, driving past a billboard, or looking at a city bus, some random person is trying to sell something to you and other random people. No one except you really knows your wants and needs, but that won't stop people from trying to convince you to buy their products. In order to be financially successful and tailor your finances to your own unique goals, preferences, and risk appetites, you need to take the time to understand what you need and the nuances of each of your options. Let's review a few common purchasing blunders to understand why this is so important.

Mortgage mishaps

Purchasing a home is an enormous commitment. The subsections below discuss some common purchasing errors and the consequences that follow.

Borrowing too much

Have you ever heard the term "house poor"? It refers to someone who has a nice (or at least expensive) home, but because of their mortgage payment, is otherwise broke. Excessive debt — even productive debt like a mortgage — is not a safe choice for your financial health. Borrowing too much is always a bad idea, even for a dream home.

Buying before you're ready because "now is a great time to buy"

Buying a home is swimming in the deep end of the pool. No one should dive into the deep end until they know how to swim; but once they're ready, the deep end is the *best*. Homeownership is worth it, but it needs to be earned, even if it's allegedly a great time to buy. Even if Great-Aunt Gladys dies and leaves you a stack of cash that would seem excessive for a 2000s rap music video, don't buy a home until you're actually ready.

Remember the famous pool scene in the classic 1990s movie *The Sandlot*? A bespectacled young boy named Squints knows that he can't swim, but intentionally goes into the deep end of the pool in hopes that heartthrob lifeguard Wendy Peffercorn will have to rescue him and give him mouth-to-mouth resuscitation. Wendy falls for the trap and saves Squints, and even though she's furious when she realizes he's trying to kiss her, the closing credits inform us that Squints and Wendy eventually get married and have nine kids together. Nine. Unfortunately, that strategy will not work for your finances. When it comes to homeownership, there is no Wendy Peffercorn to save you from your mistakes and then love you forever. Don't get in the deep end before you can swim.

Assuming prices can only ever increase

Due to inflation, prices have historically trended up over time. But that doesn't mean they go up every day, week, month, or year. Look at the global recession that started in the late 2000s, after years of people buying homes in a housing bubble. Their home values were reduced by 50% after the market crash. Don't validate a purchase you're not comfortable with or ready for by assuming that it's going to be even more valuable tomorrow. That does happen sometimes, but not always.

<u>Using a loan that you don't understand</u>

Fixed interest rate mortgages are the way to go. You know what you're signing up for, and if rates lower drastically, you can refinance. The contracts aren't nuanced, nor are they subject to future economic conditions that are difficult to predict. Keep it simple.

The never-ending contract

Read cellphone, membership, apartment lease, and other contracts before you sign them. I realize that it's annoying to read technical legal language and ask a bunch of questions, but it's imperative that you do so anytime you sign up for something. Put extra focus onto cancellation and forfeiture terms, contractual commitments not stated in the ad, data usage, and the rights of the other party (e.g., ability to raise rates etc.).

Losses on leases

Step into a car dealership and you'll quickly be told by a salesperson how smart it is to lease a brand new car. The likelihood of that being true is slim. As slim as a thru-hiker after 2,000 miles on the Pacific Crest Trail. Before you sign up for *any* lease — car or otherwise — make sure to do the math and relate your decision to your financial situation and goals. When I recently bought my truck, I was able to easily cease the pressure to lease by explaining my goals and taking out paper to literally write down the calculations to show why it didn't make sense for me. Remember, lease payments are rental payments — you don't build any equity and you don't walk away with anything when the lease is done, unless you end up buying. And even then, the deals I've seen for lease-to-buy aren't advantageous. Always do the math independently of the salesperson when making a major money decision.

There are a few scenarios in which it makes sense to lease a car, but not many. For example, if you need a reliable commuter vehicle right now but expect to need a minivan in three years, maybe a cheap 36-month lease could make sense — *maybe*. Calculate the total cost of the lease and compare that to the expected outcome of a responsible purchase. Which is better for your net worth, your goals, and your needs from the vehicle? Avoid leasing expensive vehicles or vehicles that retain their value, and avoid leasing when your goals tell you to own. The following are *not* financially savvy reasons to lease a car: it's an expensive car you can't afford to buy; you want a brand new car every few years; a salesperson or commercial is putting the pressure on you to lease *right now*.

The risk of botching a lease-vs.-buy decision — whether a vehicle or something else — is signing up for a bad contract and not being able to get out of it. This could be bad for your wallet and not meet the intended use of the purchase. Make sure you understand lease contracts before you sign up, so that you can compare them with your current financial position and goals.

Falling prey to fear and emotion

Certain industries rake in the dough by appealing to human vulnerabilities like fear and emotion. They aim to make potential buyers feel threatened or insecure, and assure them that they'll be better off with a simple purchase. I often like to mock ads by summarizing them in a one-sentence takeaway, and then using a funny voice to say that sentence out loud. It can be pretty amusing (for me at least). Give it a try if you want extra entertainment and help in understanding the way you're being targeted by marketers. For example: "Buy this pizza and your family will finally appreciate you!"; "Buy our fragrance so you can be hot, rich, and mysterious!"; "Click here or you and your loved ones will *DIE!*" Anyway. If a sales pitch is designed to make you feel unsafe or extremely emotional, try to step back and look at things objectively before you invest too much more time or money into what it's selling.

The wedding industry is notorious for taking advantage of emotions in order to upsell couples on things they "didn't know they needed." Sales people say things like, "This is the most important day of your life!"; "You'll be looking at these pictures for the rest of your life!"; "So what if most people just wind up divorced, this is *your only wedding!*" I know of at least one vendor who has called a future bride in the middle of a workday urging her to send a $2,500 nonrefundable venue deposit prior to providing a contract. The vendor implored her, "You need to pay before the other couple takes your special day away from you!" First of all, if there really had been another couple, would the vendor have been so desperate for the bride-to-be to pay? Secondly, as it turned out, the actual contract that was provided later was about 50% more expensive than what had been advertised. The bride-to-be walked away and never gave that pushy vendor a penny. My point is, do your best to identify when fear and emotion might be driving up prices, increasing desire for unnecessary purchases, or validating bad contracts. It's a classic tactic because it works.

Defend your dough with knowledge

It's difficult to make smart choices if you aren't informed on the subject matter. Imagine you're at the grocery store trying to pick out bananas to snack on during the week. You notice that some of the bananas are sort of green, and some of the bananas are brown-ish, and some are just plain yellow. Clearly you have choices, but which to choose? If you want to avoid a banana-buying-blunder, you need to understand what a ripe banana looks like; otherwise, you may just be spending your hard-earned money on something you won't be able to use. Banana buying is a pretty low-stakes scenario. If you buy bananas that go bad before you can eat them, you may be throwing away a few dollars and feel bad for wasting money and food. You may even be able to salvage them for use in banana bread. But the stakes for many purchases are bigger than bananas. Think about buying a car, buying a home, paying for school, renting an apartment, buying a mattress, or anything else that ain't cheap and is supposed to last. The best way to avoid bad deals, from banana-buying-blunders to mortgage mishaps, is to defend your money with knowledge.

Most major purchases aren't like buying bananas in an open market because you'll be working directly with a human salesperson, often someone who works on commission. Someone will always be willing to take your money if you're willing to make it available, and not all deals are fair or wise. Understand what you're buying before you buy it. Make a plan for how you expect the discussions and negotiations to go. Ask questions about *anything* you don't understand, including anything related to the product/service or the contract itself. One side effect of doing this is that it really helps narrow down the "wants vs. needs" conversation. You don't have to be cynical or defensive, you just need to be prepared and firm.

Trust but verify

When I was an auditor I learned one of my all-time favorite phrases: "Trust but verify." To trust but verify means to assume that the information you've been provided is complete and accurate, but to verify on your own to confirm that conclusion. It's basically saying, "I believe you, but I'd like firm evidence." An example you might be familiar with in the "trust but verify" application is employers requiring job candidates to provide official school transcripts when applying. They don't ask for transcripts because they assume everyone is lying about having gone to college; they do it because they'd prefer to have objective evidence over reliance on universal honesty. Seeking clear and documented answers is also extremely important in the financial world.

Get comfortable asking clarifying questions to confirm understanding. Don't just assume you understand — check in to make *sure* you understand. For example, if you're signing an apartment rental agreement and the cancellation language is unclear or concerning, you might ask the property manager, "Can you please confirm the options and costs associated with an early cancellation?"

If you're ever given something to sign, make sure you understand the ins and outs of what you're signing. Depending on the stakes, it might make sense to have trusted friends or professionals read it as well. This will allow you to discover any questions you may have, find hidden fees and commitments, and determine the suitability of the contract for your purposes. Ask the questions you come up with and you may be surprised at how often a sales pitch isn't as good of a deal "on paper" as it was made to seem in an ad. You don't have to be rude, untrusting, or aggressive when asking questions — you just need to politely and objectively make sure you understand anything you sign. Make it known that you don't sign anything until you've thoroughly vetted the terms; you'll set the tone for the interaction. You don't have to be dishonest or mean to be clear.

In a retail setting, you may not have a formal contract to review, but you can still do some light due diligence. For example, if you're shopping for machine washable slacks, you can't ask the sales clerk to sign an attestation that you'll never have to go to a dry cleaner — you just pay for your clothes and take them home. But the simplicity of such a transaction doesn't necessarily mean you have the right-of-way to buy the wrong thing. You can easily read the tags to make sure you understand the cleaning instructions. Reading tags and labels doesn't take long and it's always a good idea.

WAIT on large purchases

Mindful purchasing will help you spend an appropriate amount of money on things that are essential or otherwise important to you. Having the right mindset may even block foolish spending before it happens, and that's pretty neat. No one wants to spend money on something that's not important to them. Would you buy a birthday gift for your cousin's landlord's nephew? Of course not — it's not important to you! But when it comes to significant and potentially emotional purchases, it can be difficult to understand what's important, and why, without putting a little bit of time into it. For that reason, I suggest adopting a template to help map the right moves. If you're considering a major purchase, try the method I call *WAIT*.

W is for "W questions"

A is for research "Alternatives"

I is for "Investigate options"

T is for "Think on it"

This *WAIT* strategy is meant to be used when considering a major material purchase, such as a residence, vehicle, vacation, expensive recreation, school, furniture, contracts, electronics, and so on. No need to use it for every purchase. If you tried to use *WAIT* for grocery shopping, you'd get frostbite in the frozen food aisle.

It's up to you to define a material dollar amount for your personal *WAIT* threshold. I recommend matching it up against your wages, which allows your materiality to be scalable. The absolute floor should be equal to one day's worth of work. For example, if you make $20 per hour you may set your *WAIT* threshold at $160 (eight hours at $20 per hour). Using this threshold, you can contextualize the personal labor cost of the purchase, and ask yourself, "Is this worth an entire day of my labor?" or, "Can I afford to spend an entire day of wages on this purchase?" If your *WAIT* threshold is a week of wages ($800 in this example), "Is this purchase as valuable as a week's worth of wages?" Comparing your potential purchases with your salary can be especially powerful in vehicle purchasing due to the cost range and variety of vehicles to choose from. If you're making $20 per hour — about $41,600 gross income per year — and considering a vehicle that would have total a cost of $50,000, you may realize that the vehicle isn't worth well over a year of gross wages, and nearly two years of net wages.

Let's dive into the script for how to *WAIT* on large purchases.

W: Ask the "W" questions to clarify your objective

Have a money monologue with yourself anytime you're thinking about shelling out a bunch of dough. Asking yourself the "W" questions — who, what, where, when, why, and how — can add clarity to challenging choices. By asking yourself the right questions right away, you may be able to turn down unnecessary spending without stressing too much about it. Writing these things out adds value to the exercise, since it forces you to slow down your thinking and allows you to read what you've written (it's the same concept as journaling). Write out your questions and write out your responses, answering these questions in order:

- What benefit am I trying to obtain with this purchase?
- Who am I intending to benefit with this purchase?
- Where/When/Why/How will this provide the benefit I want to obtain?

This first question is where you'll define the objective for the purchase. Defining the objective for an essential purchase is likely to be easy, since by nature the purchase is essential (however, you may find that there will still be a lot to consider in the forthcoming "research Alternatives" and "Investigate options" steps).

Defining the benefit of a nonessential purchase may allow you to realize that what you're thinking about buying doesn't really address the desired benefit after all. For example, if a man is considering the purchase of a $1,000 wristwatch, he may determine that the benefit of the flashy wristwatch is added confidence in his physical presentation. He may then realize that he's attempting to fix his self-image issues with a material possession, and conclude that what would really give him confidence would be getting back in shape. Don't stop at the easy answer when defining the benefit — try to find the deepest underlying level of what you're actually seeking.

The next step is to define the beneficiary, which is likely to be you or your dependents. The remaining W (and how) questions are meant to sharpen the objective.

There's no need to overcomplicate things, but make sure to answer your questions honestly. If you ask yourself, "What benefit am I seeking from this purchase?" and your honest answer is "babes," then maybe it's not a good time to buy.

A: Research Alternatives

After you clarify your objectives in the first step, it's time to research alternatives. What are the different avenues available to you to pursue that objective? Consider the purchase of a cooling system for your home: you will have many alternatives to choose from, possibly even the alternative to not buy at all. This is why the first step is to ask questions to clarify your objective. Once you know the objective, you can research the various alternatives that may be able to meet it. For example, you can start researching central air conditioning versus portable air conditioners versus natural cooling methods. You're not picking a model yet, but deciding which method makes the most sense.

You may find it helpful to create a pros and cons list for each alternative. Also, your deep dive into alternatives should always include a review of what it would be like to *not* make the purchase. This is another opportunity to consider wants versus needs and stymie unnecessary spending.

I: Investigate options

By this point, you've clarified your desired benefit, chosen which alternative best suits the objective (if any), and are now comparing specific options. In this step you might shop around, read reviews, research reliability and longevity, compare prices, and so on. Remember to compare add-on costs for things like maintenance, insurance, accessories, or other possible spending requirements.

I speculate that some people consider themselves good shoppers so long as they investigate their options, even if they don't bother defining an objective or considering reasons not to buy at all. In my mind, that's like a football offense that's bad on first and second downs, but average at third and long. It's tough to have success that way. Investigating options is about finding a quality deal on a smart, value-based purchase, not just getting a good deal on a random, unnecessary purchase. If you handle the first two steps correctly, you may realize you don't need to buy anything and don't need to bother investigating options.

T: Think on it

At this point, you've likely made up your mind, and have a plan of what you want to buy. Whenever possible, I recommend stopping to think on it for a bit. Take a day off from planning, and then revisit your notes and ideas. Are you still passionate about the benefits of buying? Does it still seem like a quality deal on a well-informed purchase? If so, and if you can afford it — go get it! The point of thinking on it is to have a second check, and a chance to reset and react, to make sure you're comfortable with your choice. If you follow each step, you should be more confident in what you're buying and why.

Example: *WAIT* to get in the water

Carlos is at his happiest when he's out on the water. He grew up going fishing with his family, loves swimming and paddling, and believes that the local lake is his ideal place to recharge. When he was a kid, the whole family used to load up into their motorized fishing boat and hit the lake at least a couple times a month, and those are some of his most favorite memories from his youth.

Carlos is a young adult now, and still lives close to the lake he loves so much. He finds himself missing the calmness of being on the water, so he's looking for a way to get back out there. He is in great financial shape and has no debt on his reliable car, so he decides it's a reasonable time to buy some sort of watercraft. Like he does with all major purchases, Carlos chooses to clarify his objectives and think through what his best option may be.

The first thing that Carlos does is ask himself: What benefit do I expect from this purchase? At this point in his life, he doesn't want to have to call and ask his parents if he can borrow the family boat each time he wants to get on the water. He realizes that what he really wants is to find a consistent way that he can access the lake, since it's his favorite place to be. Being the savvy young man that he is, Carlos also chooses to dig one layer deeper and ask himself, "What specifically do I get out of being on the lake?" Having now asked the right question, the real reason he craves lake access becomes apparent: the lake is his favorite place to recharge. It's where he feels most calm, present, and reflective. He can now easily summarize what he really wants out of a potential purchase: a way to access the lake so that he can get on the water and recharge whenever he wants to. With that in mind, Carlos moves to the next set of his "W" questions.

He contemplates "who" the purchase is for, and realizes that it's really just for himself — he doesn't need to think about anyone else's interests for this particular purchase. Because he's been a diligent saver, Carlos finds it to be reasonable that his "when," as in, when he wants to get out on the lake, is as soon as possible. He also confirms "when," or how often, he will use it

— in his mind, it's whenever he possibly can. He's already clarified "why" he wants it. He compiles the different ways he wants to use a watercraft, such as casual paddling and fishing near home, but knows he'd like to be able to take it to other destinations as well.

He also asks himself how his life would be if he didn't have an option to make the purchase of a watercraft. He asks himself, "What other ways could I recharge if I weren't able to purchase a watercraft to take to the lake?" There are a few other self-care habits at his disposal, such as journaling, hiking, or taking a "solo day" to keep to himself and relax. These habits are mostly free, and they do help him renew his energy, so it's good to know they are there as an alternative to a big purchase. He knows he'd be fine to continue without buying some kind of boat, but he really thinks that being able to get in the middle of the lake at a moment's notice would add value to his life. At this point, he's feeling ready to go buy something, because being on the lake sounds amazing; however, he continues his purchasing process and begins to consider which "alternatives" might meet his objectives.

There are quite a few products that float. The first thing that comes to mind is a motorboat similar to the one he grew up with. It *would* serve as a great way to hit the water, but after he considers that his "who" was defined as solely himself, he realizes he doesn't really need a big boat. Plus, his car wouldn't be able to tow that kind of boat, so he would have to purchase a different vehicle to transport it (not to mention pay for storage, maintenance, and fuel!). Since the ticket price and add-on costs of a big motorized boat don't seem necessary or reasonable in order to meet his objective, he moves on to nonmotorized options. He has friends with canoes, but hasn't really liked the feel of canoes as much as he's liked kayaks. Plus, canoes are quite a bit bigger and may also pose a problem with hauling. Carlos decides that the best alternative to meet his objective is a fishing kayak.

Now that he knows what he wants, Carlos spends a bit of time "investigating" his options for fishing kayaks. The inflatable options are cheapest, and would break down to fit in the trunk of his car. But as much as he likes swimming, he doesn't really like the idea of his sharp fishing gear in an inflatable boat. He realizes that he'd like to get a hardshell kayak. Buying a hardshell would mean an added cost to buy a roof rack for his car, but he thinks that it will be worth it to have the best option to meet his objectives. He checks out a few different options and finds the 'yak and roof rack that he thinks he will buy. He opts for a higher-end rack because he'd like to take the rig for longer hauls such as camping trips. It's not cheap, but neither are car accidents. His next move, as usual, is to walk away and "think on it."

After a good night's sleep, Carlos wakes up still feeling that the purchase of a hardshell fishing kayak is the best option to meet his objectives. He decides that even though it's a large purchase, and he has cheaper options, that the value of being on the water whenever he wants is worth more than the cash he will trade for it. Carlos chose to *WAIT* on this major purchase, and because of that, he's confident in his choice. He appreciates that his kayak is not just a hunk of buoyant materials, but a vessel that allows him to get into nature and experience the world around him. The kayak is simply a practical means to get what he really wants, which is the healthy benefit of finding peace on the lake.

Example: *WAIT* on your wheels

Dewayne loves being a dad, and he loves basketball. So naturally, one of his greatest joys as a parent is supporting his kids and their competitive select basketball teams. He has a fifth grader and a seventh grader, and both play for the big local club, the Grit City Defiance. He's been deployed off and on throughout his U.S. military service, and now that he's retired and settled, he doesn't want to miss a thing. The kids' basketball schedule is pretty intense and involves frequent travel. Because of this, the parents of the players often rely on other parents to drive their kids to practices, games, and tournaments if they aren't available to do it themselves.

Dewayne earned his full military pension, and the deciding factor in choosing his first civilian job was schedule flexibility to allow him opportunities to participate in his kids' activities. He helps out the other parents as much as he can with providing transportation, because that's just how he rolls. He's considering buying an SUV with a third row of seats so he can carry even more kids when needed. Dewayne takes good care of his money and knows that he doesn't need luxury or excess to be happy. He has worked hard and overcome obstacles to earn his pension, and wants to be sure he's making good use of his civilian wages as well. He considers the validity of this purchase using the *WAIT* technique.

It takes Dewayne a bit to be sure, but he determines that the desired benefit of purchasing an eight-seater SUV will be to provide value to the basketball program. The intended recipients of the value (the "who") are the parents, players, and coaches — and himself, because having a nice new car will be kind of cool. He likes that his current rig is paid off, but he does kind of wish it had some of the features a new land yacht SUV has. He thinks through "when" the car will provide value, and the only times he can think of are when two or three more kids will need to be hauled — there's nothing else that his current car, a midsize SUV, can't already do.

Dewayne considers whether or not there may be alternative ways to provide value to the parents, players, and coaches, rather than buying a $60,000 vehicle. It occurs to him that there are a significant amount of planning and logistics required to keep the basketball program running, and that right now each team is in charge of their own organization. He expects to have two kids in the program during the next couple of years, which will ensure he's involved for a while. He comes up with a different way to provide value: he can volunteer as the program coordinator. He can help with scheduling, setting up carpools, and managing contact info, and he can be the point person for communications among the team's parents.

The next steps of the *WAIT* method aren't necessary for Dewayne, because he has already found a better alternative to the purchase he was considering: he will provide value to the parents, players, and coaches by giving his *time*. This choice bears no financial burden and is a much better alternative to spending significant money on a vehicle that wouldn't have provided much new value. That money can be so much better spent saving for his kids to go to college, although, he speculates, they may have athletic scholarships in their future. And if the team ever really needs a giant vehicle, he can arrange (and pay for) a commuter van rental.

Dewayne is happy that he has decided to *WAIT* on his wheels, and instead will provide other benefits to the team in a way that is basically free.

Example: I need a laptop, but I'll *WAIT*

Breanna recently read a fantastic — no, phenomenal — personal finance book called *Healthy* — never mind. The author encouraged her to improve her earnings potential and find fulfillment, which fueled her energy to make some career moves and pursue a major life goal. When Breanna was younger, school had never really been her thing, and she dropped out her junior year of high school while going through some tough personal times. She's worked hard at her job in retail ever since, but wants to feel more fulfilled and earn more money. Breanna decides that her combination of personal experience and genuine compassion will make her an excellent guidance counselor. Her career will take some grit and patience, and will be a long process even before she gets a foot in the door, but she thinks it will add more than just financial value to her life.

Since she didn't finish high school, Breanna needs to obtain her General Educational Development (GED) certificate as an equivalency to use for her college application. On an early September morning, she maps out her plan: she will earn her GED certificate between January and June, then pursue a cost-savvy associate degree for her first two years of college, and eventually get her bachelor's degree in counseling.

The money and time required to complete college is intimidating, but not impossible. Breanna gets comfortable with her plan by researching her options and finds a route that will supply her with the most financial aid and flexibility. As a bonus, the guidance counselor jobs she is interested in have federal loan forgiveness programs, so she feels comfortable that she will be able to afford her student loans. She will need to keep working throughout her schooling, and plans to take 100% online classes whenever possible.

Breanna uses her phone for most internet activities, so she doesn't currently own a personal computer. She realizes that she'll need computer access to achieve her goal, and decides to use the *WAIT* technique to evaluate her options.

The first question Breanna asks herself is, "What benefit do I hope to obtain by purchasing a laptop?" She concludes that the value of a laptop is that it allows her to complete her schooling remotely and on her own schedule. This being a worthy objective, she moves onto her other "W" questions. She asks herself, "Who is this purchase intended to benefit?" and recognizes that she will be the only user of the laptop, so she can buy one tailored solely to her needs. She considers "when" the laptop will serve its intended purpose, which is the next four to five years beginning in January. This is good news; even though she's eager to start school shopping right away, she can wait for the big holiday sales to get a great price on a laptop.

By now, Breanna knows she needs a laptop. She considers her alternatives to making the purchase, such as using the computers at the public library. She realizes that for how often she will need access and the flexible times she will require, the library isn't feasible. It's also not feasible to go without a laptop, considering that she will primarily take online classes, and even in-person classes likely require access to a personal computer. She needs to buy the laptop no matter what.

Breanna waits patiently until the holiday sale ads start showing up in November. She sets an approximate budget and investigates her options in the ads. For each option within her budget range, she looks at the different capabilities and features to make sure she is buying a computer that meets all her needs, without overpaying for flashy features she won't use. She makes a list of her top few picks, knowing that sometimes special deals have limited stock. As a savvy buyer, she gives herself time away from her research to "think on it." Her time away from reviewing specific products allows her to focus on general needs, the most important need being reliability. With that in mind, she realizes that she had previously underrated her most reliable option because she thought it was ugly. In her defense, it isn't cute. But since her objective in buying a computer lives in function, not fashion, she buys the ugly one.

Breanna is confident that she is making a quality purchase with her personal computer, and it pays off as she uses it to achieve her life-changing goal. Looking back, she didn't spend much time planning her purchase or obsessing over options — she merely defined her intended benefit and made a purchase that seemed to best serve her objective. Since she had a framework in place to make smart purchases, her decision-making was easy and effective.

Example: Worth the *WAIT*

Hannah and Kelly just celebrated their third wedding anniversary, and life is going quite well for both of them. Hannah is a rock star at selling high-end accounting software, and Kelly is the director of a youth program at the local health club. Their financial forecast is strong, and they've found a great mix of saving money and treating themselves. They have wonderful families and friends, and a healthy marriage built to run forever. Hannah and Kelly are generally very happy, and are appreciative of this time in their lives. For the past several years, they've hoped that life stays about the same for a long, long time.

That all changes after Hannah volunteers at Kelly's health club for Family Fitness Night. After seeing how amazing she is with the kids, it occurs to Kelly that Hannah would be an incredible parent. Kelly has always thought she could fulfill her love of nurturing children through her work, but suddenly she realizes that she wants to start a family with Hannah.

When they get home after Family Fitness Night, both are slightly quiet and awkward, despite having had so much fun at the event. After some small talk, Hannah finally spills: spending time playing with the kids and teaching them the different games was some of the most fun she's ever had, and seeing how loving and natural Kelly was with the kids somehow amplified her adoration. Kelly is relieved, and shares that she left the event feeling the same way. They each admit that they were nervous to bring it up, since it could throw a curveball at a pretty wonderful existence; but they are on the same page and understand things will never be the same after how they feel today. They talk for a long while, and decide that in the morning they'll look into their options for starting a family.

Hannah and Kelly know that raising a child is going to change their financial picture, so they research the estimated annual costs and update a draft of their written budget accordingly. The up-front costs of childbirth and adoption are both high, so they'll be spending money no matter which route they choose. Caring for a new dependent will materially increase their subsequent monthly spending as well. The *WAIT* technique is standard practice in their other big spending decisions, so they apply it to this scenario as well.

They each have their own individual "W question" monologue and ask themselves the clarifying question, "What benefit do I hope to obtain with this decision?" This is the easiest answer for both of them, because what they seek is the joy of being a parent. When defining "who" they hope will benefit from the decision, they each jot down that they want it to benefit themself, their partner, and a child in need. By clarifying this, they realize that they'd prefer to adopt rather than carry. There are already plenty of children in the world who need love and care, and they have the hearts and resources to make a difference for at least one of those children. They both feel the "when" for their objective should be soon, but not rushed — adoption can be a long, heart-wrenching process and there are lots of different options.

The realization that they want to adopt gives them enough information to breeze through the "research alternatives" step of *WAIT*; they don't believe that any amount of volunteering, mentoring, or other activities that are alternatives to parenthood will provide the value they seek from being moms.

The "investigate options" stage is when Hannah and Kelly review the different adoption methods available to them. They can adopt locally, nationally, or internationally. There are so many adoption agencies, and they see a huge range in costs. They determine that they'd really like to adopt locally if possible. After looking into some local agencies, they stumble across a foster parenting program that offers affordable adoption placement options. The foster-to-adopt options they review are 60% to 90% cheaper than some of the other adoption options they've seen, and it will also provide great opportunities to ensure a good fit for the adults and kids alike. Relief sets in as they realize this is their route — they plan to start as foster parents with intention to adopt.

As with all big decisions, Hannah and Kelly "think on it" to make sure they're comfortable with their choice. This is first and foremost a huge life decision, but it's also a big financial decision, so they take their time. They confirm that the foster-to-adopt program is their favorite option, and it's also by far the most affordable. They follow the process and eventually get matched up with a brother and sister to foster, and they adopt both kiddos as soon as they're eligible. The family lives a happy, healthy life together full of love, support, and a true appreciation for having one another.

Protect your money with wellness

As I said at the beginning of the book, being unhealthy is expensive. This warrants a line in the game plan. Take care of yourself to spend less, earn more, and maximize your quality of life. Enough said.

Insure things you can't afford to replace

Could you afford to replace your car if it burned into ashes? If you broke your leg, could you pay thousands in cash for medical treatment? Would you be able to replace your roof if a ruthless storm smashed your house like a 1-year-old eating a birthday cake? Since the answer is probably no, we need to talk about insurance.

Insurance is an important safeguard for your assets. Maintaining proper coverage can mitigate the financial losses associated with damage or the loss of costly assets such as a home or vehicle, as well as protect against other harmful financial burdens such as health issues. But should you buy every policy you see on TV, as long as the commercial is funny? Maybe not. The quick and simple rule I recommend is to only buy insurance for things you can't afford to replace.

Home insurance

Home insurance is a must, because the cost of a home is incredibly high. Unless you can afford to lose 100% of your home and possessions in a house fire, home insurance should be considered mandatory. Even if you *could* afford to lose it all, the policies are still worth having.

Health insurance

Go online and search for leading causes of bankruptcies in the U.S., and you'll find a plethora of sources revealing that approximately two-thirds of U.S. bankruptcies cite medical issues as a key factor. I attribute this to three main factors: First, most Americans don't have three months' worth of emergency savings to cover a surprise medical bill; second, the significant presence of certain underlying health factors such as obesity are known to lead to increased rates of illness and health complications; and third, many Americans are underinsured in regards to health care coverage. Health insurance is imperative in mitigating overwhelming health care costs, but it won't cover all of them. In the current U.S. health care system, staying clear of medical debt nightmares requires a commitment to staying healthy, adequate cash savings for unexpected costs, *and* adequate health insurance. Significant financial problems await those who aren't prepared with all three. Even citizens who commit fully to all three run the possibility of a medical issue becoming a money pit. But if you control the factors that you can, you'll improve your odds of avoiding disaster.

Auto insurance

Car insurance is mandatory in almost all states, but should probably be a no-brainer for most vehicle owners. Even if you drive a junker that you could easily afford to replace, you might have an at-fault auto accident that could be severely more costly without decent auto insurance.

Life insurance

Life insurance should be carried if you have a family or have any debt. Life insurance is intended to replace your income in the event that you die. And at some point, you're going to. Some employers offer life insurance coverage at little to no cost to the employee, and it can also be obtained through traditional insurance companies or specialty institutions. I personally opt for term life insurance rather than whole life insurance. Term life is a policy for a specific term, and only pays out if the insured party actually dies. For example, a five-year term life policy would only pay out a benefit if the insured party dies in that five-year term. If they die one day after coverage lapses, the insurance company doesn't owe anything. Whole life pays out no matter when you die, and has a cash value associated with it. It acts like a quasi investment account, but I think it's generally too expensive to be worth it. Buy term life insurance to replace your income in the event that you die unexpectedly, and place other quality investments rather than seeking multiple benefits from whole life insurance.

The reason life insurance is so important to those with families or debt is because when you die, you stop earning money. This means that new income isn't available to pay the bills and debts, which could put loved ones at severe financial risk. Guardian angels and pesky poltergeists do not earn United States currency that they can give to their living loved ones. I personally choose to purchase term life insurance that would be enough to cover the cost of paying off my house in full, and round up to cover funeral costs. Debt may transfer to loved ones when you die — it doesn't just automatically go away. Some lenders will forgive certain debts upon death, such as student loans, but others will pursue collection from the family. Aren't these pleasant thoughts? Planning for death is grim to think about, but less grim than knowingly putting loved ones at risk.

Other insurance

You can also purchase insurance to protect your income if, for some reason, you find yourself unable to work. There are a variety of options that are likely to have different product names and coverages, and they're often offered through employers. Look into your options and see if a product makes sense for you. Do the math.

Skip insurance coverage on minor rentals, minor appliances, or anything else you can easily replace in cash. Remember, only buy insurance for things that you can't easily afford to replace. Some homeowners prefer to buy insurance for major appliances such as refrigerators, furnaces, washers, or dryers. These plans could be worth it to those who have concerns over the reliability of their appliances, and can't easily afford to replace them, but it all depends on the rates and coverage. If you're curious, do your research and shop around. Those in a good financial position with adequate emergency savings should be able to skip this form of insurance, but if there truly is a great deal floating out there, there's no shame in taking advantage of it.

Identity theft protection is another form of insurance. Some financial institutions offer free coverage to account holders, and there are also vendors that specialize in identity protection. Do your research to determine coverage requirements, find out where else you have existing coverage, and figure out the potential costs of identity theft in both time and money.

Add value to your life without spending money

What's your favorite way to have fun for free? Are you able to appreciate life without being entertained? Can you enjoy social situations without having to invite Benjamin Franklin? Well, you need to be able to do those things if you want financial health.

Learning to enjoy life without spending a bunch of money might be the very most important attribute of a good defense. No matter what the TV says, it is very possible to find hobbies and social circles that don't require constant splurging. Americans tend to believe that money and fun are inseparably linked, but I think that's a dangerous perspective to have. It's more dangerous than a pissed-off shark in a saltwater swimming pool. We literally have a hobby called "shopping" — during which people pick a venue and hope to come up with a reason to part with their money. You can find fulfillment, fun, and value without giving all of your money away.

This section intentionally comes after the *WAIT* examples because enjoying life all comes down to finding out what is really valuable to *you*. Individual preferences may vary, but the underlying concepts of what provides value to humans are consistent. Like all other living creatures, we share the basic needs for nutrition, water, and safety, so all of those things obviously provide value. They are basic needs that keep us alive, but not things that *add meaning* to our lives. The things that add the most meaning and value to our lives are things that humans have been doing since the beginning of time. Acting like a natural human is a low-cost way to have a wonderful life. But before we explore that, let's go into a simpler example and learn how to be a dog.

Bandit and Ginger are two dogs who live on a farm with a family of humans. Each of the dogs has their basic needs met daily, with plenty of access to food, water, and shelter when necessary. They spend their days wandering the farm grounds, sometimes in leisure and sometimes with relentless curiosity. Bandit's favorite game is fetch, while Ginger thinks her purpose in life is to play tug-of-war. They chase each other around and wrestle at least once a day. They both get some solitude as well, and have been known to pick up a scent and follow it around the pasture for hours, trying to learn what it is and where it went.

Bandit's favorite special treat is leftover meat, and Ginger feels extra blessed on the days she gets to have some peanut butter. Each of them has a couple of durable chew toys that they've had forever. They only really ever get in trouble when their attempts to catch rodents result in too much digging in the garden. When they're worn out, they tend to curl up right next to each other and take a snooze. And oh *boy*, do they love their humans.

Bandit and Ginger are each living a wonderful dog life because they are getting to live a life meant for a dog. When they play, sniff, and explore, they are using their bodies and their brains. They're also picking activities that come naturally to dogs, like running, digging, chewing, and hunting. Their pack animal instincts are satisfied by having a family. And they aren't preoccupied or trying to do too many things at once — they're just focused on the task at hand, and simply being dogs.

Have you ever noticed how happy dogs are when they get to do dog things like walk, run, chase, chew, cuddle, socialize, play-fight, and sniff? That's because dogs are *built* to do those things, and living your intended purpose is satisfying for all creatures.

Just like dogs, the most meaningful things in our lives are the things that are natural to us; therefore, tapping into your own humanity will give you value. Our brains, bodies, and socialization are what make us uniquely human. In those ways we're a lot like dogs, just quite a bit more complicated.

We need to do things that are naturally human in order to enjoy being humans. Use your brain. Move your body. Socialize and apply your complex human emotions such as love, compassion, empathy, and joy. Learning to recognize the value in these things will add meaning to your existence while also improving your financial health.

Do you think an eagle would be living its best eagle life if it tried to act like a penguin or an ostrich? Of course not. What if a husky tried living like a sloth, or a sloth tried living like a cheetah? If you want a great human life, act like one! You are a human, therefore a mammal, therefore an animal — and that's actually really cool. Embrace your inner animal!

Use your brain

The human brain is quite possibly the most complex organ in the natural world, and it requires stimulation to function properly. It is powerful beyond belief, and in addition to opposable thumbs, the brain is the flagship trait of humankind. Eagles use their wings to fly, fish use their gills to breathe underwater, and people use their brains to think, learn, and create. We are so complex that we're capable of metacognition, which in simple speak is "thinking about thinking." The fact that we can actually *study* the organ responsible for thought is just bizarre. A human using their brain is a soaring eagle — it's what they are built to do.

Finding low-cost ways to stimulate your brain will add value to your life. Learn and create. Seek mental challenges and solve puzzles. Engage in stimulating conversations. Observe the world around you, ask questions, and find answers. Make connections. The world has unlimited opportunities for observation and creativity.

Move your body

People who are physically active tend to lead happier, healthier, more fulfilling lives. There are hundreds of studies I could cite, and they'd explain the science of how our body mechanics, endorphins, dopamine, serotonin, and other hormones have scientifically proven that the human body is meant to be active. Using our bodies feels good because it is a natural part of our human existence, and it's not hard to find anecdotal evidence to support the science.

Humans are built to move, and we have an extraordinary arsenal of capabilities. Run, jump, climb, dance, lift, throw, stretch, roll, carry, crawl, swim, push, pull — it's all very human and it's all very satisfying. Enjoy what your body can do and the experiences it can provide.

We all vary in our physical abilities, but I bet you can find healthy ways to use those you currently have. If you can run, get out and run. If you can walk, then walk as much as you can. If you can't walk, do everything else that you can do. If you can swim, stop taking pool selfies and go play in the water! Next time you're looking for a new series to binge-watch, search your favorite streaming website for videos of para athletics, such as the Paralympic Games. Your inspiration and motivation will reach new peaks once you see a swimmer with limb difference power through an Olympic-size pool, or witness a basketball star sink the game-winning shot from a wheelchair. The viewing experience is like eating name-brand potato chips — it's hard to stop at just one. These remarkable athletes give everything they can with everything they've got, and you can do the same to enjoy your own abilities.

Think about how much exercise you're currently getting, and ask yourself, "Is this a human amount of exercise?" Exercising will help you save money because it is satisfying and fills the time and space that would likely otherwise be spent trying to buy happiness. Walking, hiking, running, swimming, dancing, and bodyweight exercises are basically free once you have basics like shoes and clothing. A gym membership or home gym equipment aren't always cheap, but they can provide hours of physical, mental, and social health benefits. Assume someone goes to the gym three days per week for one hour per session, which equates to about 13 hours per month. For a $50 gym membership, that means that all of the value provided by going to the gym costs less than $4 per hour. The cost per hour will only go down with more usage. Someone earning $20 per hour (approximately $3,467 per month) would only be spending about 1% of their monthly earnings on a gym membership of $50 per month. Worth it.

Physical activity provides entertainment, stimulation, and confidence. There is no substitute, and any attempt to find one is going to be very expensive. Do what *your* body can do. Go explore, and challenge yourself, and be as happy as a dog, without breaking the bank.

Socialize

Humans are uniquely social creatures, and we have complex social relationships that are highly influential on our overall well-being. Throughout our history, humanity has formed communities, tribes, and cities. We don't pick our biological family, but we do have choices in our social circles. Healthy socialization is part of a balanced and meaningful life.

It's fun to do things like go out to dinner or go to the movies, but healthy socialization shouldn't always cost money. Fact: a healthy social circle should be able to interact and bond without excessive spending. I don't mind spending money to acquire a shared experience, like travel, concert tickets, or even a little luxury here and there, but those should be treats, not requirements. A social relationship that requires consistent spending and entertainment might not be a very strong bond. I'd rather eat Top Ramen in a rundown apartment with my best friends than eat surf and turf at a five-star resort with people I can't stand. Find people and communities who add value to your life, and you'll find that you don't crave material things quite as badly.

If you have healthy relationships, you should be able to add meaning and enjoyment to your life simply by being with your loved ones. In a world in which having internet and a cellphone are basically required, simply communicating with friends shouldn't ever add much cost to your base budget, no matter where they are. On top of being affordable and fulfilling, being able to socialize also makes it easier to get jobs and work effectively, so it might even help you *make* money.

Learn, engage, teach, debate, share stories, and just enjoy your people in general. Use your body and your brain to provide value to your social circles and your community, and you'll get tenfold your investment in return.

Value-added ideas

The ideas below are some of my favorite ways to add value to life without spending money. For each, we will review which human characteristic it satisfies, and what the potential costs are. Fill your life with humanity and purpose and you may find that you don't have to spend as much money to feel OK.

Think about the *Four Circles of Health* diagram from Chapter 3, and how the circles overlap. Imagine where to plot each of these activities in the overlays of the shape. Do any fall into the true center, where the activity provides value to physical, mental, social, *and* financial health? Let's take a look.

Walking, running, and wandering

Value: body, brain, and sometimes socialization

Potential cost: footwear and weather-compatible clothing if necessary; park passes if necessary

Tip: be mindful as you wander. Observe your surroundings and take it all in, and appreciate the life and world around you. This can also be a great way to connect with people.

Other physical exercise

Value: body, brain, and sometimes socialization

Potential cost: fitness club dues and/or equipment

Tip: use this as an opportunity to improve self-esteem by setting and achieving goals that are meaningful to you.

Reading

Value: brain and sometimes socialization

Potential cost: nonrecurring purchase of book

Tip: read for free by using a public library or book exchange, and don't be afraid to buy used.

Bonus tip: consider joining a book club to add a socialization component.

Board games and puzzles

Value: brain and sometimes socialization

Potential cost: nonrecurring purchases of games or puzzles

Tip: acquire games that allow for creativity and fun, so that they don't get too repetitive. A onetime purchase of a great game might cost $20 up front, but can provide hours of entertainment for years on end.

Other outdoor recreation

Value: body, brain, and sometimes socialization

Potential cost: varies, but sometimes totally free

Tip: enjoy your parks and public spaces — your taxes already helped pay for them! A great purchase of outdoor recreation equipment can go a long way. Buy a basketball or soccer ball (or anything you can throw or kick) and take good care of it, and it can provide hours and hours of joy, entertainment, and exercise. Even a larger purchase like a self-propelled watercraft may add enough brain, body, and social value to be worth it; just take care of it and use it to go amazing places!

Create something

Value: brain, sometimes body, and sometimes socialization

Potential cost: varies

Tip: find inexpensive ways to use your creativity to express yourself. Writing and art may only cost as much as the supplies used. You can learn an instrument for free using online instructional videos, and for the cost of the instrument you could literally change your life. See if a community center has resources available such as instruments, woodshops, art studios, etc., that will allow you to create. Try cooking, baking, gardening, or other interactive and creative hobbies. Make your own game with things you already have. Honestly, some of the most fun I've had has been from creating games with what's been available, regardless of whether I've been a kid or an adult.

Listen to music

Value: body, brain, and sometimes socialization

Potential cost: music player, speakers/headphones, and albums or streaming service

Tip: putting music on the FM radio or free version of a streaming service can provide hours of no-cost entertainment, exercise, and fun. Have a dance party with your friends and/or partner. Heck, sing and dance along by yourself — who cares!? Rock out while you talk to friends. Invest in a decent paid streaming service if you really do listen to music all day. I pay $130 per year for my favorite streaming service because I listen to music at least an hour a day, every single day, and I love being able to pick what I want. I've been listening to music for over half the time I've worked on this book! With the right mode of delivery, music can be a cheap and sustainable way to experience life as only humans can. The cost is worth it to me, and may be worth it to you.

Volunteer

Value: brain, socialization, and sometimes body

Potential cost: zero

Tip: find something you care about and help the cause. It will add value to your community, offer you a chance to meet like-minded people, and add fulfillment and purpose to your life.

Talk to someone

Value: brain and socialization

Potential cost: zero

Tip: conversations can range from nonsensical (like most of my interactions with friends), to emotionally rewarding, to educational, and beyond. Daily investments in quality conversations will provide you with value for which there is no substitute.

Chapter 20: Intangibles

As with any game, sport, team, family, organization, or otherwise, success is undeniably influenced by intangible qualities. Intangibles are the "X factor," aka the "it factor," that cause some people to maximize their potential, and others to fall short. Intangibles are abstract and not objectively measurable. You can't touch an intangible quality, but you can absolutely associate it with success. Whether it's in sports, academics, business, fashion, or music, it's often the intangible qualities that consistently sweep victory to the same highly successful people.

The following is a selective list of intangible qualities to get us started: leadership, toughness, charisma, decision-making, "clutch" performance, ethics, confidence, attitude, desire, tenacity, cleverness, poise, grace, observance, and adaptability.

Even people who aren't basketball fans tend to know who Michael Jordan is, and that he's considered by many to be the greatest basketball player of all time. Air Jordan was incredible at both offense and defense, but I think the reason he earned more rings than a jewelry store is that he also had the "it factor." He was an unbelievably gifted athlete – 6 feet, 6 inches tall, loaded with lean muscle, and somehow explosive and graceful at the same time; but that's not the only reason he had such extraordinary success. Jordan had all the intangibles — things that are impossible or difficult to measure — that a competitor needs to succeed. His goal was to outwork *everyone*. There's no reliable stat for "hustle" in the box score, but he made hustle a hobby and it clearly contributed to his greatness. He had an intense love for winning. He was extremely knowledgeable about the game and understood what to do and when to do it. And Jordan was extremely "clutch" — he made positive impacts in situations that would have proven too challenging for most of his competition.

Intangibles show up in all of life's arenas. Organizational leaders need a high code of ethics, or they are more likely to abuse their power. An interior designer needs charisma, confidence, and a subjective cool factor to generate demand for their business. It's possible for a less gifted runner to edge out their more naturally talented competition, as long as they compete fearlessly and run a smarter race. Parents need poise, grace, observance, and toughness to care for a child.

Financial intangibles are what turn knowledge and employability into financial health. If offense and defense relate to technique and skill, intangibles relate to behaviors and mentality. At a minimum, you need to be tough, observant, adaptable, ethical, and have a good attitude. The following subsections will discuss a few key intangible qualities needed to build a winning game plan in personal finance. If you want to consistently play good offense and defense, you're going to need the right intangibles.

Get tough

Defining toughness

There comes a scene in every saga when it's time to get tough. Whether it's an athlete, a fictional hero, or a lovably awkward romantic comedy lead, the story can't conclude positively unless they overcome some challenging times. The protagonist may develop new abilities, or they may just summon their existing perseverance; but positive endings always require toughness. In movie plots, novelistic apexes, and even real life, the story is the same — toughness is a requirement for success.

Think of toughness as energy available to deal with challenges. There are four sources of energy to fuel toughness, and the great news is, you control of all of them.

Energizer 1 - Purpose

Finding a good reason to do something will always make that thing easier to do. People find energy to do amazing things because they can connect them to a purpose, whether it is to help others, to be the best version of themselves, to support their families, or to find fulfillment. Think about the intended outcome or reward of a given action, and you'll find the energy to do it.

It's easier to save money when you know what you're saving for. That's why it's so incredibly important to be thoughtful and have financial goals.

Understand the purpose of healthy choices and you'll be tough enough to make them consistently.

Energizer 2 - Positivity

Staying positive can power people through incredible challenges. Adopting an attitude of "I can do this" will block out the cold of limiting self-doubt. Positivity is really about belief. It's nearly impossible to beat a deadly disease, lift a heavy object, finish school, or even just be kind to others, if you don't believe you can. While some choose to slog through thick, slimy, suffocating negativity, masters of positivity and belief continue to overachieve in wide open country.

In personal finance, the belief that you will achieve your goals will give you the energy to stick to them. If you consistently say, "I'm never going to be able to afford a house," you're certainly going to be right. But if you believe you can find ways to make it happen, you're going to find the energy and toughness to do it. Find the positives of working and saving, and both will be easier and more enjoyable.

Energizer 3 - Gratitude

Being grateful will give you more energy than a pink bunny playing drums in a battery commercial. Find a reason to appreciate any given challenge, and you'll smile through the adversity. I live in a region with frequent rain, cool temperatures, and big, steep coastal hills that abruptly lead to one of the most prominent mountain peaks in the entire world. That may turn some people off from running, but I think it makes it more fun. That's because I choose to run gratefully. When my knees start hurting, I decide to be grateful for the use of my body. When it starts dumping rain, I look at the trees and I'm grateful to have fresh water to support the life around me. When I feel like my legs are frozen in carbonite, I choose to be grateful for the beautiful parks and safe streets I get to run in. When I start the climb up yet another massive hill, I'm grateful for the chance to get stronger, and I smile like a great big idiot. In all those opportunities to stop or quit, I find energy to keep going instead, because I know how lucky I am to have the chance.

Being grateful will put more money in your pocket, and help you keep it, too. Workers who are grateful for employment are more likely to try their best every day and produce more quality work. People who are grateful for what they already have are more likely to resist buying things they don't need. People who are grateful for their challenges find the energy to thrive.

Energizer 4 - Determination

Determination is the most classic source of extreme energy. Determined people can tap deep into their reserves and summon courage and brutal endurance. It's what gets a single mom through night classes. It's what gives athletes just enough energy to finish an event before collapsing immediately after. It's the energy to nurture a relationship, even on the days when it's not convenient.

If you're determined to reach your goals, you're going to. Being determined to properly serve yourself, your dependents, and your community will give you plenty of energy to pursue financial health.

Stress management

Stress management and discipline are both major intangible inputs into financial health, and each requires significant energy, so it helps to be tough.

Stress management and self-improvement are vital in maintaining employment and preventing useless spending. Understanding your challenges and addressing them will make you stronger and tougher. This will give you more energy to stay disciplined. As we think more about why this is so important, let's look at how stress resistance and stress tolerance impact your finances.

Stress resistance is the ability to handle things without experiencing stress, and stress tolerance is the ability to *endure* stress. Think of how stress resistance and stress tolerance play out for people who have a long commute to work. Some people really don't mind driving, and may even enjoy it. Those folks have high stress resistance to commuting, since it doesn't really stress them out. On the other hand, some people really don't like commuting, but do it to bridge the gap between where they want to live and where they want to work. They hate the commute and it stresses them out in the moment, but it doesn't ruin the rest of their day. That group has a high stress tolerance for commuting — they have energy to endure the stress because they think the benefits outweigh the costs.

Improving stress resistance and stress tolerance are amazing ways to become a high earner, which means these intangible factors have a direct impact on financial success. It's easier to stay employed when stress resistance and stress tolerance are high. On top of that, high-paying jobs are often considered "high-stress," so they require some toughness. Great employees need adequate energy to produce quality work, and quality work usually translates into promotions, better paychecks, and bigger bonuses. That said, I don't suggest pursuing a "high-stress" job unless your stress resistance and stress tolerance are well suited for that particular role — otherwise the job will become a net negative on your total health. I would never accept a job as a semitruck driver, even if it paid millions per year, because it would stress me out too badly to be worth it. I have limited stress resistance and low stress tolerance for driving huge vehicles, and let's be honest, after a couple of bumpy hauls, they'd probably end up paying me even more to leave. I'd probably have better luck flying a broomstick than I would keeping a semi in one lane. Anyway. If you're thoughtful about what you want from your career and you're able to get tough, earning money shouldn't be a problem.

Tough money

Everyone can get tougher, which means everyone can improve their health with a little extra work. Getting tougher requires an admission that you *can* be tougher, as well as an acceptance that sometimes life isn't easy or fair. It might also mean admitting some shortcomings or underlying issues, such as low self-esteem, insecurity, lack of focus, inflexibility, or low stress tolerance, to name a few. It seems counterintuitive that admitting weaknesses and tapping into your feelings will make you tougher, but I promise this tactic will make you more powerful if you use it to learn and grow. Have you seen *Star Wars*? It works for the Jedi and it can work for you too. *Search your feelings. You know it to be true.* Approaching mental and emotional health with a mindset focused on continuous improvement will enrich your daily life and optimize your financial outcomes. It can help you enjoy life, earn more, and spend less.

So, how would you rate your mental health? What are your coping strategies, and are they sustainable and healthy? Are your coping strategies expensive in more ways than one? Nagging mental and emotional health issues can be a huge drain on energy that could otherwise be used to stay tough and disciplined in more productive ways. Life is better when those things are addressed, whether independently or with professional help. Some people think counseling is for whiners and wimps, but I'd bet the farm they only think that because they've never really gone through with it. Take it from me — therapy requires brutal toughness. It takes serious guts to relive trauma, admit to screwups, uncover insecurities, confront fears, process losses, or face debilitating pain. A lot of people won't go to therapy, or go but dismiss it as soon as it gets hard. I think that's because they're secretly afraid they're not strong enough to address their problems, and would rather just pretend the problems don't exist. I've been that person, and I've known that person. I bet we all know someone who is incredibly strong, successful, and resilient in most situations, but ironically is terrified of dealing with fear, feelings, and weakness. In my opinion, that's self-limiting. Investing in personal growth takes discipline and energy, and though it can be a drain on the front end, the resources given are awfully small compared with the resources received.

You may sometimes have to say "not now" or "never" to certain things that could be fun or convenient. You may even have to say "not now" to a great investment opportunity if the timing doesn't align with your situation at that moment. Sometimes saying no is annoying or downright upsetting, but you just have to get tough. □As a society, we overvalue instant gratification and undervalue impulse control. This leads us to overspend, overconsume, and underperform. We're so buried in convenience and indulgence that we become clinically anxious when we have to demonstrate patience or restraint. Instant gratification doesn't make life easier, but being tough *does.*

Getting tough might mean doing things that aren't your first choice, but are still a good choice. Think of it *exactly* this way: it's not your *first* choice, but you've determined it to be a favorable choice overall. An obvious example that demonstrates this mindset is the choice to maintain full-time employment. Going to work may not be your first choice of ways to spend your time, but it's often a much more favorable choice than *not* working.

Personally, I think it *is* fair that we have to work a little bit for prosperity and health. Until recently, no human could have ever survived while they were being physically and mentally apathetic. Put some humanity into your work ethic, and get tough. To be honest, sometimes I get very, *very* annoyed about going to work. I sometimes worry that I'm wasting my life feeling overwhelmed and stressed, flirting with an existential crisis. All I really want to do is wander around, think creatively, lift heavy things, and still have my basic needs met. But that's not possible in the modern developed world. Hunter-gatherer is not a sustainable career path in a world painted in pavement. So I just have to remember to fix my attitude and appreciate the opportunities I *do* have. Life is pretty damn good, when you slow down to notice.

If you think you will be able to meet your health and financial goals without significant discipline, you're incorrect. Some of the concepts in this book may identify *reasons* people spend the way they do or struggle to maintain employment, but these aren't excuses to continue the pattern. They are meant to draw connections among underlying issues that cause people to behave in ways that make them broke. The issues need to be fully addressed, or they'll negatively impact your financial health in the present and future. If you had water dripping from your ceiling, you wouldn't just dab it and hope for the drywall not to rot — you'd fix the leak before you have bigger problems! By the way, I'm giving myself bonus points for that analogy because it has financial relevance for homeowners.

You're doing the right thing by pursuing your financial education, but book smarts will only get you so far. You need discipline. You should never go without basic needs, but meeting financial health goals might sometimes mean skipping a night out, postponing a big purchase, or saying no to a vacation with friends. Learn to be proud of these times when you've toughened up and learned to deal with missing out sometimes. You *get* to work. You *get* to exercise and eat well. You *get* to save money. Financial goals take effort, and you need to be tough enough to put in the work even when it's inconvenient.

Be a student of the game

You may have heard the term "student of the game" used to describe an athlete whose brain contributes as much or more to their success as their physical gifts. Their knowledge, cleverness, and recognition of patterns and tendencies help maximize their natural abilities. They genuinely love and respect their craft, which gives them energy to pay attention and find ways to win. This really hurts to say, but the ultimate example of a student of the game is NFL legend Tom Brady. After years of counseling, I can finally admit that Tom Brady is a good football player. In three different decades, he has consistently outperformed other quarterbacks who, in many cases, were bigger, stronger, faster, had a better arm, or had a higher IQ, and often some combination of those things. But old Tommy has paid attention and sought every advantage — on and off the field — to help him achieve his goals. His style of play has been so consistent and dependable that some have even accused it of being boring. He has always looked for the best blend of reliability and reward, just like you should do with your finances. You may not become the Tom Brady of personal finance, but you too can make the most of your natural gifts by becoming a student of the game.

Adopting a studious mindset makes it quick and easy to find opportunities to improve your financial health. Just pay attention to the patterns and behaviors of yourself and others. No need to judge, but feel free to be thoughtful and analytical through a lens of interactive financial health. Recognize patterns you want to follow and those that you *never* want to follow, because success and failure are both accredited teachers. If you find yourself having a reaction to something you observe — whether you don't like it, you like it, or you don't understand — take a few minutes to think about the patterns and circumstances so that you have a chance to learn. This will help plot the map to your financial goals.

A student of the game is adaptable and competitive in any setting because they're clever and they know what they're doing. Wouldn't you like to be informed and clever when it comes to managing your money? Tax codes, economic conditions, laws and regulations, and untapped opportunities will never stop changing. Try to stay informed on the financial environment you exist in, so that you can apply your skills and knowledge toward advantageous outcomes.

Maintain quality credit

How much money would you be willing to lend to someone you didn't think was going to pay you back? What would you want to be aware of before lending to someone you didn't know? Would you front your neighbors $10,000 so they could buy a VIP booth at a nightclub? Picturing yourself as a lender can help bring logic to the reasoning behind why some folks can borrow as much as they want, while others can't get approved for a credit card.

When lenders sort through credit applications, they need a reliable way to guess how likely someone is to pay back their loan in a timely way, even though they probably don't know the applicant personally. Banks and other lenders assess a person's likeliness to pay by obtaining their credit score. A credit score is an objective estimation of how likely an individual is to pay their debts. The score is calculated by credit rating agencies, and calculations may be different by agency and loan type. But one thing is consistent in all credit situations — the better the applicant's credit, the better deal they get.

When you apply for a loan, a lender will want to know information about your income, rent, scheduled debt payments, etc., but this is in *addition* to your credit score, since the score itself isn't affected by any of those things. Someone with an excellent credit score isn't necessarily able to afford payments on a megayacht, even though they've shown quality credit behaviors in the past. Conversely, someone with poor credit behaviors may be less likely to get approved to borrow, even if they earn a lot of money.

Credit ratings impact financial opportunities, and adequate credit is a requirement for financial health. It's not just lenders who are interested in credit ratings; it's any party who needs to guess the financial reliability and potential risks of doing business with an individual. The following list includes several common scenarios in which an individual's credit rating may be considered.

Loan terms: The better your credit score, the better your interest rates and other terms will be, meaning cheaper loans when borrowing is necessary.

Employment: Some employers such as banks require credit checks as part of their employment screening, which means that bad credit can literally keep you from getting a job.

Housing: Landlords may require prospective renters to agree to a credit check, and will not rent to those who don't meet their standards. Not to mention, getting approved for a mortgage in order to make a responsible home purchase is virtually impossible without adequate credit. That means someone with bad credit may struggle to find a desirable place to live — regardless of renting or buying — if they have a low credit rating.

Other opportunities: In addition to its impact on loan terms, employment, and housing, credit may impact other opportunities. Who knows — maybe someday, premium online dating sites will list a credit score right next to each user's flirtiest headshot. More seriously, there may be other opportunities that are impacted by credit ratings. For example, it may be hard to obtain a small loan to start a business if the applicant has unreliable borrowing history. Credit reports may also be reviewed as part of applications to establish phone contracts or utilities. The most likely vendors to require this information are those who provide services in advance and then bill later. For example, a utility company may provide two months of service before sending a bill, which means that they need some assurance that they'll be paid for what they've provided.

Cash flow and credit

Having quality credit provides cost savings and even cash-back opportunities. Lenders offer interest rates to applicants that directly relate to how they perceive the applicant's ability to pay (as well as the character of the loan). The irony is that the people who are most likely to pay are charged less, while the folks who are least likely to pay are charged more. This is one of the reasons why bad credit and overwhelming debt are so challenging (but not impossible) to overcome.

Comparison of interest expense

A lender makes money by charging the borrower interest and fees in exchange for the use of the lender's money. The more creditworthy a borrower is, the lower the interest rate they're offered will be, meaning their interest expense will be lower. Let's look at a simplified example of the costs of financing a vehicle using an auto loan.

Lauren and Luke each buy a quality used car from the same dealer, and their cars are identical in every way, down to the interior color, mileage, and service history. Each takes out a 60-month (five-year) auto loan of $20,000. Lauren has excellent credit and is able to take out a loan with AB Credit Union (ABCU), bearing an annual interest rate of 5%, compounding monthly. Luke has below-average credit due to unfavorable history that includes missed payments on his student loans. Because Luke's history shows he's not always a reliable payer of his debts, he is offered an interest rate of 8% from ABCU. Since the credit union is less confident that they'll receive timely payments from Luke, they want more money from him throughout the process. They need their reward to exceed their risk. No one is necessarily lining up to lend Luke money, because they just aren't sure how it's going to go. On the other hand, Lauren's credit history makes ABCU very confident that she will pay them back in a timely fashion. Since Lauren is likely able to borrow from any lender she chooses, they have to offer her a lower interest rate to earn her business. Responsible, reliable borrowers are easy money for the credit union, so they feel safe enough to offer her a cheaper financing option.

With her 5% interest rate, Lauren's monthly payment (prior to lender fees) is $377.42 per month. With his 8% interest rate, Luke's payment is $405.53 per month. Luke is outraged when he finds out that he has to pay more for the exact same thing as Lauren. Red-faced and crying, he calls ABCU to complain. I mean, snot-on-the-collar-of-his-shirt *bawling*. But ABCU explains that's just how the industry works. He'll need to improve his credit to avoid the waterworks next time.

Even though Lauren and Luke bought the *exact* same product, Luke ends up paying 7.4% more than Lauren over the course of their loans. Compounding interest makes it so the 3% difference in their rates adds up to even more disparity over time. Lauren will pay $2,645 in interest in the 60 months it takes to pay off her loan, and Luke will pay $4,332. This means that in actual dollars, Luke's total interest cost was 64% higher than Lauren's.

Doesn't it seem extremely backward that financial institutions charge *more* to someone who is less likely to pay? Doesn't charging more make it even *harder* to pay? The answer is yes — absolutely. But this is why messed-up credit is such a problem, and why the credit section of this book is as thick and flavorful as a milkshake.

The choice to charge extra to risky borrowers comes down to the economic concept of supply and demand. When supply is high, prices are lower; when supply is low, prices are higher. Going back to the Lauren and Luke example, Lauren's market for loan products has very high supply. Because Lauren has excellent credit, lenders literally send her mail and promotional deals. Lenders love lending to Lauren because she is low-risk. The supply of loans is high, which means that the price of the loan (i.e., interest rate and fees) needs to be low in order to entice her to sign. Luke's loan environment does *not* have high supply, because lending to Luke has proven to be historically risky; so no one is overly eager to lend to Luke. The supply of loans to Luke is low, so the lenders can stay competitive at higher prices.

In addition to the impact of loan supply on interest rates, another reason lenders might charge more to riskier borrowers is to accumulate more cushion in the event of nonpayment. We can draw up an oversimplified example that can help prove the point without causing a headache.

AB Credit Union offers members a 12-month personal loan of $1,000, bearing simple interest ranging from 10% to 20% depending on credit rating. Principal and interest are due in full at the end of the 12-month term. ABCU categorizes potential borrowers into five tiers according to the risk associated with their credit rating. Tier 1: minimal risk; Tier 2: low risk; Tier 3: moderate risk; Tier 4: high risk; Tier 5: maximum risk. They never lend to applicants who fall into Tier 5 because their research says the risk exceeds the reward. They hire an actuary to help with the math, and together they pull up their arithmetic-patterned dress socks and crunch the numbers. They determine that applicants who fall into the Tier 1 category are 99.3% likely to pay back the principal and interest at the end of the 12-month term. At the other end of the spectrum, they estimate that borrowers in Tier 4 are 91% likely to pay back the principal and interest at the end of the 12-month term. Figure 3-10 below shows that in order to earn a 9.2% margin on the $1,000 loans ($92 average per loan), the lender can charge 10% to Tier 1, but needs to charge 20% to Tier 2. Even the seemingly small difference in likelihood to pay requires the interest rate to double in order to achieve the same outcome. For this reason, lenders charge more to those who are less likely to pay, even though higher costs make it even harder to pay.

Figure 3-10

Credit Tier Comparison for a $1,000 loan

Tier 1		Tier 4	Calculation Steps
99.3%	Likeliness to pay back	91.0%	A
1,000	Principal	1,000	B
10%	Simple interest rate	20%	C
100	Scheduled interest earned over 12mo	200	D=B*C
1,100	Amount due in 12mo	1,200	E=B+D
1,092	Average expected realization per loan	1,092	F=A*E
92	Average expected margin per loan	92	G=F-B
8	Expected loss outcome per loan	108	H=E-F
9.2%	Average expected margin %	9.2%	I=G/B

Better credit, better deals

In addition to receiving better interest rates on loans, those with quality credit will qualify for more favorable credit products, especially when it comes to credit cards and other consumer credit products. Credit card companies usually offer perks such as cash back on purchases, airline miles, additional savings for cardholders when shopping with partner vendors, and more. Additionally, someone with quality credit may even be offered free financing (0% interest), payment-free periods, and other options. It's nice to have a handful of decent financing deals to choose from, even if you eventually wind up choosing to pay cash.

Let's do the math on how a cash-back credit card can positively impact someone's finances. Imagine that a program offers 2% unlimited cash back on all purchases made using the card. The cash back is characterized as a reduction of expense rather than a source of income, meaning the cash flow is tax-free. If the cardholder and their dependents spend $5,000 per month ($60,000 per year), they will have saved $100 per month and $1,200 per year from the cash-back program. They pay off the card routinely and never *ever* carry a balance, so they never owe a cent of interest. Could they also take that $100 savings and invest it to make it work for them, say, over the course of 30 years? In this scenario, the person would save $100 per month for 360 months, making a total amount saved from the cash-back program $36,000. If that same $100 per month were to be invested in a fund that earned 6% annually, the earnings would be nearly $65,000 during those same 360 months — which would mean that 2% savings on routine purchases could conceivably turn into over $100,000 in extra dough over that time span.

That scenario — which is shockingly realistic for someone with excellent credit — demonstrates how perks and rewards are an incredibly valuable benefit of having quality credit. Just remember to never ever carry a balance, and to not let rewards or 0% interest trick you into buying things you don't want or need.

Lender pretender

Credit ratings can seem convoluted, and honestly, sometimes they seem stupid at first glance. You get dinged for opening accounts, you get dinged for closing accounts; if they could, they'd probably ding you for overcooking a pot roast or having elbows. Here's an example of a seemingly silly credit score adjustment. Someone with excellent credit history will take a hit to their score if they don't have many (or any) active accounts. For example, when I sold my first house and was 100% debt-free at age 29, with no missed or late payments, my credit score immediately went down 10 points because I "no longer had any active installment accounts." My score was still plenty high, but I was pissed off like a bull at the Rose Parade. It seemed about as logical as a teacher docking me 10 points on a science project solely because I turned it in early. But when I thought about it from the perspective of potential lenders, it made a *little* more sense. Lenders may see a lack of accounts as a smaller sample size, meaning they can place less reliance on the data. Still annoying, but at least not totally random.

In this section we will play lender pretender to start understanding credit from the perspective of the money source. Pretending to be a lender helps you stop to think about how different variables affect a lender's confidence that a prospective borrower would actually pay them back timely (or at all). Let's look at the nuances of credit measures through the eyes of various lenders.

Payment history

<u>Concert cash advance</u>

You, Brad, and Beth want to go to a concert. Brad and Beth say that if you buy the tickets, they'll pay you back. You aren't really worried about covering up-front for Beth. She used to be roommates with a mutual friend, and you know that she always paid her share in a timely manner. You're also friends with Brad's roommate, and the roommate has complained to you that Brad frequently forgets to pay his share of the bills. You also remember other times when Brad was supposed to pay for something, but didn't. There was one time you ordered pizza with Brad and his roommate, and even though Brad said he would pay for one-third of the pizza, he refused to pay his share when it was delivered. Then he had the nerve to eat two slices, and you didn't talk for a few days. Then there was the time you let Brad borrow your hiking poles, and he never gave them back, claiming he didn't have them anymore. Because Brad has a history of not paying things timely, refusing to pay, and not returning things that he's borrowed, you are a little nervous about buying Brad's concert ticket in advance. You have no problem "lending" the money to Beth by buying her ticket before she pays you, because she's proven over time that she's reliable. But it's harder to trust that you'd get the money from Brad, because he has a history of delayed and missed repayments.

<u>Takeaways for payment history</u>

Lenders don't want to lend to people they don't think will pay them back. This is why people with poor payment history and poor credit ratings may not be approved for certain loans and will likely suffer less favorable terms such as higher interest rates, collateral requirements, smaller loan amounts, and other non-perks.

Length of credit history

<u>Cheesecake credit challenge</u>

You are a recent graduate, and your friends Priya and Sara are juniors in the business school at your alma mater. They are known around campus for making amazing cheesecakes, which they bring to parties and school fundraisers. They see an opportunity to make some extra money during the summer by selling their cheesecakes at local farmers markets, fairs, and festivals. They might even be able to sell their cheesecakes as street vendors outside of sporting events. If all goes well, they'd love to try to launch a full-blown dessert shop after they graduate.

Priya and Sara will need a portable generator and a portable refrigerator in order to keep their cheesecakes at the right temperature. Food poisoning is bad for business, because not even cheesecake tastes good a second time. They'll also need a business license. The total cost of equipment and licenses will likely cost a few thousand dollars. They know you have some savings stacked up from your new job, so they approach you with an investment opportunity. Priya and Sara ask if you'd be willing to lend them each $500, with simple (non-compounding) interest of 10% per year, due one year from the date of the loan. So the deal offered to you is to give them each $500 now in exchange for $550 a year later; they'd be giving you back 10% more than you gave them, in order to make it worth your while. You see their entrepreneurial spirit, and you know firsthand how ridiculously delicious their cheesecakes and other treats are. You think they can make it, but before you'll fork over the dough you want to think through the risks, which are mainly that you won't get your money back. You know that Priya has been paying her monthly bills throughout college, including rent, utilities, and other living expenses. You use this information to conclude that Priya has learned how to manage her money, and will be sure to have already set aside the $550 she'd owe you when the loan comes due. You also know that Sara, who is a scholarship soccer player, has never actually paid her own bills. Between her full-ride scholarship and assistance from her parents to pay any leftover expenses, Sara has never actually managed her own money before. You know and like Sara, but you're hesitant to give her a $500 loan knowing that she has no experience managing money. Whereas Priya has always had to be sure to spend less than she earns, Sara hasn't ever had to think about it. You are very willing to lend to Priya, since it seems like easy money and you want to support your friend. But since Sara has no experience and no history, will you be comfortable lending her money?

Takeaways for length of credit history

Someone with no credit history can't be rated as an excellent borrower, because they haven't proven themself yet. As you think through the scenario of lending to Sara, even though she has limited formal financial history, you would at least have the advantage of knowing Sara personally and having a general opinion of her capabilities and reliability. Commercial lenders don't know every single applicant, and they would go bankrupt if they didn't have robust credit policies that incorporate credit history heavily into risk assessment.

I applied for my first credit card when I was in college, and was quickly denied because I had no credit history. In hindsight, I should have asked a family member with quality credit to cosign with me, which would have given the bank extra assurance of timely repayment. I was in college during the Great Recession, when financial institutions were extra stringent with their lending policies in response to the credit crisis. I remember how infuriating it was that I was denied for having no credit history. I knew that I had no intention of even carrying a balance, let alone missing a payment if I did have a balance. I knew I had a good monthly savings plan based on a reasonably thorough budget. I was working while in school, and I expected a professional job with quality pay after I graduated. With my career goals I was expecting to double my salary within six to eight years, and I was actively researching personal finance so that I could make the most of my earnings. As it turned out, the credit card company didn't care about my life plans — they just cared if my profile indicated whether I would be a financial risk or not. And because I had no history, they concluded I was too risky. This scenario was ridiculous in my opinion, but I get it. Lenders can't reasonably assess the potential reliability, judgment, decision-making, and other unique personal factors of each credit applicant.

The credit rating agencies make people *earn* a high credit rating. You can't have quality credit without consistently proving that you're a reliable borrower — they don't know you, and you won't be given the benefit of the doubt. You don't start out with an "A" grade, you start out with nothing.

Credit utilization

The Rocky Road of lending to Hot Rod Ricky

You work in a local coffee shop, and you're chatting with Richard, who is a coworker and friend. He's talking about how much he loves his car, and all his plans for making it even faster. His car is a recently-purchased used muscle car that he loves to tinker with, which is how he earned his nickname "Hot Rod Ricky." Richard's nickname isn't his favorite, but hey, he could be called much worse. You were with him when he bought the car last year, and he tells you pretty regularly that the $500 per month car payment isn't a big deal since the car brings in more babes than a beauty pageant (his words, not yours). Hot Rod Ricky tells you he really wants to add a new exhaust to his car, but just needs someone to front him the money. He tells you that you can borrow the car for a weekend if you can help him pay for the exhaust, and assures you timely repayment. When you ask how much the exhaust kit will cost, he says that the cost is $250, and he can save by doing the install himself; however, he only wants to borrow $100 from you since he's already borrowed $150 from your mutual friend Keisha. You tell Ricky that you're not sure you're comfortable lending the money, since you don't really think he needs to take on more debt to add a new exhaust to his car. He tells you he's good for it, and to ask the other people he regularly borrows money from. He mentions that he's never missed a payment to his grandma, and pays her back $50 per month for when she helped him buy his upgraded sound system. He tells you about how he paid his ex-girlfriend back for random things when they broke up, although he did need to borrow a few bucks from his new girlfriend Meg to be able to do that. He suggests that you check with your mutual friends DeShaun, Han, Amir, and Alex, since he's borrowed money from all of them and has always paid them back — even if it meant borrowing a little more from a different friend to do so. This long list of references does not bring you comfort — it makes you realize that Ricky is constantly spending more money than he has. If he misses a paycheck, nobody is going to get paid back. You don't want to buy an exhaust for a car that seems likely to be repossessed by the bank if people stop lending him more money. You conclude that because his debts are so consistent and so high, you are very skeptical of his ability to pay you back, even if he's never missed a payment.

Takeaways for credit utilization

Too much debt means extra risk and too little flexibility, and that's unattractive to lenders. Credit utilization is a simple calculation used by lenders to determine the proportion of outstanding debt compared to approved debt limits. For example, if someone's only credit account is a $10,000 limit credit card, and they have a balance of $1,500, their credit utilization is 15%, which is calculated as follows: $1,500 outstanding / $10,000 total available = 15%. This metric is important to lenders because it can indicate an ability to manage money, or it can raise red flags for potential debt overload. A person with high credit utilization is riskier to lend to, which means that a credit rating agency will ding their score accordingly. The more money someone owes, the more difficult it is to meet all repayment obligations. Credit utilization highlights how close a person is to not having access to more money. If someone has 100% credit utilization (borrows every dollar available to them), they have maxed out and don't have options to get more cash unless they convince another lender to lend to them more. This means that they're forced to either start paying down debts — which is especially difficult due to interest — or go bankrupt. In the example with Hot Rod Ricky, he and his many lenders are in trouble if he ever misses a paycheck or stops getting cash advances, because his utilization appears to be 100%. He spends every dollar he earns and every dollar he borrows. This example also highlights another credit score factor, which is that having too many credit accounts may indicate poor financial management, and in turn harm your credit score.

Lenders don't want to chance not getting paid back, and by way of simple math, they know that the more someone owes, the harder it is to make all payments. They also view borrowing near maximum limits as a sign of potential financial distress, which is cause for concern.

I recommend never carrying a credit card balance unless you truly have no other viable options. It's OK to carry a balance on worthy debt products, such as a mortgage, educational loan, responsible car loan, or loan for essential home improvements. These things do drive up credit utilization — especially at the beginning of the loan — but they won't hurt too bad. Use of revolving credit, such as credit cards, is where managing utilization is most imperative. Pay off your card regularly, or if you find that having a credit card leads to overspending, stick to debit cards only. The lower your daily, weekly, or monthly balance is, the better your credit score will be at any given measurement interval. Personally, I use my credit cards as often as I can, due to the cash-back and mileage programs, but I pay everything off in advance so that my monthly statement balance is $0.

Credit mix

Borrow-B-Q

You and 20 other family members are at your cousin Todd's house for a family event. Todd and his wife Angela own a catering business specializing in spicy grilled chicken and clever southern-themed sides. Angela is a rock star on the grill, and Todd is a master with the sides. Todd just finished prepping his specialty Cajun-fusion baked beans, homestyle mac 'n' cheese, and a loaded green salad that somehow makes people forget that they're eating vegetables. Angela is working her magic on the grill, and the family is mingling and enjoying life. Todd pulls you aside and asks if you have some time to talk about a private matter involving money. You are so well-versed in finances at this point that you're excited to have a chance to talk shop. Todd asks if you'd be interested in investing in a specialty grill that he needs some help paying for. He explains that the grill is enormous, has state of the art features, and was the top-rated grill on the market last year; consequently, it costs $12,000. He mentions that paying cash would nearly deplete their cash reserves, so he's hoping to finance it. The store he wants to buy the grill from offers financing, but their interest rates are pretty high, and it's even more expensive to use a credit card. After more explanation of how special the grill is, Todd lets you know that he and Angela were wondering if you'd like to invest in the grill and earn 5% simple interest per year for the next three years, with interest payable monthly. You do the math in your head, and realize that his offer means you'd be earning $50 per month in interest for the next 36 months, and you'd be helping your family expand their catering business. It seems like a good use of your excess cash.

You reply by saying that you'll think about it overnight, and that you can totally see how the new grill could pay off for their business. It could allow them to cater bigger events, enable more variety, and maybe even improve the taste of their food (as if that were possible). Todd interjects and says that it isn't actually for the business, and that it's just for his and Angela's house. They think it would be nice to have for hosting parties and enjoying family time. You are a little startled. You had originally thought you were being asked to lend money for the catering business, which you were confident was a reasonably safe and symbiotic use of your funds. In that case, the grill would help Angela and Todd generate money, which could bolster their ability to pay you back for the full cost of the grill plus the interest payments. But when you realize the grill is for personal use, you grow concerned. It sounds like they can't really afford the grill right now, and because it's for personal use only, it does *not* improve their cash flow; in fact, it's guaranteed to do the exact opposite. If it's already too expensive for their current situation, how can you be assured that you'll get your investment back, let alone the interest money that was agreed to be paid? You explain to Todd that it would be one thing if the grill were going to be used as an investment for their business, but that you aren't comfortable lending that much money for a nonessential personal item. Todd points out that he would put up the grill as collateral for the loan — if they can't pay, you get the grill. You point out that you have no use for a $12,000 grill, it doesn't have a great resale market, and besides — you couldn't bear the thought of repossessing a grill from your own family. You let Todd know that you're sorry to say it, but you're just not comfortable making the deal.

Takeaways for credit mix

Not all debt is created equal, and this fact shows up in credit scores and borrowing arrangements. Lenders like to have extra assurance that their investment will pay off; they are just a type of investor, after all. They loan out money in exchange for interest and fees, which means that to them, lending is investing. Lenders know that debt is a bet that the borrower will have more money later, and they don't want to fund reckless gambling.

Lenders tend to prefer investing in borrowers who will use the money to pay for something productive. For example, lenders consistently lend to individuals pursuing career advancement opportunities such as college or trade school, because these things increase their likelihood of employability and financial success. The hope is that these people will have no trouble paying back the money since they are using it to improve their "offense." On the other hand, they're not likely to give a decent deal to a borrower who wants to buy personalized cookie jars.

Lenders typically only give large loans that are collateralized, which means that the loans are "secured" against nonpayment. The most common forms of this can be observed in mortgage loans and car loans, which are collateralized by the asset the loan is used to acquire. In other words, if you don't pay your lender back timely for the money you borrowed to buy a house, they have legal recourse to foreclose the loan and repossess the house. If you have an auto loan and don't make your payments, your lender will legally repossess the vehicle. Housing and used vehicles are highly marketable assets. This means that if a lender forecloses on a collateralized loan and takes possession of a house or car, they expect to be able to sell the asset for cash on the open market and recoup some, or all, of their losses. Since the loans are secured, lenders can afford to offer decent loan deals specifically for the purchases of homes or cars.

Lenders are *not* eager to dish out significant cash for an uncollateralized loan that does not improve the borrower's ability to pay. Going back to the Borrow-B-Q example, it seemed reasonable to lend to Todd and Angela so that they could buy an asset for their business, but it seemed much less reasonable to lend money for a personal luxury that wouldn't increase their cash flow. And even though Todd offered the grill as collateral, it didn't really matter, since a used supergrill isn't highly marketable like a house or car. This same logic is applied by commercial lenders — they like to know that their investment will acquire assets, or at least improve their likelihood of getting paid back. Interest rates and credit ratings follow suit with this concept. Loans for a specific purpose, such as a home, auto, or education, will come with higher approved amounts and lower interest rates because they're viewed as productive and secured by lenders (well, educational loans aren't secured because, despite the conspiracy theories out there, "the man" can't repo knowledge). Non-collateralized personal loans, and loans to purchase non-assets (i.e., a personal use grill) are more likely to have higher interest rates and lower financing ceilings, because the lender doesn't have the same security.

Do your best to only take on debt for essentials, and preferably only to invest. This will give you a favorable credit mix in the eyes of lenders, and you'll get cheaper loans when you need them.

Live a lifestyle that aligns with your goals

Lifestyle may be the most important aspect of financial health. As noted in Section 3, it doesn't matter how much you score if your opponent outscores you. Famous musicians, actors, and athletes may earn a lot of money, but someone is always willing to take it from them if they spend frivolously. I'm not out to humiliate those folks by listing them by name, but if you're drooling for the drama, look it up yourself.

There are numerous studies that explain how many lottery winners have to declare bankruptcy due to reckless spending. I have read that approximately one-third of lottery winners go bankrupt, and that they are more likely to go bankrupt than average citizens. I acknowledge that the lottery puts a target on the back of the publicly announced winner, and for all I know some of the people give all the money away to good causes; however, I'd guess most bankrupt lottery winners have simply spent more money than they've won. That's pretty remarkable.

It's easy to avoid luxurious temptation when no one is offering the bait. As it stands right now, I don't have to show any restraint to avoid buying a $10 million mansion on the shores of Kauai. I don't have the money for it and I couldn't get approved for that big of a loan if I wanted it. Of course, a $10 million mansion seems ludicrous when it's so far out of reach that I'd get turned away by the guards. But what about a home that's at the very top of my range? Suppose I get approved for a mortgage loan of up to $1 million — should I use the full amount to get my dream home? Probably not. In general, most people shouldn't take out 100% of the debt options made available to them.

If I had $50,000 in my savings account, and I spent it all on a wakeboarding boat, I'd end up with $0 in savings. It's no different than a celebrity or lottery winner who has $10 million and spends all $10 million on a yacht. Zero is zero, no matter what you started with. And until you're at $0 and your credit accounts are maxed out, someone will always be willing to sell you more.

Your lifestyle doesn't have to cost you every dollar you earn, especially as you earn more over time. It's an amazing feeling to receive a raise, promotion, or bonus, and use it to save and invest more. My general rule about buying new things that are lifestyle choices is that if something was good enough yesterday, it's likely good enough today and tomorrow. Sure, have some fun with extra money when it comes in; but think about all the work it took to earn the extra reward, and where you want that dough to go. Your taste buds don't change when you get a raise, so it's OK to keep eating chicken even if you can suddenly afford crab. You don't have to immediately quit camping once you can afford to stay in a luxury hotel. Think about how challenging and demanding work can be, and remind yourself that saving and investing is a requirement to be able to comfortably retire. I've observed that people who skip the constant lifestyle upgrades tend to be happier than those who don't.

Play to your strengths, address your challenges

Imagine a singer-songwriter trying to get her big break as a solo artist. Her lyrics are poetic, her voice is angelic. Unfortunately, she only knows four chords on the guitar, so people say her songs all sound the same. What can she do to become a better musician?

In the short term, she can ensure that her vocals and words are heavily featured in her music. That's really where her talent and passion are. But if she truly wants to make it big, she needs to get better at playing the guitar so she can become a more dynamic composer. If she advances as a guitarist, she will have more opportunities to create interesting, original sounding songs. She will always make her vocals and lyrics the foundation of her tunes, but she can develop her musicianship so that it doesn't hold her back. She should play to her strengths, and address her challenges.

If you want to build a winning financial strategy, you must play to your strengths and address your challenges. Playing to your strengths means building a strategy around *your* most reliable attributes. Addressing your challenges means understanding which things are barriers to your goals, and taking action to hurdle them with the grace and power of a show horse. I envision this method to be like managing a grade point average (GPA) in school. If I have an "A" in math and a "C" in history, I need to spend my extra energy on history. I already have the highest grade in math, so extra calculator cuddles won't improve my GPA. But if I put in an extra 15 minutes a day to improve my history grade to a "B," my GPA will jump significantly. I can keep doing what's working for math, and find more energy for history. This method is just as effective for health and finances.

Some people hate wasting money like I hate taffy. Their game plan can rely on consistent defense, and they can give extra focus to developing their offense. On the other hand, someone who earns big but spends big should supply more energy to mindful purchasing; they earn plenty of money, but have the most room for growth when it comes to keeping it. Some folks love to read financial articles, and consequently find themselves making frequent micro-adjustments to their strategies. Their passion is a strength, but they may need to work on staying patient. We all have our own aptitudes and ineptitudes; strengths and challenges. Figure yours out and build your plan accordingly.

Section 4: Ten task finale

Chapter 21: Action steps

The concepts in Section 3 intended to teach you a winning strategy; consider the Ten Task Finale to be your basic playbook to execute that game plan. I hope you'll give some of these ideas a try. Each one has worked extremely well in enhancing my own financial health and daily satisfaction.

1: Create a budget and review your spending

Protect your money by creating a budget and reviewing expenses (see Chapter 19 for example templates). Without knowing what you're actually earning, spending, and saving, it's simply difficult to make informed financial decisions. Don't approach your finances with a drunken piñata swing. That's fun at parties, but has no place in money management. Reviewing spending patterns is the best method to enlighten yourself on the financial impacts of your decisions and habits. Since most bills are on a four-week or monthly cycle, reviewing monthly is the most natural cadence to go over spending. Purchases made with a debit or credit card typically come with reporting that makes it very easy to review where money went during the month. Some people prefer to utilize applications to track and analyze spending, while others prefer to do it by hand. There's no right way, so long as you understand what you're looking at and can form conclusions on the data.

2: Start journaling

Journaling means different things to different people, and it can support a variety of objectives. Don't discount the value of journaling just because it makes you think of a sixth grader writing "Dear Diary ..." Writing down thoughts and ideas is a very productive method of seeking clarity on any given topic. Taking the time to think and write things out can support your financial goals both directly and indirectly.

The use of journaling can support successful outcomes when considering large financial decisions such as career plans or a major purchase. It also provides a readily available medium to analyze nonfinancial factors that interfere with financial results.

Journaling is frequently recommended by therapists as a way to support mental health. That's how I got my start. And as you know, supporting strong mental health will indirectly support financial success as well. Processing stress and emotions in a healthy way will free up energy to prioritize other focuses and goals, including financial management.

I personally use journaling to vent, process results and decisions, find clarity, and express gratitude. Having this monologue with myself has helped me respond properly to critical situations regarding all *Four Circles* of my health. Taking the time to write my thoughts down with pen and paper helps me reduce the speed of my highly active and anxious brain. My maximum thought speed becomes the fastest I can write, and that helps me unjumble tricky thoughts and evade intrusive ones. This mitigates the overall drain on my batteries by reducing stress, and has been a game changer for my mental health.

Journaling also helps me process positives and negatives in my social relationships, as well as puts less pressure on relationships than if I were constantly venting to those same people. Self-soothing and finding answers via journaling saves me from wasting energy on stress, which helps me stay more diligent in my career and financial life.

Even my physical health has benefited from journaling. Writing things down that may seem obvious can still be quite valuable in reaffirming physical goals and habits. These may not be verbatim, but I've benefited from writing things down such as: *Working out so hard that I get injured is counterproductive; I wish I hadn't drank so much last night; My depression is affecting my energy;* and *It felt good to run without worrying about my stats.*

There has been more than one occasion on which journaling has saved me money, or allowed me to keep earning. The financial benefits typically come in the form of expressing gratitude and renewed energy to grind it out through employment frustrations. I've had some workdays when I wanted to just quit my job on the spot, but cutting out 10 minutes to journal about the positives of that job helped me stabilize. I've also used it when considering major purchases, or to process why I think I'm spending too much money. It's helped me realize how many things in my life are wonderful, and how many are nonessential. Journaling can help you identify what's really important to your quality of life, and in turn, reduce urges to spend money.

Your homework is to start keeping a simple daily journal in which you write down one good thing. This could be something that went well, or one thing that you're thankful for, and why. You may be amazed how much light this can bring into your life. Finding fulfillment and joy in things that really matter will translate into less spending and more smiles.

Additionally, use journaling next time you need clarity on a financial matter. Remember that the *WAIT* purchase strategy from Chapter 19 works extra well if you take the time to write it all down. Maybe you're considering a major purchase, or you need to *really* understand toxic spending patterns. It's helped me, and it can help you.

3: Use a personal progress report

Create a personal progress report and complete it weekly, monthly, quarterly, or annually. Similar to journaling, this is intended to help you be mindful of how you're doing and how you're feeling. Try it out weekly to start, so that you can get some practice. Your objective is to be aware of how you perceive your health to be at a given point in time. You may decide that you want to evaluate as of the given day you do the exercise (point in time), or review the entire time period since your last evaluation (cumulative time period). It won't take more than 10 minutes per measurement period; so if you start with weekly, it isn't likely to cost you more than 10 minutes per week. The format is as follows:

For each of the *Four Circles of Health* (physical, mental, social, and financial) you will:

1) Rate your health on a scale from 1 to 4, with 4 being the best and 1 being the worst.
   > Score of 4: I am thriving, and wouldn't change a thing
   > Score of 3: I am doing well, with few areas to improve
   > Score of 2: I know I need to improve, but some things are going well
   > Score of 1: I need a lifestyle change
2) Determine the successes and the challenges:
   a. Pick one positive thing associated with your health
   b. Pick one thing you'd like to focus on improving
   c. Choose a reasonably attainable healthy action item that will address the thing you'd like to improve

3) Once all four scores are completed, average them to find your *Total Health Rating* for the measurement period.

Each score should be considered individually in addition to the *Total Health Rating*, and any lagging area should get extra focus as you move forward. Don't get discouraged if you don't like your scores — the good news is, you've brought light to where you can focus your effort! And remember that the review is merely a progress report. As we've discussed earlier in the book, you're never "done" managing your health. Taking the time to figure out where you stand and where you want to be will be time well spent. Let this process light the path to the life you deserve.

When determining your scores, consider whether you agree or disagree with these statements, and other relevant statements you may come up with.

Physical health

I have healthy exercise habits (not too little, not too much)

I have healthy eating habits (not too little, not too much)

I am getting adequate sleep

My body can do the things I want it to

My body is functioning properly

Aches and pains do not cause me much difficulty

I feel in control of my cravings

I feel physically healthy

Mental health

I have healthy coping strategies

I feel in control of my behaviors

I can focus on a task when I need to

I have positive self-esteem

I am getting adequate sleep

I feel in control of my cravings

I feel safe expressing my feelings and emotions

I feel valuable

I am comfortable "being myself"

I feel genuine

I don't have undue emotional attachment to material things

I have joy in my life

I feel mentally healthy

Social health

I have positive self-esteem

I have healthy relationships with my family

I have healthy relationships with my friends

I have healthy relationships at work

I have a healthy romantic relationship with my partner (if applicable)

My perception of myself is more important to me than how others perceive me

No person or group has undue influence on my well-being

I am comfortable "being myself"

I feel genuine

I feel socially healthy

Financial health

I have enough resources to meet my basic needs

Most of my spending is on essentials, but I treat myself occasionally

My pursuit of money is a net positive in my life

My financial health occupies a proportionate part of my self-esteem

I don't attempt to use spending as a coping strategy

I don't have undue emotional attachment to material things

I feel financially healthy

Bringing awareness to your successes and challenges will do nothing but help you in the long run. A low score doesn't mean you've failed — it means you have opportunities to develop. Monitoring your health is worth your time, and it will amplify your ability to earn, save, and grow your money.

You may find that you don't like where you currently are, and that's OK. I've been there too. Don't let it get you down; let it get you *going*. That said, if reflecting on your health has you seriously concerned, overwhelmed, or down, please seek professional support. I've done it, and it's been the best choice I've ever made. Mental health management is a display of strength, not weakness.

If you find that you like where you are, I have good news and bad news. The good news is, you're very fortunate! Keep up the great work. The bad news is, you still have to pay attention, because it ain't over till it's over. Stay diligent and stay well.

4: Make a three-year career plan

Make a plan for your "offense" by thinking about what you want out of the next three years of your career. The standard for career planning used to be five years, but the world is moving too fast for that to be as effective as a three-year plan. If my dream of this book becoming a personal finance classic comes true, you may be reading this in a distant future when even three years is ambitious. Company ownership, work environment, coworkers, bosses, job duties, and personal interests all change rapidly in the modern world. So think about the next three years and tailor your plans and goals accordingly. Do you expect to earn a promotion? Do you expect to transfer to a lower-stress but lower-paying company? Do you expect to transfer to the highest bidder? Will you be paying for additional career advancement such as a new degree or professional certification? Do you want to retire? Do you plan to open a business? Do you think you'll need to move so you can work in a bigger market? Will you suddenly become so good-looking that you'll be able to work from home as an internet influencer? Do you just want flexibility and stability, so that you can be off work in time to coach your kid's soccer team? Will you want to find a new job the second you pay off your grad school debt? Do you want to switch from full-time to part-time or vice versa? These are all questions that you may need to ask yourself in order to drive your financial plan.

Map out what you want the inputs and outputs of your career to be. What do you want your career choices to give you, and what will your career goals require from you? Start thinking about how lifestyle affects career choices, and how career choices affect lifestyle. Weighing yourself down with burdensome debt and hefty bills can force you to stay in a job or field that is a net negative in your life. On the other hand, responsible spending will give you much more choice in the way you conduct your offense. My point is, make sure that your spending patterns aren't negatively influencing, or even controlling, your career planning. Your career plans should be built around finding your own personal balance of compensation, fulfillment, stress, and time. Maybe a better budgetary plan could help you safely leave a toxic workplace when you need to. Or maybe the increased influence of a promotion will boost your career fulfillment. There's no right answer, so you're going to need to be thoughtful about how you sort through the ambiguity.

A quick caution related to factoring career plans into financial plans: don't assume that your plan is guaranteed to happen. Things can get weird and life can change in a hurry, which can screw up even the most reasonable and diligent plan. If your career goals do include promotion, advancement and higher compensation, that's great. I have followed that path up to this point, and have been relatively happy with it. Just make sure that when you get more money, you keep it. Be careful if you're drooling over lifestyle upgrades that depend on new money associated with your career plan. And never ever layer in a lifestyle upgrade for a financial change you merely *think* is going to happen. If you've just deposited a giant fully vested sign-on bonus and plan to use the cash to buy a boat, good for you! Please let me know when you have time to take me inner tubing. But don't go spend a raise or bonus before you actually get it in your bank with no contingencies. And don't assume that new money should be spent. If it wasn't a need yesterday, is it really a need tomorrow? Trust me — it feels incredibly good to get a huge raise and actually keep it.

5: Spend less money using the *Healthy Dough Diet*

You can go a long way with a simple plan. Opportunities like the *Three Keys to Financial Freedom* and reducing junk spending are ripe for picking. There's no need to get out the rickety old ladder until you've picked all of the "low hanging fruit" — the obvious, highly reliable options. A clever way to start spending less money is to triage poor spending habits using the *Healthy Dough Diet*.

In a medical setting, triaging is the method used to determine what needs to be addressed in what order — basically, giving higher priority to greater "emergencies" first. For example, a trauma victim who is severely bleeding is going to be seen before someone with a twisted ankle, no matter who arrived first. In the *Healthy Dough Diet*, you'll work to reduce your consumption, or spending — hence the term "diet." Urgent issues should be addressed first, similar to a triage. Anything that is actively causing financial problems needs to be fixed right away. Beyond that, you can focus on the spending that provides the least value. Think of a person trying to lose weight — they might make great progress by simply cutting out dessert, rather than launching into a severe overhaul of their diet. Dessert is unnecessary and doesn't provide much nutritional value, so it can be the first to go.

By nature, this approach is primarily focused on effectively managing nonessential spending. It should never cut out anything that has value, such as meeting basic needs or other reasonable essential spending. The "diet" assumes that basic needs are met, but junk spending could be reduced. Don't you dare try to lie to me — you know you can find *something* if you really try. Identify the biggest problem, and focus on that (and only that) until it is resolved. This shouldn't just be a "yo-yo" diet that you stick to briefly before resuming old habits, like trying to lose a beer belly before a beach vacation and then gaining it back on your trip. The *Healthy Dough Diet* should result in a lifestyle change with reasonably consistent adherence.

My favorite example of junk spending relates to a habit that is bad for both financial and physical health: the delicious, unfulfilling and disgusting world of junk food. Cavepeople would be blown away by doughnuts and cheesy poofs. Let's be honest — I dig it, and so does almost everyone else, because our brains and physiology haven't actually changed that much since the days before electricity. Fake ingredients that don't decompose over time, high in the sugar, fat, and salt that our ancestors craved — yum! To our primitive brains, it's the perfect survival food. When cavepeople were hunting and gathering, they would have wanted calorically dense fuel that didn't go bad. But in the modern sedentary world, junk food is a serious problem, and a lot of people would earn huge benefits from quitting it immediately.

Quitting (or at least reducing) junk food is one excellent application of the *Healthy Dough Diet*. Candy, desserts, assorted crunchy salt bombs, soda, and all their ultrapalatable cousins are more than just physical health busters — they're also unnecessary and counterproductive uses of money. They should be special treats and not staples; when you do treat yourself, try to buy from local businesses rather than stacking up big-box store family packs. Countless people fail their diet goals because they have access to saboteurs like junk food. And as you've learned, poor physical health tends to mean less money. You could start the *Healthy Dough Diet* by simply ceasing the purchase of junk food.

We overspend because of cravings. People might spend too much on physical cravings such as food, drinks, or drugs. Some overspend to try and satisfy social cravings like acceptance. Other may spend excessively on entertainment, since they crave distraction from depression and anxiety. Identify the root of your cravings, and you'll find the right things to triage in your *Healthy Dough Diet*.

The *Healthy Dough Diet* can have compound health benefits, as shown with the junk food example. I suspect that for a large proportion of the population, the least valuable, yet most troublesome, habits involve spending money to acquire temporary "rewards." Things like junk food, gambling, drugs, alcohol, and tobacco all provide temporary ignition of the brain's reward centers, and have been proven to be highly addictive as a result. You can save substantial money and prevent scary problems by decreasing or completely eliminating these vices. This may not be easy, especially if addiction is present, but it comes first in the triage queue. If you or a loved one is dealing with addiction, please seek professional support.

Lower-risk overindulgences can still be highly problematic, and can be cut out or reduced using the same triaging system. Significant nonessential spending is part of an attempt to seek luxury, entertainment, or comfort. Pick one spending choice, evaluate the "why" of the current pattern, and work to reduce or eliminate it. Figure out what's not worth the money, what you can live without, and which reasonable alternatives are available. Focus on one source of spending at a time, and once you've mastered that, you can move to the next most urgent spending issue in the queue.

You may find that you simply didn't realize how much you were spending on certain things, and the choice to alter the habit is easy. You may also realize that you need to get tougher and learn to enjoy living without certain luxuries. In some cases, you may find that the excessive spending is an attempt to compensate for insecurity. Ask yourself, "What am I really seeking from these choices, and what am I *actually* getting?"

Some other easy targets for excessive spending to triage and resolve first are entertainment packages, retail shopping (especially online shopping, with no socialization), dining out, unnecessary convenience products, and other luxuries. Maybe you don't need every new gadget or video game. Maybe your hair and face don't need to cost $1,800 per year. Maybe it's OK if your neighbor's car is faster than yours, especially if all you do is sit in traffic anyway. Everyone can find one thing that they can spend less on.

Figure out how much you're spending per year on watching TV and movies — encompassing all platforms — and try to scale down your entertainment contracts. Set a limit for how many times you can dine out or order in each week. Even simple changes like that can really add up. Cutting back $20 per month on TV and movies will save $240 per year. Spending $10 less per week by restricting takeout food orders will save $520 per year. Saving $100 per month by reducing retail spending on clothes, decorations, or whatever else, will save $1,200 per year. Making a decision to not purchase any new furniture, electronics, or other major items for a year can make a hefty impact as well.

The *Healthy Dough Diet* is intended to remove or reduce nonessential spending, but can also reduce essential spending where appropriate. Remember, essential spending will have slight nuances for every unique person. Art supplies may be essential spending for people who create artworks as part of their career, self-care routine, or fulfillment activities. These people should not cut out art supplies, since they are essential in these unique cases. However, there could be opportunities to reduce costs.

Art supplies will just belong lower in the triage, unless current spending is severe enough to make it an urgent cut. The same rule applies to anything that qualifies as essential due to its total health or fulfillment value, whether it's gardening, outdoor recreation, baking, or anything else. Don't remove these things if they are truly valuable to you, but don't be afraid to reduce the cost if it won't negatively impact your quality of life. Consider a cheaper cellphone or internet plan, or making easy substitutions in your grocery shopping. Make the most of the gear and supplies you already have. Simple stuff.

Find ways to spend less money by triaging the most urgent issues using the *Healthy Dough Diet*. Start it as a diet, but let it become a lifestyle change. Extra spending isn't likely to materially improve your quality of life nearly as much as saving toward financial freedom.

6: Monitor your credit score, and run your credit reports periodically

Monitoring your credit report and credit score can help prevent fraud and inform you about your financial picture. You are entitled to one free copy of your detailed credit report from each of the three major bureaus (Equifax, Experian, and TransUnion) every 12 months. A common method is to review one every four months, alternating through the three different sources. Credit reports are what drive your credit score, which influences your borrowing rates and opportunities. Make sure you understand how you're being evaluated.

7: Set health and fulfillment goals

Setting goals to support health and fulfillment can result in some serious savings. I don't actually know many people who have formal, written personal goals, and that seems to me like a lost opportunity. I assure you it's pretty easy, as long as you find something you care about and a reason to do it. I'm not just talking about New Year's resolutions that fail by 11 a.m. on Jan. 1 due to hangover-related complications. I'm talking about goals that mean enough to you that you will actually try to achieve them. Building goals related to health will always be meaningful, and will provide value that will make them worth sticking to.

"I want to lose 10 pounds" isn't a goal that means much to anyone on its own. Sure, I think most people wish they were a little bit leaner, but most don't actually care enough to do anything about it. Include me in that mix, by the way. Heck, I want to lose 10 pounds *literally* as I type this, but not enough to put in the work amidst my other current goals, especially since I'm close to that stubborn "last 10" that takes 12 times the effort as the first 10 (triage!). But a goal to lose 10 pounds can become meaningful when supported by a healthy reason.

I will lose 10 pounds *so that my knees feel better*. I will call my mom once a week *to keep our relationship strong*. I will restrict dining out to once per week *so that I can save for a down payment*. I will go to counseling once per month *so that I have a safe outlet for my depression and anxiety*. I will deposit $50 per month into a college savings account *so I can help my kids get a healthy financial start*. These are all actionable items that can improve at least one component of total health.

I also suggest writing fulfillment goals. We all risk getting snared into the trap of trying to find fulfillment by spending money, or conversely, fulfillment from maximizing savings at all costs. Actively seeking fulfillment can alleviate those risks, and even when it's not 100% free, it's still a good allocation of funds (think about your *PFE* activities — passion, fulfillment, and empowerment). Bonus points if the goals support other healthy pursuits as well. Visualize the pride and joy of doing something that makes you truly feel human. Dream of the possibilities of your journey and destination. I will climb a mountain *so that I can connect with nature*. I will participate in a park cleanup once per month *to preserve the resources in my community*. I will lose 30 pounds *so I can keep up with my kids*. I will create content *to teach people valuable skills*. I will complete a Spanish language course *so I can improve communication with my in-laws*. I will run an obstacle course race *to celebrate what my body can do*. I will reduce my spending $100 per month *to save for a trip to see the northern lights*. I will complete a woodworking class *so I can make custom gifts for my friends and family*. I will lower my water bill by $10 per month *to save water and donate the savings to charity*.

Notice that all of these goals were written as "I will" statements. Your brain is more convincing than anyone else's, so start using power statements like "I will" to influence your results. Those two simple words are the ultimate fuel for hope and motivation.

In summary, pick a performance period, and pick a goal. It makes sense to choose clean time blocks when choosing a performance period: daily, weekly, monthly, quarterly, or annually. At first, it could make sense to just focus on *one* daily goal for a month to get into the groove.

Warning: Achieving goals that support health and *PFE* can result in certain side effects such as increased well-being, higher self-esteem, and more money. Go get after it, and have fun with it!

8: Find a money-friendly hobby

Identify at least one way you can bring joy and fulfillment to your life without touching your bank account. Refer back to section in Chapter 19 regarding how to add value to your life without spending money. Use your brain, move your body, and socialize.

Simply going outside more often could become a money-friendly hobby. There's no replacement for being outdoors, and you'll never be able to get the same magic from anything else. Focus on connecting with nature if that's your jam; if not, just enjoy the fresh air. It's cost-effective and all-around healthy. If you're not already doing so, here is your first new money-friendly hobby: find a way to get out into the fresh air, and make it a habit.

9: Extend your battery life to support healthy habits

In the *Five Truths of Financial Health*, I discussed that discipline is an exhaustible resource, and healthy financial habits take discipline (truth number 3). Your homework is to find some ways to supercharge your ability to stick to healthy habits by upgrading your batteries; in other words, finding ways to have more physical and mental power, and improving their efficiency.

Upgrade

Willpower requires energy. If you upgrade your batteries, you'll inherently have more energy available to support healthy habits, because your willpower will be, well, more powerful. Humor me and pretend that we can reasonably quantify energy using "points," and that a fully charged battery means maximum points available. Every stressor drains points from the self-discipline battery. All else the same, a battery capable of a 90-point charge will last longer than a battery that maxes out at 60 points. The more resilient and flexible you are, the more powerful your battery is — the more points you have available to expend before completely running out of energy. So when it comes to self-discipline batteries, bigger is better. I know of three major ways to upgrade your battery power: improving physical health, getting tough, and diversification.

The first way to increase battery power is to improve physical health. Energize yourself with exercise, healthy diet, and other quality choices. Then reinvest that extra energy into supporting your other fun, wellness, and fulfillment activities. How many times have you heard, "Oh I just love to exercise in the mornings, because it gives me so much more energy for the day!" Or, "I've just had so much more energy since I cut out sugar!" I bet you could even enjoy the benefits of developing more energy without having to seek praise and validation for it. Healthy activities increase energy in the long run. Adopting a healthy lifestyle will give you more energy — and probably more money — but feel free to skip telling everyone at the office (unless they ask).

The second way to upgrade your battery power is to get tougher. Strain and pain take a toll, but the tougher someone is, the more energy they have to endure those challenges. Consider the extreme toughness of people who battle perilous diseases such as cancer. They show up energized for life day in and day out, despite the extreme strain of illness and treatment, because they're tough as nails. Start thinking of toughness as energy available to conquer challenges, and how you can grow your toughness with purpose, positivity, gratitude, and determination. These ingredients provide the fuel that allows single parents, soldiers, endurance athletes, and survivors of all kinds to find ways to continue onward — their toughness gives them energy. If you want to be tough and disciplined with your finances, do this: identify your purpose for financial health; stay positive and determined as you pursue your goals; be grateful for where you are and where you're going.

The third way to upgrade your battery power is to diversify. The goal is to create a universal battery with energy that's flexible enough to support a variety of needs. You can't power a car with AAA batteries, and you can't use your car battery for your TV remote. It's the same story when it comes to wellness. Some people have an amazing amount of energy for physical activities, but a subpar fuel source to support social relationships. Sure, sometimes you can channel physical energy into work or healthy mental and social activities. But kinetic energy can't manage your money, stop a panic attack, or maintain a relationship. Different wellness factors require different types of energy. To be healthy, you need to be able to power all sorts of activities. The first step is to accept that, and then start finding ways to energize each factor individually. Your brain, heart, and muscles all need unique fuel. So go find the fuel that works for you.

Recharge

Find healthy ways to recharge your batteries. Things like going for walks, getting some rest, talking to friends, being alone, bonding with pets, reading, writing, or playing in general are among the many healthy ways to recharge. Different things work for different people, and different methods work for different situations. I can share some of my own examples. If I'm drained from a 10-mile hike with a long commute, I recharge by getting off of my feet and resting my mind. If I'm drained from a 60-hour workweek, I recharge by moving and getting some fresh air. Most would identify me as an extrovert, because I'm loud and friendly like a partially trained Labrador retriever. But my extroversion can drain my batteries, and I really need quiet time alone to recharge. When I'm really struggling, journaling is a great way to get some juice back (or at least reduce the energy dump). There's no single or correct answer, so just figure out what really brings your energy back to you. You may be surprised when you think about it. Finding the right ways to recharge your battery back to full (or at least close) will give you enough energy to stay diligent.

Conserve

Energy should ideally be used for things that add value to your life — healthy activities, fun, employment, hobbies, and supporting others. You'll always have to use energy to support less fulfilling things such as routine chores and daily minutiae; but you can conserve energy by automating and planning out those mundane tasks. No one wants to spend all of their energy scrambling and being constantly behind. It's stressful and wasteful. So take the stress out of everyday responsibilities and stick to healthy habits by automating tasks and planning in advance. Make it easy to make good choices and hard to make bad choices.

Making decisions and feeling urgency all day is strenuous. It's why presidents always looks 20 years older after a four-year term and why parents lose their hair. Plan quality choices in advance (some ideas are listed below), and you'll be less tired and more healthy.

Being unprepared is stressful and expensive. Studies have shown that people who shop without a grocery list spend significantly more than those who go in with a plan. The folks with a plan probably also spend less time wandering around trying to remember if they have mayo and paper towels at home, which means more time for value-added things like fun and exercise. Extending the grocery example, people are more likely to need to stop for coffee or dine out if they aren't stocked up at home, and that's expensive and time-consuming as well.

Here is a rapid-fire list of easy things you can do to be prepared, conserve your energy, and get better outcomes. Lay out your work clothes and gym clothes the night before. Prep coffee and lunch the night before. Use a grocery list. When traveling, pack your bags in advance so you have time to remember everything — you don't want to pay airport prices. Write down a list of what you need to do the following day before you go to bed. Make a chore chart. Set a routine for basic errands like grocery shopping. Follow a workout plan. Set consistent alarms. Use journaling to prepare for and process challenging conversations and decisions. Use checklists for *anything* you can think of. Schedule days to review your finances. Create a bill pay schedule. Use a calendar or a planner. Write goals. Take small steps to keep yourself organized at work.

You can also conserve energy (and money) by removing temptation. Keeping unhealthy options out of sight and out of mind works wonders with reducing the strain of staying disciplined. I am someone who can stand in the kitchen for several minutes without blinking, staring at a plate of cookies. I argue with myself about whether or not the deliciousness of one cookie is worth the calories, and if I would really only have one. Because sometimes if I get a taste, the whole stack is gone within minutes, as though a top secret agency hustled in and made it look like the cookies were never even there. Just a whirlwind of dark suits and sunglasses, and the cookies were gone before I could even ask questions.

I can waste so much time and energy resisting junk food that it's better not to have it around in the first place; I just pray my grizzly bear cravings are somewhat comical and endearing. I save myself a lot of time, energy, money, and diet days by simply not buying junk food. If advertisements get you itching to spend, consider paying the extra few dollars to get commercial-free streaming services — it may cost you less overall. Better yet, reduce screen time and exposure to ads in general. Keep your favorite stress snacks out of the house, or at least out of sight. Delete shopping apps from your phone, which can make it a little less convenient to make impulse buys. You don't have to say no to temptation as often if it's not looking you in the eye.

Better battery life

Find ways to supercharge your batteries, and you'll have more time and energy for fulfillment and healthy activities. Figure out what works for you, and don't get discouraged if it doesn't solve all your problems right away. More energy will help you stay disciplined with your finances and prevent unnecessary scramble spending. Better battery life, better life in general.

10: Say thank you

The best way to spend less is to need less. You will realize you need less once you reflect and realize you have enough. I've found that the best way to realize you have enough is to be actively thankful for what you have. Try to reflect on positives and gratitude. That feeling of nothing ever being enough is expensive and it drains your batteries.

Being grateful and saying thank you may not seem like much, but you'd be amazed what a difference it can make on your physical, mental, social, and financial health. My favorite methods of saying thank you are verbal expressions, handwritten cards, thankfulness journaling, and prayer.

Your best life is a healthy life

If you only remember one thing from this book, let it be this: your best life is a healthy life. Give yourself the care and attention you deserve. Invest in yourself every day, live gratefully, and focus on wellness. Learn to love being a human, and enjoy living out your own personal human potential. If you do these things, health and success will follow in every phase of your life. You can do it, I can do it, and your neighbor can do it. We're all inherently capable of being our very best. You are good enough today, and you'll be even better tomorrow.

You now have the ingredients to make your own *Healthy Dough*, and maybe even an idea of the flavor you're going to pursue. I hope you continue to follow *Healthy Dough*, and I want to thank you so very much for supporting my brand and my dreams. Your healthy future awaits you. Go get it!

Appendix: Terminology crash course

401(k): the most common tax-advantaged employer-sponsored defined contribution retirement account. The employer (and other parties) are responsible for oversight of the plan as a whole, but individuals (employees) own and manage their own accounts. If the employee ceases employment with the employer, they are entitled to all of their contributions, earnings, and any vested employer contributions.

403(b): the tax-advantaged employer-sponsored defined contribution retirement plan offered by governmental and nonprofit employers

Accrual:

Accrual accounting: the standard method of accounting in which revenues are recorded when earned and expenses are recorded when incurred, as opposed to recording transactions only when cash changes hands. This method is required for businesses that publish financial statements used by investors, since it provides greater visibility into future cash flows of the business, such as payments expected from customers and amounts owed to others.

General: an accumulation of transactions where cash has not yet changed hands. Example: an employee may "accrue" paid time off (PTO) as part of their employee benefits package, and thus have an "accrued PTO" balance with their employer, and at the same time the employer has an "accrued PTO" balance owed to the employee (the employee accumulates time off as earned, even though cash doesn't change hands until the employee is actually paid by the employer — in this case, in the form of time off from work).

Appreciation: increase in the value of an asset due to time or market changes

Asset: something of use or value; something that improves or protects cash flows

Bank account: the common term for a financial account consisting of cash funds deposited with a financial institution

Checking account: a bank account that is intended to be used for day-to-day purchasing. Funds may be accessed through payment vehicles such as checks (hence, checking) or debit cards.

Savings account: a bank account that is intended to accumulate cash savings. The account is not intended to be a primary payment account used in day-to-day purchasing, and as such, does not typically come with checks or cards.

Bond: a common form of debt security issued by corporations, governments, or other institutions. The issuing institution raises capital from investors without sacrificing ownership, and pays the investors interest for use of the capital.

Capital: a broad term, similar to asset, that describes something of use or value to the owner. The term is more widely used in business, but is sometimes used in personal finance as well.

Cash, currency: both words are synonymous with "money." Cash and currency represent a medium of exchange, typically issued and regulated by a government. In the modern world, currency may be tangible, such as bills and coins, or intangible, such as virtual currencies and cryptocurrencies.

Cash flows: inflows and outflows of cash. Cash inflows will typically be in the form of income, and cash outflows may be to pay bills or purchase assets.

Credit:

As a purchasing arrangement: a borrowing arrangement in which the borrower promises to pay the lender back at a later date, often with interest (i.e., purchasing on credit)

As a score: an abbreviated reference to a credit score or credit rating

As a reduction in expense: a transaction in which an amount owed is reduced, often related to a discount or correction of an error. Example: your phone provider "credits" your account balance $10 to resolve an overcharge.

In accrual basis accounting: a credit is a bookkeeping entry that decreases assets, increases liabilities, increases equity (net assets), increases income, or decreases expenses. The opposite of a credit is a "debit."

Creditworthiness: an assessment of a borrower's likeliness to pay back debts

Credit bureau: an agency that tracks consumer (personal) credit activities and provides information to potential lenders regarding that individual's creditworthiness. This comes in the form of a credit report and a numeric credit score. Credit bureaus may sometimes be referred to as credit rating agencies, but the proper technical differentiation is that credit rating agencies evaluate businesses while credit bureaus evaluate individuals.

Credit card: a payment vehicle attached to a credit account. Money is advanced by the lender (issuing financial institution), and then paid back by the borrower (cardholder) at a later date. Credit card issuers often charge interest and fees to the borrower in exchange for the advancement of funds.

Credit rating agency: an agency that provides objective analysis to a potential lender regarding the creditworthiness of a business

Credit report: a report showing payment history, loans, current debt, and other financial information. The report may also show personal information such as job history and certain legal history that is deemed relevant to creditworthiness.

Debit card: a payment vehicle funded by a depository account (i.e., checking account). Funds available on a debit card are restricted to the funds in the account.

Debt: a contractual liability, typically bearing interest. In other words, money owed associated with amounts borrowed from a lender. Student loans, mortgages, auto loans, and credit card balances are some common forms of debt in personal finance.

Debt securities: financial securities in which the issuer borrows money in exchange for future cash interest payments to the investor

Defer: to postpone to a later time

Deferral: in the context of personal finance, the term deferral typically refers to the postponement of a cash exchange. This may be the delay of a cash outflow, such as with deferred taxes, or delay of a cash inflow, such as with deferred compensation.

Defined benefit plan: an employer-sponsored retirement account plan in which individual members (employees) are part of a pool that is administered by the employer. Individual members do not have their own accounts. A pension is the most common example of a defined benefit plan.

Deferred compensation plan: A deferred compensation plan withholds a portion of an employee's pay until a specified date, typically retirement. These may take the form of a defined benefit plan (i.e., pension), defined contribution plan (i.e., 401[k]), or other benefit programs such as employee stock options.

Defined contribution plan: an employer-sponsored retirement account plan in which each individual participant (employee) owns their own account and determines their own contribution amounts. Retirement savings plans such as 401(k) and 403(b) plans are common examples.

Depreciation: a reduction in the value of an asset due to time and usage. An asset's value may decrease with time due to its "useful life," which is an estimate of how long the asset will last or maintain financial value. It may also decrease due to actual usage. Consider the used car market. Older cars with higher mileage cost less because vehicles are expected to eventually stop working.

Dividend: a payment to owners of an equity security

Employer-sponsored benefit plan: a benefit plan offered to employees by an employer at lower or no cost to the employee. The common forms of employer-sponsored benefits are retirement plans, health insurance plans, and other insurance plans.

Qualified deferred compensation plan: an employer-sponsored deferred compensation retirement plan that must comply with the Employee Retirement Income Security Act (ERISA), and as such, have special rules such as contribution limits and certain withdrawal rules.

Non-qualified deferred compensation plan: other employer-sponsored deferred compensation options consisting of a written arrangement between the employee and the employer, and not subject to compliance with ERISA.

Equity:

Personal finance: the share of ownership in an asset (i.e., equity in a home).

This is calculated as the value of the asset, minus any amounts owed.

Business finance: the calculation of assets minus liabilities (also referred to as "net assets"). This represents the value of assets unencumbered by liabilities.

Equity securities: financial securities in which the issuer offers stock or shares of the issuing institution in exchange for capital. This means that the investor is acquiring equity (ownership) in the issuing institution.

Exchange-traded fund (ETF): a common form of investment security consisting of a variety of individual securities, such as stocks, bonds, or both. Rather than transacting with a firm or brokerage, individual investors transact with each other directly, and can do so anytime markets are open.

Expense: money or value going out

Income: money or value coming in

Index: a method of tracking the market performance of a group of assets to approximate the performance of the broader market they exist in. Popular indexes in the United States are the Dow Jones Industrial Average ("the Dow"), the NASDAQ Composite Index, and the S&P 500 Index.

Index fund: a fund designed to track a certain index, such as the S&P 500. The fund aims to consist of the securities in the index it's tracking, and changes over time to closely follow the underlying index.

Individual Retirement Account (IRA): a common tax-advantaged retirement account that is administered by the accountholder. The account is not associated with an employer.

Inflation: a decrease in the purchasing power of money, as reflected in increased prices of goods and services. For example, $1 in 1970 would generally buy much more of a given good or service than $1 in 2020, because the prices of goods and services increased during that 50-year period.

Intangible assets: assets without physical presence. Common examples of intangible assets might include investment ownership or intellectual property such as copyrights or patents.

Interest: a fee charged on borrowed money. Interest and other lender fees are what incentivize financial institutions and other investors (like you) to lend money. Think of it as the cost of borrowing money and the incentive for lending money.

Compounding interest: an interest calculation method in which interest is applied to the total of principal plus accumulated interest, meaning that interest outstanding is also subject to interest charges.

Simple interest: an interest calculation method in which interest is paid only on principal and not accrued interest

Interest earnings: interest earned from holding a debt security

Interest rate: the percentage and method of interest charges, consisting of the expressed percentage rate, calculation period, rate type, and calculation method. For example: "4% annual fixed rate compounding daily."

Annual percentage rate (APR): an expression of the total cost of borrowing including interest and fees.

Fixed interest rate: a stated interest rate that does not change

Variable interest rate: an interest rate that is subject to change, based on terms defined in the applicable borrowing agreement

Investing: exchanging a resource to acquire a resource of greater benefit

Investment: something that can improve or protect cash flows

Investment earnings: a broad term referring to the performance of an investment; typically refers to earnings from interest, dividends, and appreciation

Liability: amounts owed to another party; an expected burden

Loan: money borrowed, usually in exchange for interest and fees paid to a lender. A loan is a liability to the borrower, and an investment asset for the lender.

Margin: the general term to describe the difference between income and expenses

Market:

As a place: a place where goods and services are exchanged

As an environment: a general term to describe the broader economic ecosystem. This might not be the word's technically correct usage, but prepare for people to use it in this context.

As value: An abbreviated use of the term "market value" (see below)

Market value: the expected cash value of a good or service. Market value may not be measurable until or unless an actual transaction occurs, thus, estimates are often based on completed transactions involving similar goods or services.

Mortgage: a loan acquired to obtain real property. Mortgages are common because the high costs of home purchases often require buyers to borrow money to pay the full purchase price.

Mutual fund: a common form of investment security consisting of a variety of individual securities, such as stocks, bonds, or both. Mutual funds transact with a firm or brokerage, which then transacts with investors. Mutual funds can only be transacted once per day after a net asset value calculation.

Net worth: in personal finance, the calculation of assets minus liabilities. This is the standard measure of wealth, because it represents the value of assets unencumbered by debt. Think of net worth as the amount of money a person would have if they sold all of their assets and paid all of their debts.

Nominal:

As a stated value: when you think nominal, think "named." For example, the nominal interest rate and nominal value of a debt security are "named" (stated) in the contract.

As a rate: nominal may refer to a rate that is unadjusted for inflation

As immaterial: nominal may refer to an immaterial or negligible amount, such as used in the term "nominal fee." Be sure to differentiate between a nominal fee and a nominal interest rate. As mentioned above, a nominal interest rate simply means the rate is stated (not necessarily negligible).

Note: a form of debt offering that may be classified as a debt security, but not always. Notes that are not considered debt securities may not be subject to the same regulations as other debt products such as bonds.

Par: the face value (stated value) of a debt security (defined below)

Pension: an employer-sponsored defined benefit plan in which individual employees are part of a larger pool and do not hold their own accounts, nor do they determine contribution and distribution amounts.

Personal balance sheet: a summary of an individual's assets, liabilities, and net worth

Principal: the amount borrowed in a debt transaction

Real property: also known as real estate. Includes land and any permanent fixtures, such as homes, buildings, and natural or added resources within the land.

Return:

Nominal return: the net profit or loss of an investment expressed in the amount of dollars (or other applicable currency) before adjustments for taxes, fees, dividends, inflation, or any other things that may influence the true change in value and purchasing power

Real return: the net profit or loss of an investment adjusted for changes in prices due to inflation or other external factors. This method expresses the nominal rate of return in real terms, which keeps the purchasing power of a given level of capital constant over time.

Securities: financial instruments issued by companies, financial institutions, or governments in order to raise capital. Securities are tradable, and may be issued privately or on an open market exchange. Securities are regulated by applicable authorities in an effort to ensure that the issuing institutions provide potential investors with accurate, relevant financial information in order to make informed purchase and sale decisions.

Stock: an equity security issued by corporations or other institutions in exchange for capital from investors. Rather than borrowing money from investors, the issuing institution allows investors to acquire ownership.

Tangible assets: assets with physical presence. Buildings (either residential or commercial), land, and vehicles are common examples of tangible assets.

Tax: a charge imposed by a government in exchange for goods and services supplied to the public

Tax-advantaged account: a personal financial account that receives special tax advantages for investing in a specific purpose determined by the taxing authority. The standard purposes of tax-advantaged accounts in the United States are to support individual retirement and health care costs. The more an individual has saved for their own retirement and health care, the less that individual will rely on Social Security, Medicare, and Medicaid, which are all programs that account for a significant amount of annual federal spending. Common examples of tax-advantaged accounts intended to support retirement savings efforts might include 401(k), 403(b), or 457(b) plans. Tax-advantaged retirement accounts tend to be named after the applicable section of the Internal Revenue Service (IRS) tax codification. For example, the rules related to a 401(k) account are described in section 401(k) of the IRS tax code. Common examples of tax-advantaged accounts intended to support health care costs might include Health Savings Accounts (HSA) and Flexible Spending Accounts (FSA).

Vesting: a type of schedule used to determine the timeline for when a benefit is partially or fully earned by the beneficiary. The beneficiary becomes fully entitled to the benefit when the vesting period has completed. For example, if an employee receives quarterly 401(k) contributions from their employer, and the contributions are subject to a two-year vesting schedule, the benefits would become fully vested after two years. If the employee left the organization prior to meeting the two-year vesting requirement, they would forfeit the prior contributions from the employer, and any earnings associated with those contributions.

Yield: refers to the earnings generated and realized on an investment over a particular period of time. It's expressed as a percentage based on the invested amount, current market value, or face value of the security. Yield includes the interest earned or dividends received from holding a particular security, and is often used as an objective measure to compare security performance.

References

[i] American Psychology Association & Harris Insights & Analytics LLC. (2022). Stress in America. https://www.apa.org/news/press/releases/stress/2022/october-2022-topline-data.pdf

[ii] Obesity is a Common, Serious, and Costly Disease. (2022, July 20). Centers for Disease Control and Prevention. https://www.cdc.gov/obesity/data/adult.html

[iii] Konish, L. (2019, February 11). This is the real reason most Americans file for bankruptcy. CNBC. https://www.cnbc.com/2019/02/11/this-is-the-real-reason-most-americans-file-for-bankruptcy.html

[iv] Shaw, G. (2021, October 5). These are the 11 most common reasons people get divorced, ranked. Insider. https://www.insider.com/why-people-get-divorced-2019-1

[v] Hutchinson, A., & Gladwell, M. (2021). Endure: Mind, Body, and the Curiously Elastic Limits of Human Performance (Reprint,Updated). Custom House.

[vi] Food Loss and Waste. (n.d.). USDA. https://www.usda.gov/foodlossandwaste

[vii] USDA ERS - Key Statistics & Graphics. (n.d.). https://www.ers.usda.gov/topics/food-nutrition-assistance/food-security-in-the-u-s/key-statistics-graphics/

About the Author

Dan Wickens is a certified public accountant who consistently meets his goals, but he's not as dull as you may fear. Dan's dynamic delivery will keep you awake through topics that might otherwise be literary sleeping pills. Born into a family of teachers and coaches, he continues the tradition by developing timeless financial education. His writing will speak to you like a real person and friend. He will challenge you to be your best self and find out what really matters to you.

Dan's own health and money stories shared in the book range from cringeworthy to inspirational, bridging the gap between textbook knowledge and life in the real world. His passions for fitness, sports, nature, and music flow throughout the content.

In addition to financial education, Dan finds fulfillment from playing guitar, being with loved ones, and moving his body. He is one of those weirdos who loves lifting heavy things, running for hours at a time, and wandering mountain tops and ocean waves alike. He believes that health is freedom, and that you deserve to be free.

Made in the USA
Las Vegas, NV
23 October 2023

79602264R00122